MAKE YOUR STORY MATTER

ALSO BY ABBIE EMMONS

100 Days of Sunlight

Tessa and Weston: The Best Christmas Ever

Snapshots of Sunlight: A Tessa and Weston Collection

The Otherworld

PRAISE FOR *MAKE YOUR STORY MATTER*

"A hands-on, practical, and effective manual for anyone building a powerful story. In an age of AI cookie cutters, Abbie's approach gives you the power to make your story fully human."

—Seth Godin, *New York Times* bestselling author of *The Practice* and *The Dip*

"Understanding why stories move us is one of the most powerful things a writer can learn. *Make Your Story Matter* brings the psychology and heart of storytelling to life in a way that will transform how you think about your characters and your craft. Abbie Emmons has built something special here—the kind of book that doesn't just teach craft, it reignites the reason you started writing in the first place."

—Jessica Brody, author of *Save the Cat! Writes a Novel* and founder of Writing Mastery Academy

"Abbie Emmons's *Make Your Story Matter* is a generous gift to aspiring authors. Emmons has thoroughly deconstructed the elements of an effective story—particularly the complex interplay between internal conflict (character) and external conflict (plot)—and rebuilt it from the ground up as a working tool kit, a guide as accessible as it is thorough. Had *Make Your Story Matter* been available when I was writing my debut, I suspect I would have saved some time and heartache!"

—Virginia Hume, *USA Today* bestselling author of *Haven Point*

"From the beginning of time, story has been at the heart of what it means to be human—first carried through oral histories, and later through the written word. We all live stories, yet not all of us know how to faithfully and powerfully place those stories on paper. That is about to change with Abbie Emmons's *Make Your Story Matter*. Abbie truly hits it out of the ballpark with this book. While *Make Your Story Matter* stands powerfully on its own, it also beautifully complements her YouTube channel and courses. Unlike many books in this genre that feel formulaic or dry, this one is refreshing in its presentation, practical in its guidance, and creative in its approach. It is well-written, deeply encouraging, immediately applicable, and genuinely empowering. Writing a book can feel overwhelming, but Abbie breaks the process into a clear, accessible structure that invites writers forward with confidence. I believe *Make Your Story Matter* will become a trusted resource—one writers will return to again and again. Reading this book has been an empowering experience for me, and I am confident it will be for many others as well."

—Susanne Reed, PhD, educator at the University of Arizona

MAKE YOUR STORY MATTER

An Interactive Guide to Unlocking Your Brain's Storytelling Power and Writing a Book Readers Love

ABBIE EMMONS

BENBELLA

BenBella Books, Inc.
Dallas, TX

BenBella Books, Inc.
8080 N. Central Expressway
Suite 1700
Dallas, TX 75206
benbellabooks.com
Send feedback to feedback@benbellabooks.com.

BenBella is a federally registered trademark.

Printed in the United States of America
10 9 8 7 6 5 4 3 2 1

Library of Congress Control Number: 2026005005
ISBN 9781637748909 (trade paperback)
ISBN 9781637748916 (electronic)

Copyediting by Shelby Harbour
Proofreading by Jill Kramer and Jenny Bridges
Text design and composition by Aaron Edmiston
Cover design by Jason Arias
Printed by Lake Book Manufacturing

To the person who has a story burning in their heart,
but no idea how to bring it to life.
This one's for you.

CONTENTS

PART 3: BRINGING YOUR STORY TO LIFE

INTRODUCTION

(Do not skip . . . even though you want to.)

Are you struggling to write an emotionally engaging story? A book so enthralling that your readers stay up all night flipping pages because they just can't put it down?

Is there a story idea burning in your heart, begging to be written, but you're too intimidated to take that first step and put your pen to paper?

Have you read all the books and absorbed all the advice you could find on creative writing, only to be left feeling overwhelmed and underqualified to write a book?

Do you feel like that spark of inspiration has flickered out because you've become so buried by the avalanche of writing advice that you no longer feel any passion for the idea you were once so excited about?

Have you ever felt like you're stuck in a cycle of endless revisions and rejections, while other authors effortlessly soar to the top?

Do you ever catch yourself saying, *I don't know if I can do this*?

If you answered yes to any of the above, don't worry—you're not an imposter, you're not crazy, and you're not alone.

As a professional writing coach and YouTuber with a growing community of over half a million writers, I have witnessed firsthand the struggles and obstacles they face when embarking on the overwhelming feat of writing a book.

You see, many books on the craft of writing get bogged down in theory and rules that can kill a writer's creativity, leaving them feeling confused, burned out, and defeated before they even begin. (As if being a writer wasn't already lonely and discouraging enough as it is.)

But what if I told you that writing doesn't have to be like this?

What if I told you that by tapping into simple, everyday rules of psychology, you can hook your reader from the very first sentence and make them care about your characters enough to keep flipping pages late into the night?

In this book, I'm going to introduce you to a groundbreaking three-step storytelling technique I call the Who, What, Why Method. Designed to harness the brain's natural storytelling instincts, this method will give you all the tools you need to transform raw ideas into emotionally compelling and unforgettable stories. *Make Your Story Matter* addresses every piece of the storytelling puzzle.

Unlike other writing guides that bury you in information and leave you to guess your way through the process, I've designed this book to be an interactive journey—complete with a companion workbook that you can follow, chapter by chapter, as we build an unforgettable story from the ground up. That's right: You don't have to read this book cover to cover before you can start implementing what you learn. Instead, you'll make progress on your story *while* you read, and by the end, you'll have a failproof road map to follow—and all the confidence you need to bring your story to life.

Throughout this book, you will discover science-backed techniques and eye-opening insights designed to help any writer become a master of storytelling. We'll look at story examples that illustrate these powerful principles in action, helping you visualize how they play out in some of the best-loved stories of all time. With its easy-to-use templates for crafting conflicted characters and structuring a powerful plot, this book will provide you with a storytelling framework you can use again and again to turn your rough ideas into polished masterpieces. My goal is to help you harness your inner creativity to create stories with heart, power, and impact—stories that will matter not only to you but also to your readers.

If this sounds too good to be true, let me tell you a secret: Being able to write a compelling story has nothing to do with innate talent. It's about understanding how your reader's brain works.

Storytelling is science . . . but not the boring kind

Millions of pieces of information compete for our attention all day, every day. "The brain is bombarded with 11 million pieces of information every second from our senses, but the conscious mind seems to process only about 50 bits per second," according to Dr. George Markowsky, a professor at the University of Maine.[1] That seems like a lot of information to not even be aware of, doesn't it? You might be wondering, *Who authorized this decision?* And you would be right if you guessed the subconscious mind.

You see, your brain has a sophisticated neural network called the Reticular Activating System (RAS), which helps you focus on a specific task while filtering out irrelevant stimuli. This is also the part of the brain responsible for keeping you awake and alert by modulating brain rhythms. Because only about fifty bits of information (or less) will matter to you at any moment, your brain's RAS brushes the rest aside and says, "TMI."

This is how we navigate everyday life without feeling overwhelmed by input. Your subconscious mind is actually quite brilliant—it's hardwired to distinguish between what matters to you and what doesn't, making you consciously aware of only the need-to-know information that affects you on a personal, immediate level.

Renowned author and psychiatrist Dr. Bessel van der Kolk explains it like this: "Lacking a filter, [individuals] are on constant sensory overload. In order to cope, they try to shut themselves down and develop tunnel vision and hyper-focus."[2]

Why is this important to understand as a writer?

Because you need to know how your reader's brain works if you want to write something that sneaks past their extremely vigilant subconscious mind and says, "Hey! Pay attention—this story matters to you!"

Sure, countless things distract us all day, every day, grabbing our attention momentarily. But what truly captures and *holds* our attention?

What pulls you into a story?

Why do you stay up way past your bedtime because you need to know what happens next?

Writers have been asking these questions for thousands of years. However, most writers fail to find the answer because they don't consider how a reader's brain works. And this is why so many stories fall flat and lose our interest.

To capture and hold our readers' attention, we need to sneak past their vigilant subconscious by making this story personally *matter* to them. And that brings us to the most important question you will ever ask yourself about your story: Why does it matter?

WHY DOES IT MATTER?

Most writers don't know how to answer that question. Not before they write their story, not after. And that's why many stories lack the emotional punch needed to make readers care about what's happening on the page.

Ten years ago, I didn't know the answer to that question, either. I had always loved writing, but I felt like my stories were missing something—the secret, magic ingredient that sucked me into a book and made me forget that the real world existed.

I knew it was all about the characters, because that's what I've always loved about *my* favorite books and movies. I could spot well-written characters when I saw them, but I didn't understand what it was that made a character lovable.

Was it what they did? How they behaved? Their personality? Their sense of humor? Was it that they were the victim of something bad? Or that they were fundamentally good and pure at heart?

What about morally gray characters who did bad things for good reasons, or characters who had absolutely no redeeming qualities, but I still found myself caring about them, rooting for them, wanting them to be happy?

That was when I realized something.

My readers had no reason to care about my character's personality, their sense of humor, their job, or their interests. Because all these things are only relatable to *some* people. But I wanted *anyone* to be able to pick up one of my books and instantly empathize with the main character.

And that led me to a single burning question that kept me up at night: What is it that *every person in the world* can relate to?

The answer was staring me right in the face:

INTERNAL CONFLICT

Aka: the subconscious battle between what we want and what we're afraid of.

Every single human being struggles with an internal conflict. *You* have an internal conflict. There's something you desire in life—perhaps to be a bestselling author or award-winning screenwriter—and there's also a little voice in your head holding you back. That voice is fear: *What if I don't have what it takes to be a great writer? What if everyone hates my book? What if my screenplay never gets turned into a film? What if I fail?*

This is an unavoidable part of the human condition. We can't escape it, no matter how many therapy sessions we go to or how many chocolate bars we eat. Therefore, if you want your characters to be relatable and believable, they must also experience internal conflict.

As I began to explore this concept of internal conflict, my whole perception of storytelling crumbled apart and rebuilt itself—this time through the lens of *characters* rather than *plot*. I began to revisit some of my favorite books, movies, and TV shows with fresh eyes, seeing the hidden storytelling framework that was there all along, just beneath the surface.

With my excitement for storytelling rekindled, I couldn't keep these new discoveries to myself. I had to share them with other writers who were struggling as I had been. So I started a YouTube channel, where I posted weekly videos breaking down my process and perspectives on creative writing.

As fellow writers from around the world began to discover my channel and connect with my videos, I became even more excited. I started receiving countless comments, emails, and messages from writers who had college degrees in creative writing or put themselves through years of rigorous self-study by reading all the writing manuals out there, only to feel confused, overwhelmed, and no closer to actualizing their dreams of becoming authors. However, after watching my videos and shifting their focus to internal conflict and the all-important question "Why does it matter?," these writers started to look at storytelling from a new perspective—and everything changed for them.

Now, eight years later, my YouTube community has grown to over half a million creatives with a burning passion for story and a revolutionary new understanding of how to make their audiences fall in love with their characters. I now receive countless messages every week from writers who have successfully completed novels, signed major publishing deals, and seen their screenplays win awards. What once seemed like an impossible dream to them has now become an effortless flow of natural creativity—all because of the simple mindset shifts I'm about to share in this book.

Ready to make your story matter?

Are *you* ready to unlock the creative power within you and bring your ideas to life? You already have everything you need to begin—so let's embark on this life-changing journey together.

In part 1, we'll explore the art of creating characters. I will show you how to craft deeply conflicted characters that your reader will instantly empathize with. You'll learn to weave powerful themes seamlessly into your character's journey in an emotionally engaging way that leaves a lasting impact.

In part 2, we'll craft a brilliant plot outline using my character-based three-act story structure. Unlike other story structures, this storytelling method is based on psychologically proven principles. Our primary focus is always on the characters and why what's happening matters to them. As we walk through each beat of the structure step by step, I'll show you (with story examples) why this method works.

In part 3, we'll bring your story to life. I'll provide you with the most valuable tools and insights into the writing process—freeing you to not only transform your ideas into a masterpiece but also to make the writing process fresh, fun, and creatively fulfilling.

By the end of this book, you will have a detailed story road map that makes you excited to get out of bed every morning. A story you want to cancel all your plans to spend time with.

A story that matters to you,

to your characters,

to your readers,

and, ultimately, to the world.

So grab a cup of tea (or coffee), and let's get started. I promise that this will be fun!

DOWNLOAD YOUR COMPANION WORKBOOK

Make Your Story Matter is designed to walk you through every single step of the storytelling process and leave nothing to guesswork. That means you don't have to read this book from cover to cover before you start implementing what you learn! Instead, you'll make progress in real time as you read. Scan the code below to download your companion workbook and follow along.

https://abbieemmonsauthor.com/mysm-companion-workbook

This companion workbook can be used again and again for every new project you write. Simply print it and fill it out by hand or open with your PDF editing software of choice. Once you've completed the workbook, you'll have a failproof road map that will guide you along the journey of bringing your story to life.

Part 1

CRAFTING CONFLICTED CHARACTERS

"In each of us, two natures are at war – the good and the evil. All our lives the fight goes on between them, and one of them must conquer. But in our own hands lies the power to choose – what we want most to be, we are."

—Robert Louis Stevenson

Chapter 1

CRAFTING A STORY FROM THE GROUND UP

What if I told you that storytelling was not invented to be an entertainment device? Would it shock you? Believe it or not, it's true: Storytelling originated as a creative way to impart truth and wisdom to the reader or listener.

If you go back far enough through human history, you will find that some of the oldest stories were oral traditions handed down from generation to generation. Perhaps the first stories ever told were designed to help people navigate this world and avoid as much pain and danger as possible—teaching our ancestors how to avoid being eaten by a saber-toothed tiger, for example. Some were likely inspired by true events, and others were imagined. As a civilization, stories have helped us steer clear of threats, some of them tangible and others unseen—such as the danger of being consumed by pride, resentment, and jealousy.

Some of the oldest fables, epics, and myths tell stories of animals, humans, and mythical creatures whose actions may not match what we see in the real world—yet they all contain what we find satisfying in a story today, whether in a novel, a play, or a movie. These stories carry a specific theme—a message or a big idea that transcends the story itself. These stories have been immortalized because they were built to *matter.*

Since the dawn of time, stories have been a sacred vehicle to transport us out of our everyday routines and impart truth to us. Only in the last few centuries have they come to be overly valued for their entertainment factor. We refer to authors and screenwriters as part of the entertainment industry. And while stories *should* be entertaining, that is not their main function. They entertain us simply to draw us in, to pry open our souls so we can discover the story's *meaning.*

An entertaining story will only affect you for however long you are engaged with it. But a story that *matters,* because of the characters' emotional, internal transformation, will affect you long after you reach the final page.

Perhaps you've heard something different—that to make a story unputdownable, you need to include shocking twists and turns that add up to a super-exciting plot. Maybe a creative writing teacher told you that driving the plot forward was the number one goal. But what if I told you that plot is not as important as you think it is?

Now, don't throw this book across the room if that comes as a shock! I want to let you in on a secret. To write a story that is truly unputdownable, you must find an equilibrium between characters and plot. Do we need both? Of course. But here's the thing: *Characters* are what truly drive the story. Not the plot.

> If you want to make your story matter, remember this: Story is not about what happens. It's about *how* what happens affects and transforms the characters.

Think about one story that left a lasting impression on you. It could be a book, movie, TV show, musical, stage play—anything. Now, looking back at that story, think about whether the characters had an internal transformation. Did they end up different from the way they were at the beginning of the story?

Chances are, this story left a lasting impression on you because the protagonist (the main character) changed as a result of their journey. You didn't simply watch a series of exciting events happen to them . . . you watched them transform from the inside out. This transition might have been so subtle, you didn't even notice it was happening. But when you compared the protagonist at the beginning with the protagonist at the end, you saw the difference.

This is the heart and soul of a well-told story, and it's what will leave a lasting impression on your audience.

But how do you write a story like that? How do you craft a story that matters not only to you,

but to the reader,

and to the characters,

and to the world?

I know what you're thinking: *Wait a minute, Abbie . . . This sounds like a tall order! To do all this, I'd have to be a creative genius! Maybe I'll just take up knitting instead? I have ideas for a novel, but I'm not sure they're interesting enough to keep readers flipping pages late into the night.*

Yes, creativity is extremely important in coming up with an exciting, meaningful story. But here's some good news. You don't have to worry about whether you're creative enough. As the following scientific study shows, you have all the creativity you need.

You're More Creative Than You Think

In 1968, Dr. George Land conducted a study over several years. He tested the creativity of 1,600 children, using the same sort of test he devised for NASA to help select innovative engineers and scientists. The children's assignment was to look at a problem and come up with *new, different, innovative* ideas for solving it.[3]

Dr. Land tested the same children at five, ten, and fifteen years of age. Here are the percentages of children whose ideas scored at the genius level, according to their ages:

- **Among five-year-olds:** 98%
- **Among ten-year-olds:** 30%
- **Among fifteen-year-olds:** 12%

When Dr. Land tested 280,000 adults (average age of 31), only 2 percent produced results that scored at the genius level.

Dr. Land's research revealed that there are two kinds of thinking: convergent and divergent. Convergent thinking refers to the process of evaluating and criticizing ideas, measuring them against those that have already been tested and proven, all of which takes place in the conscious mind. Divergent thinking involves imagining original ideas that differ from anything done before; it may be messy to start with, but this kind of thought originates in the subconscious mind. This is the type of thinking Dr. Land was testing for.

The younger you are, the more likely it is that you will be able to think divergently as a natural response to a challenge—and as a result, your ideas may be especially original. (What happens to creativity as people age is a topic for a different book.)

I'm sharing this information to reassure you that your subconscious mind still has that spark of creativity. You just need to pull it out, dust it off, and use it. Believe it or not, you still possess those imaginative tools you had as a five-year-old.

The secret to coming up with a brilliant story idea is simply a matter of asking yourself the right questions. Let's explore those vital few questions now and start crafting a unique story idea from scratch.

GATHERING STORY INGREDIENTS

To begin, I'm going to walk you through a tried-and-true method for brainstorming your ultimate book. I have used this framework many times, and I've watched other writers use it with great success. The best part? It's super fun, easy, only takes a few minutes, and there are zero skills or writing experience required.

If you're not sure what you want to write a book about, but you know what story ingredients you *love,* now is the time to make a list of those specific elements. You're going to draw inspiration from this list and combine all your favorite ingredients to craft a story you'll be excited to write every day.

(Turn to page 1 of the workbook for the complete template of prompts to build your ideal story from scratch!)

Step 1: What Is Your Favorite Genre?

If you don't know what your favorite genre is, here's a pro tip: Locate your closest bookshelf (Hint: You may have more than one!), and take a quick inventory of your books. What genre is taking up the most real estate on your shelf? This is likely your comfort genre—the section of the bookstore you always wander to on autopilot. For me, that genre is contemporary—stories that take place in the real world—with a side of romance, a dash of humor, and a pinch of family drama.

Your favorite genre might be:

- Fantasy
- Science fiction
- Mystery
- Thriller
- Romance
- Historical fiction
- Or something else!

Step 2: What Are Your Favorite Timeless Tropes?

A trope is a plot device used across a wide variety of stories to the point where it has become easily recognizable by the audience. For example, rags-to-riches, enemies-to-lovers romance, an epic fantasy quest for a magic artifact, or a city girl moving to a small town are all tropes commonly used to promise a certain conflict for a story. To build your list of story ingredients, start listing all the tropes you enjoy reading. Don't worry if you've seen this particular plot device used many times before. If you love it, add it to the list.

When I was brainstorming my novel *The Otherworld,* I started by writing down a few of my favorite tropes:

- Enemies-to-lovers romance
- Buried family secrets

- Fish out of water
- Found family of misfits
- Forbidden love
- Brothers who are best friends

Keep in mind: not all the ingredients you write down will make it into your story, and that's okay. Just like creating a recipe, the brainstorming process will reveal which ingredients complement each other.

Step 3: Vibe and Mood

The overarching vibe or mood of a book is what gives you a certain feeling when you open the pages and step into that fictional world. It could be cozy and comforting, dark and tense, mystical and dreamy, or something totally different. In a few words, write down the vibe, mood, and setting that gives you the most escapism when you read a book.

When I was developing my ideas for *The Otherworld,* this was the vibe I chose:

- Cozy and nostalgic
- Rainy, moody coastal vibes
- Pacific Northwest in the 1990s
- Feels like snuggling a dog by a snapping fireplace

Step 4: What Is Your Favorite Type of Romance?

Even if romance isn't a main part of your story, it can add lots of conflict and depth to your characters' relationships with each other. Take a moment to reflect on your favorite romance plots (from books, movies, or TV shows), and list out the tropes that *always* pull you in and make you interested in a story.

For me, those romance ingredients are:

- Love triangle
- Reluctant allies in a time of crisis
- A couple stranded together

- Class gap
- Age gap
- One saves the other's life

Again, not all these ingredients made it into my final concept for *The Otherworld*—and that's okay. The next few steps will reveal which ideas are compatible with each other and which ones are not.

Step 5: Build Your Main Characters

As you'll discover throughout this book, characters are the lifeblood of a compelling, memorable story. We'll dive deep into character creation in the following chapter, but for now, I want you to quickly sketch out your favorite character traits using the following prompts:

In a few words, describe your ideal main character:

- I love a main character who is struggling with:
- I'm drawn to a character whose greatest strengths are:
- I'm drawn to a character whose greatest weaknesses are:
- Choose a look for them:

When I was brainstorming *The Otherworld,* I knew I wanted the story to follow three main characters—a girl and two brothers. I personally love a female main character who is free-spirited, compassionate, loyal, and stubborn. For the two brothers, I knew I wanted a dynamic of the serious, responsible older brother and the fun-loving, hotheaded younger brother. With these few character traits in mind, I started to get a clearer idea of *who* this story would be about.

As I jotted down these rough ideas, I could see the story coming together in my mind—which is one of the best feelings in the world.

- The main female character has lived in a lighthouse on a remote island her whole life.
- Her father is a super-protective lightkeeper and the only person she's ever known.

- The love interest is a bush pilot who crashes his plane near the lighthouse.
- His younger brother is searching for him and meets the girl through a cell phone washed up on her beach.

Now it's your turn. Are you ready to start brainstorming ideas for your story? If so, jump right in. Don't worry if your ideas are messy to start with. They *should* be unformed and full of possibility—ideas that will get *you* excited to sit down and write. This is the brainstorming process—your chance to be recklessly and wildly creative. No ideas are too outlandish to bring to the table. Take risks! Be imaginative! Don't let fear stop you from coloring outside the lines, where real creativity originates. If you need to scrap some ideas and start again, you haven't failed—you're still just warming up. (Turn to page 1 of the workbook for prompts to help you along.)

Or if you'd rather wait, that's fine, too. Keep reading to get a clearer sense of the creative process before you plunge in.

WRITE THE BOOK YOU WANT TO READ

As I write this book, approximately 158,464,880 book titles exist in the world. Each year, about 2.2 million new titles are published. This number might make you wonder: *Does the world really need my book? Do I have anything unique to offer that hasn't been done before?*

Here's my clear and unwavering answer: YES.

You have a gift that no one else has. You have an idea that no one else has. Your story is unique to you, and this world has never seen anything quite like it. As you just saw in my examples above, it doesn't matter if you're using ingredients that thousands of other writers have used before. There are many, like enemies becoming lovers in a romance, or ancient prophecies and epic quests in a fantasy. It's the way you arrange and mix these elements that will make your story truly original and inspired.

Don't worry about genre expectations, oversaturated markets, or appealing to specific niches or publishing trends. If you write a book with the single goal of appealing to a certain audience, you will only disappoint yourself.

Instead, write the book that would appeal to *you.* The book you'd like to give to your past self, if you could travel back in time. Write the book that would have changed your life five years ago.

I hear what you're thinking: *Abbie . . . Where do I go from here? All I have are rough ideas!*

Don't worry! The techniques I'm about to share with you will revolutionize your writing process and change your life. How do I know? Because thousands of writers have already been using this method through my video lessons and have seen incredible results. I promise this book is going to spark your creativity and leave you feeling more inspired and empowered to write than ever before.

We're going to take this one step at a time. And I *promise* it's going to be fun.

THE WWW METHOD

Once you've brainstormed some promising story ingredients and can sense that they're starting to come together, it's time to take the next step in developing your story. If this feels overwhelming, don't worry. I've created a way to kick-start the process that has proved successful again and again. I like to call it the WWW Method. Here's what those Ws stand for:

1. **The Who:** These are the characters, including the protagonist.
2. **The What:** This is the plot—both the actions that characters take and the things that happen in their world.
3. **The Why:** This is the theme, the big idea that lies at the heart of the story.

These three Ws will be your guiding compass as you bring your story to life.

ASK YOURSELF:

- **Who do I want to tell a story about?** What inner conflict is my protagonist, or main character, dealing with? What are their desires and fears? How have their experiences shaped them into the person they are today?
- **What journey will I take this character on?** What actions will they take, and what will happen as a result? How will they be forced outside their comfort zone and ultimately transform?
- **Why do I want to write this story?** Why does it matter to me? What are the big ideas I want to share with my reader?

It's perfectly fine if you don't have a clear vision for each of these elements right now. Your ideas will continue to develop and evolve. We'll dive deeper into these three groups of questions throughout this book.

If all of this sounds a little theoretical, here's an example to show you how the WWW Method played out as I started to develop my novel *The Otherworld*. All the details aren't worked out yet—and that's exactly how it should be at this point.

Here's what I came up with.

Who—The Characters

Orca Monroe is a free-spirited young woman who has spent her whole life isolated from the outside world. She's sheltered and innocent, but way stronger than she thinks. Soft but tough. Gentle but courageous. Wears her heart on her sleeve. Sings with whales. Romanticizes everything. (Also, maybe she has a cute dog sidekick that she talks to like a best friend.)

Adam Stevenson is the older, wiser, and more sensible of the two Stevenson brothers. He's a bush pilot and mechanic, always in problem-solver mode. He is a deep thinker and a truth-seeker, more logical than emotional but not totally out of touch with his feelings. He tends to put the needs of others before his own. Hardworking. Loyal. Self-critical. Perfectionist.

Jack Stevenson is the adventurous, fun-loving, golden retriever type. Fiery and short-tempered, he's a glutton for exciting experiences and afraid of missing out (feels like life is passing him by). When he falls in love, he falls head over heels . . . and when he falls for Orca, he has no clue that he's about to get caught in an impossible conflict with his brother and the girl of his dreams.

What—The Plot

Growing up in a lighthouse on a remote island, Orca Monroe has lived isolated from the world . . . until one day, when she finds a cell phone washed up on the beach. That's how she meets Jack Stevenson, a young man whose older brother, Adam, has gone missing after crashing his seaplane off the coast. While her father is away, Orca searches her island for the missing pilot, and when she finds him, she nurses him back to health. There will be a storm or some event that forces them to be stranded together on the island for several days. Orca and Adam start to fall for each other, but some obstacle will keep them apart . . . like maybe an age gap and her father's overprotectiveness.

Adam is resigned to give Orca up, so he returns to the mainland—but Jack is obsessed with her at this point and doesn't want to leave her at the lighthouse. He convinces Orca to come to the mainland, where she rekindles her complicated relationship with Adam, who, maybe, helps her dig into her past and discover some family secret that's been hidden this whole time. Obviously, it will have a happy ending, but first, there will be lots of drama and angst between Adam, Orca, and Jack as they all navigate their complex relationships with each other.

Why—The Themes

You never know how much your small, seemingly insignificant decisions will impact others and the world around you. Sometimes love means letting go and letting the person you love come back to you on their own.

See how these ingredients are coming together to create a layered and complex story—even though there are plot holes and missing bits of information? At this point in the brainstorming process, I wasn't sure what Orca's buried family secret was going to be, or how the love triangle would be resolved. But that's okay.

Remember, your ideas at this stage don't have to be complete or tidy or make perfect sense. You're going to sharpen these ideas more as you walk through each step of this process. Additionally, throughout this book, I'm going to show you more about how I developed *The Otherworld* so that you can see my science-based story principles in action every step of the way.

Are you ready to take your brainstormed ideas and try out the WWW Method? Turn to page 2 in the workbook.

Chapter 2

CHARACTERS: THE HEART OF YOUR STORY

As I have already pointed out, countless writers make the mistake of believing that all they need is an exciting *plot* to make their story interesting. But what makes us care about the plot of a story is knowing *why it matters to the characters*. If that deeper meaning doesn't shine through, we won't discover why the story matters *to us*. That's why character development is so incredibly important!

Without this strong personal connection to the characters, a reader's attention is likely to wander—because they have no emotional investment in what's happening. But what if there was a way to make sure your reader is hooked from the very first sentence? What if there was a way to capture their attention and keep them flipping pages late into the night? Good news: There *is* a proven way to create this personal connection on page 1—by tapping into simple rules of psychology.

To begin, let's look more closely at what makes characters emotionally compelling to readers. Hint: The secret is internal conflict.

WHAT IS INTERNAL CONFLICT?

Internal conflict is the key ingredient to capturing your reader's attention. It's the unseen, inner battles the characters are waging in their minds. It's the electricity that supercharges a story and makes us viscerally *feel* what the characters are feeling.

Internal conflict is actually quite simple: Your character wants something, but their fear is stopping them from going after it. And both their desire *and* their fear are based on a false belief—a lie they believe is true about themselves and the world. (A false belief is sometimes referred to as a fatal flaw.)

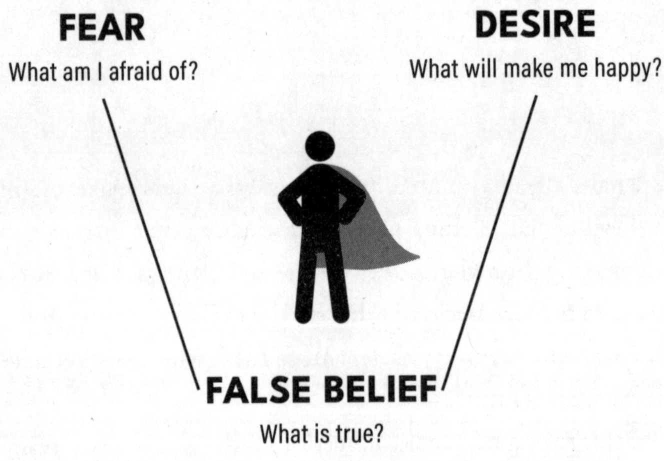

For example, let's say your character is a writer. Their desire is to become a bestselling novelist. Their fear is that putting their work out there will lead to rejection and criticism. What would their false belief be? Perhaps something like, "I am only successful if my work is admired and approved of by others." This false belief is what fuels their every decision throughout the story—it's their guiding compass, leading them from one choice to the next.

If we don't know why what's happening has *personal meaning* for a character, related to their fear, desire, and false belief, the story won't matter to us or hold our attention. It will become one of those pieces of information the subconscious shoves out the door—because we don't know why it matters to us.

At its core, story is not overly complicated. Simply put, it's a reflection of the human experience—the personal struggles that each of us face in our own way. Characters, like ordinary people, grapple with desires, fears, and their own flaws. That's what allows us to relate to them and root for them. That's what makes us find ourselves in a story. That's why stories have the power to change our lives.

Take a moment to think of another story that stayed with you long after you encountered it.

Now, ask yourself: Did a single character take center stage? Did they have deep internal conflicts that drove their actions? Did they change or grow because of this journey? Was I cheering them on, feeling their pain, and wanting to see them succeed?

If you answered yes to any of these questions . . . guess what? That story was character-driven. (Yes, even if it was a sci-fi novel filled with exploding spaceships, a thriller packed with car chases, or a fantasy swarming with fire-breathing dragons!)

That's because all compelling and memorable stories have relatable *characters* at their core—even ones with nail-biting peril and plot twists.

Am I saying that you don't need a plot for your story? Of course not. You need a plot because it provides external conflict, and without external conflict, your characters have no opportunity to change. But it's internal conflict that gives your plot meaning—and leaves a lasting emotional impact on your audience.

External conflict (the plot) is about what happens in the story, but internal conflict is about why it matters.

So, let's examine what sets the stage for a masterfully told story—a perfect combination of external and internal conflict.

Don't Let Your Characters Be the Punching Bags for Your Plot

Your characters aren't here simply to absorb what happens—instead, they must be the agents of change, with a deep desire driving their motives and a conflicting fear holding them back.

PASSIVE VS. ACTIVE CHARACTERS:

Passive	Active
✗ Passive characters are like punching bags for the plot.	✓ Active characters make choices based on their beliefs and goals.
✗ They don't make choices; they get pushed around by life.	✓ They have a deeply rooted false belief (fatal flaw) which guides their steps.
✗ They don't change as a result of their journey, because they never battled with a false belief.	✓ They ultimately choose to change their beliefs when they discover the truth at the end of the story.

While an exciting or dangerous external event can be an effective way to capture your reader's attention, it's crucial to go beyond that as soon as possible. The first event may be an act of the plot itself, but you must quickly show your reader why it means something to the characters, or you risk losing their interest.

But, Abbie, what about all the popular movies and books that fall into the plot-driven category? How do you explain their success?

That's a very good question. Perhaps you've watched movies or read books where the high-stakes action was heart-pounding and unrelenting, even though the characters didn't have much depth—and yet, it still managed to hold your attention. Why?

To find the answer, we need to return to the topic of brain science.

The Tiny Neurons That Make You Feel Big Emotions

You have some special brain cells called mirror neurons—you've probably heard of them before. They do exactly what they sound like: *Mirror* the emotional reaction of whatever the eye sees.

For example, when you're watching a movie and see a character get their hand crushed, your mirror neurons say, "Ouch!" You could even experience a physical sensation in your hand, as if *you* were suffering from the injury.

Turn around next time you're in a movie theater and watch how people physically react to what's happening in the movie. (Our brains automatically do this—we can't control it.)

Mirror neurons are incredible because they allow us to feel immediate empathy for characters, even though they aren't real people. As neuroscientist Dr. Christian Keysers discovered using fMRI research, certain areas of the brain responsible for sensing physical touch light up not only when we experience touch ourselves, but also when we observe someone else being touched.[4]

This explains why plot-driven stories hold our attention. Your brain mirrors what is happening to the characters as if it's happening to you, which means as long as you keep the perilous high-intensity survival scenes coming, your fight-or-flight instinct kicks in with the character's and *boom*! Your brain is engaged with the material. But for how long? A few weeks later, you might not even recall what happened—or why it mattered.

Because mirror neurons serve us *in the moment* as a reactive mechanism, the response is not lasting. In other words, you might be in survival mode with a character who is facing a life-or-death situation, but once the perceived threat has passed, you are no longer empathizing with that character on a deeper, emotional level.

> Finding the equilibrium between character and plot is what makes a story memorable. We can't care about a plot outside of characters, but we *can* care about characters outside of a plot.

Your protagonist's first emotional reaction grabs the reader's hand, but their internal conflict *pulls them in.* Or, as I like to say, the plot is the fist, and the inner conflict is the punch. Without the power and velocity of the internal struggle, a fist is just a fist. We need something *driving* it on an emotional level to pack a punch.

The opposite is also true. You can open your story with the character's internal conflict as your hook—in fact, I recommend that—but don't wait too long before you let some external events (plot points) push them outside their comfort zones and make something happen.

THINK ABOUT THESE QUESTIONS:

- What is my main character's motive?
- Why do they react to the beginning of the plot this way?
- What do they want in life—what is their goal?

If you can reveal the answers near the opening of your story, through what characters say and do and feel, you will be leaps and bounds ahead of most storytellers.

You don't have to trade character for plot, or vice versa. You can still have a riveting plot filled with action and peril *and* have your characters' internal conflict take center stage. Action becomes ten times more entertaining and nerve-wracking when we know and relate to the characters. It's your emotional attachment to them that puts readers on the edge of their seats. After all, if you don't intimately know and care about these characters, watching them in danger is only perilous because your mirror neurons are firing as if *you* are in that situation.

On the flip side, when you know and care about the characters, not only is your brain engaged with the action as if you're stuck in that situation, but you also have an emotional attachment to these characters—and *that's* what makes a story stick with you long after the final page.

The Importance of Internal Conflict

As we discussed in the introduction, readers have no reason to care about the protagonist's favorite food, time of day, or even their jobs or interests because all these things are only relatable to *some* people. But you want *anyone* to pick up your book and relate to your protagonist.

So, then, what is the one thing every person on planet Earth can relate to? Internal conflict (aka: desire clashing with fear).

It's important to remember that your protagonist's internal conflict begins long before the plot shows up to destroy their life. It *has* to. Because otherwise, your plot wouldn't matter. It might matter to the universe, the government, or some higher power, but who cares about that? Not your reader! We readers care about the *characters*. And if we *don't*? We won't be hooked.

Your characters, especially the protagonist, are the skin in which readers live as they experience your story. When readers open your book and steps into their shoes, you want them to feel what that character is feeling—their desires, fears, and deepest conflicts. This will make readers care about the whole story.

KEY TAKEAWAYS

- **You must find the balance between plot and characters.** Without external conflict, your characters don't change. But without internal conflict, your plot is meaningless.
- **Don't let your characters be the punching bags for your plot.** Instead, they must be the agents of change, complete with a deep desire that drives their motives and a conflicting fear that holds them back.
- **If you want your story to have an impact, it must be character-driven.** Remember, the story is about characters going on a journey to realize the truth about something—the truth *you* want to scream from the rooftops.
- **Internal conflict is what makes your characters relatable.** You don't want your reader thinking, *How would I feel if that were me?* You want them to think, *How would I feel if I were them?*

Chapter 3

MEET YOUR PROTAGONIST (AND THEIR BAGGAGE)

As we've seen, it is the characters who make us care about what happens in the plot. They embark on a journey and come to understand new truths about themselves and the world. They have a goal, but obstacles stand in the way—and these obstacles appear in the form of both internal *and* external conflict. Internal conflict ups the ante by revealing the character's emotional battle, while external conflict pushes them outside their comfort zone and forces them to make difficult choices. This is the bedrock of character-driven storytelling that pulls a reader in and sparks their empathy.

This part of the process is all about finding the balance between your characters and your plot. First, let's refresh what we've learned so far about the three key ingredients to relatable characters:

1. **Fatal Flaws:** A fatal flaw is essentially a false belief about the world or themselves that prevents a character from finding true happiness.
2. **Internal Conflict:** This is the inner, emotional battle that gives your plot meaning. Your character wants something, but they are also

afraid of something. Their fear is constantly stopping them from getting what they want.

3. **Clear Goals:** This is the momentum of your story, the driving force that makes your protagonist an active character in their life rather than a punching bag for the plot.

Bottom line: If you don't have character transformation, you don't have a story; you just have a random assortment of events happening to a random assortment of people. The character's arc, or journey of change, is what makes your story memorable, meaningful, and satisfying.

Below is my ultimate character profile, which covers every essential aspect of character creation. You can apply this straightforward questionnaire to any of your characters to help you better understand them and develop their internal conflicts.

The answers to all these questions will help you craft that gripping story opening that will pull your readers in and make them care about your characters. Let's start with the most important character of all—the protagonist.

CHARACTER BASICS

Character's name:

Role in story: Protagonist

Physical description:

Age:

Enneagram Personality Type: *More on the Enneagram later in this chapter.*

Distinctive skills/abilities: *Could be realistic (really good at math) or fantastical (really good at magic).*

What is their greatest fear? *The thing that holds them back from finding true happiness.*

What is their false belief? *The root of that fear—something they believe is true about themselves and the world.*

What happened in this character's past to make them believe this lie? *The moment in your character's past that shaped their outlook on life. (See the next chapter for more on developing this backstory.)*

What do they most often criticize others for? *Again, digging into the beliefs here. Real people have convictions, opinions, and principles, so your character should, too.*

What is their love language? *How they show love and like to be loved by others.*

How do they respond to emotional pain? *You can reference the Enneagram here; it will help you a lot.*

Inner motivation: *The deepest core emotion that drives them.*

Top three things they value most in life: *This can be physical or abstract . . . family, money, success, waffles, etc.*

Their typical outfit, from top to bottom: *How they dress should say something about their character . . . and it's a great way to show, not tell!*

Defining Your Character's Goals

- How is your character dissatisfied with life?
- What does your character believe will bring them true happiness or contentment?
- What definitive step could they take to turn their dream into a reality?
- How has their fear kept them from taking this action already?
- How does your protagonist feel they can accomplish their goal while still steering clear of the thing they are afraid of?

STRATEGIES IN ACTION: CRAFTING A PROTAGONIST

To better understand what crafting a protagonist looks like in action, let's use my ultimate character profile template to develop a character. We're going to return to *The Otherworld*, and I'll give you a behind-the-scenes look at my process.

So far, we have only rough sketches of the novel's plot, themes, and characters. We took a list of random character traits and began to scratch the surface of who the protagonist is.

Here's the brief description of our female protagonist, Orca, that we already have:

> **Orca Monroe** is a free-spirited young woman who has spent her whole life isolated from the outside world. She's sheltered and innocent, but way stronger than she thinks. Soft but tough. Gentle but courageous. Wears her heart on her sleeve. Sings with whales. Romanticizes everything. (Also, maybe she has a cute dog sidekick that she talks to like a best friend.)

Let's expand on these ideas and fully develop this character, using my template:

CHARACTER PROFILE—ORCA MONROE

Character's name: Orca Monroe

Role in story: Protagonist

Physical description: Petite and naturally beautiful, with wild sandy-brown hair and blue-green eyes.

Age: 18

Personality Type: Enneagram 2. Sweet. Idealistic. Emotional. Innocent. Curious. Giving. Introverted. She feels deeply for others and treats them with kindness and understanding. She is friendly, generous, and self-sacrificing, but can also be too trusting, naïve, and people-pleasing.

Distinctive skills/abilities: She knows how to survive off the land, grow food, make homeopathic medicine, sing with orcas, run the lighthouse, and keep her home running smoothly.

What is her greatest fear? That she'll miss out on everything that life has to offer because she lives isolated on her island. Thanks to her father keeping her away from the Otherworld, Orca fears she won't be able to face the dangers of the mainland. She feels trapped by her father, but she's also afraid of hurting him.

What is her greatest false belief? That her father is correct, and she's not strong enough to handle the harsh realities of the Otherworld.

What happened in this character's past to make her believe this lie? All her life, her father has kept her safe from harm and told her how delicate and precious she is, how she's safer on the island and doesn't belong in the Otherworld.

What does she most often criticize others for? Being cruel or unkind to others.

What is her love language? Acts of service; quality time.

How does she respond to emotional pain? Orca is very open-hearted and shares her feelings with people she trusts, but she also hates to burden others with her problems and keeps some things to herself.

Inner motivation: Needs love and connection with others to experience everything that life has to offer, but not at the expense of her relationship with her father.

Top three things she values most in life: Her father, the lighthouse, and her dog, Lucius.

Typical outfit for her, from top to bottom: A hand-sewn dress or jumpsuit, a soft cable-knit sweater, and ribbons in her hair.

All right, we have a solid foundation for our protagonist now. We understand her most important character traits, internal conflict, and false belief. We've also developed some of her hobbies, skills, and interests. However, we need more than that to create a character who actively participates in the story (and doesn't just serve as a punching bag for the plot).

As we explored in the previous chapter, the best way to make your characters active is to give them clear goals—something they passionately pursue throughout the story. So, let's continue filling out this character profile for Orca, giving her a clear goal that aligns with her internal conflict.

Orca's Character Goals

- **How is Orca dissatisfied with her life?** Living on an island her whole life, Orca is totally isolated from the rest of the world. She feels like she is missing out on life, particularly relationships with others.
- **What does Orca believe will bring her true happiness or contentment?** She longs to know what the rest of the world is like and believes that going to the mainland is the solution.
- **What definitive step could she take to turn her dream into a reality?** She could ask her father to take her to the mainland the next time he goes, but she has done this before, and he always refuses, telling her that the mainland is a dangerous place.
- **How has her fear kept her from taking this action?** Orca fears hurting her father by defying him and going against his wishes.
- **How does Orca feel she can accomplish her goal while still steering clear of the thing she's afraid of?** Orca feels she has to prove to her father that she is strong enough to handle the darker, harsher realities of life. Maybe then he'll let her go.

Great! Now, we have a distinct goal for our protagonist to pursue, which balances nicely with her internal conflict. Next, we need a better grasp of the other main characters, who they are and what they want. We know the two brothers, Adam and Jack, are going to be essential to the story and the love triangle with Orca. Let's take a minute to flesh out their character profiles and understand their goals.

CHARACTER PROFILE—JACK

Character's name: Jack Stevenson

Role in story: Love interest 2

Physical description: Chestnut-brown hair, hazel eyes, a smile that lights up the room.

Age: 18

Personality Type: Enneagram 7. Fun. Hyperactive. Spontaneous. Optimistic. Scattered. Good sense of humor. He is extroverted, restless, playful, and always up for a new adventure. He can be temperamental and undisciplined when he doesn't get what he wants.

Distinctive skills/abilities: He's a bush pilot, like his brother, Adam, who taught him how to fly. He also has an uncanny knack for avoiding responsibilities.

What is his greatest fear? Being physically trapped in one place and emotionally trapped in pain. Fear of missing out on all that life has to offer. (Compare with Orca's fear—find similarities and differences.)

What is his false belief? The thing you desire is always out of reach, happening somewhere else to someone else. The only way to gain fulfillment is to go out there and chase it. Also, Adam will always be better than he is.

What happened in Jack's past to make him believe this lie? All his life, Jack has looked up to Adam and followed in his footsteps, but he wants more out of life than his older brother does. Still, he feels like he never measures up to that standard.

What does he most often criticize others for? For being too controlling.

What is his love language? Physical touch; gift giving.

How does he respond to emotional pain? Jack is very reactionary. Unable to escape his feelings, he often lashes out in anger and blames others.

Inner motivation: Wants to have freedom and happiness, avoid missing out on exciting experiences, keep himself occupied, and avoid emotional pain.

Top three things he values most in life: His freedom; his brother, Adam; and probably his Mustang.

Typical outfit, from top to bottom: Jeans, bomber jacket, band T-shirt, aviator shades.

Fantastic! We're starting to establish Jack's identity and see how his struggles are very different from (but very similar to) Orca's. Now, let's examine Jack's goals and see if we can make him an active character—not just a victim of tragic circumstances.

Jack's Character Goals

- **How is Jack dissatisfied with his life?** Jack struggles with the potential loss of his brother when Adam goes missing in a plane crash. He isn't ready to accept that Adam is dead, and he feels unable to escape the pain.
- **What does Jack believe will bring him true happiness or contentment?** To find Adam, of course—if he's still alive. Beyond this crisis, Jack believes he needs to escape, travel, and visit places he's never seen in order to truly find himself.
- **What definitive step could he take to turn his dream into a reality?** At the start of the story, Jack's main goal is to find Adam. His chance encounter with Orca (via the cell phone washed up on her beach) gives him the perfect opportunity to pursue this goal by enlisting her help.
- **How has Jack's fear kept him from taking this action already?** Jack

is the only one who holds out hope that his brother is still alive. So far, all attempts to find Adam have failed, leaving Jack at a dead end until Orca comes along.

- **How does Jack feel he can accomplish his goal while still steering clear of the thing he's afraid of?** If he can convince Orca to help search for his missing brother, he'll be making progress toward his goal (finding Adam) and avoiding the emotional pain of accepting that his brother is gone.

Terrific! Both characters now have complex layers and clear goals they will pursue throughout the story. But we have one more character to develop—Adam, who will add more layers of complexity to the story.

Up until now, we've created a short list of Adam's character traits. Now, let's expand upon these ideas by filling out a character profile for him.

CHARACTER PROFILE—ADAM

Character's name: Adam Stevenson

Role in story: Love interest 1

Physical description: Tall, dark, and handsome. Blue eyes, messy dark hair, and an impeccable jawline.

Age: 28

Personality Type: Enneagram 1. Patient. Understanding. Empathetic. Torn between logic and emotion. Serious. Principled. Conscientious and ethical, with a strong sense of right and wrong. Introspective. Philosopher. Loner. He holds himself and others to impossibly high standards, which sometimes leads to criticism and a deep sense of dissatisfaction.

Distinctive skills/abilities: He's a bush pilot, mechanic, and entrepreneur. Though he doesn't have Jack's social skills, he can look at conflicts from everyone's perspective.

What is his greatest fear? That he'll do the wrong thing, not be a good person, and prove to be a bad influence on his younger brother, Jack.

What is his greatest false belief? Putting himself first is wrong; he must prioritize others' needs and desires above his own. What he wants doesn't matter.

What happened in Adam's past to make him believe this lie? Throughout his life, Adam has recognized how hard his parents worked and has wished to help them, to be a responsible son and a good brother. He feels a sense of duty to give back to his parents, and at a young age, he felt rewarded for being the perfect child.

What does he most often criticize others for? Willful ignorance, laziness, and lack of responsibility.

What is his love language? Quality time.

How does he respond to emotional pain? Adam is very introspective about his feelings. He's prone to internalize and hides any emotional pain he feels, even from himself.

Inner motivation: He wants to feel that he's done good for others and wants to find someone with whom he connects on an intellectual/spiritual level.

Top three things he values most in life? His family, his work, and Orca.

Describe a typical outfit for him from top to bottom. Carhartt pants, flannel shirt, bomber jacket, aviator shades.

Adam's Character Goals

- **How is Adam dissatisfied with his life?** Adam is a paradox because he isn't dissatisfied with his life in the same way Orca and Jack are. He is quite stable and at peace with life, but deep down, he does desire to find love with someone who is his equal. He finds that in Orca, but the situation is complex.

- **What does Adam believe will bring him true happiness or contentment?** While stranded together at the lighthouse, Adam finds himself enchanted by Orca's wild beauty and her unconventional perspective on life. He's going to end up falling in love with her, even though he believes it's impossible for them to be together.
- **What definitive step could he take to turn his dream into a reality?** Although Adam forges a deep connection with Orca, he is too skeptical to believe it is the kind of love that will endure. He can't pursue Orca without disrupting her life.
- **How has Adam's fear kept him from taking this action already?** Though he falls in love with Orca, he's afraid his actions might cause more harm than good, and he could never forgive himself for causing strife between Orca and her father.
- **How does Adam feel he can accomplish his goal while still steering clear of the thing he's afraid of?** When Adam returns home, he is determined to forget about Orca, believing that it is the right thing to do. His fear of causing conflict leads him to suppress his own wants.

Awesome! Now that we've developed Adam's character, we have compelling motives for all three characters—motives that directly connect to their false beliefs.

COMING UP WITH GOOD INTERNAL CONFLICT (WITHOUT OVERTHINKING IT)

At this point, you might be thinking, *Okay, I get it—my characters need to have desires, fears, and a false belief, but . . . what should those desires, fears, and false belief be?* If you're drawing a blank and not sure what your main character's internal conflict should be, don't worry—you're not alone.

Writers ask me this question all the time. *Abbie, how do I come up with good conflict ideas for my characters? I'm worried that they'll all seem the same, or—even worse—they will all sound like me, the author. Is there a shortcut to this?* Yes! As you've probably gathered by now, I'm a bit obsessed with psychology, and that obsession extends to personality types. It's fascinating how the same inner struggle can look drastically different, depending on the personality of the individual facing it. Here, I want to introduce you to a powerful personality typing tool you can use as a shortcut to develop your protagonist and the other most important characters in your story. It's called the Enneagram and centers around the idea that personality is an expression of what we believe, not just how we behave. The Enneagram is often presented in this graphic form, showing all nine types:

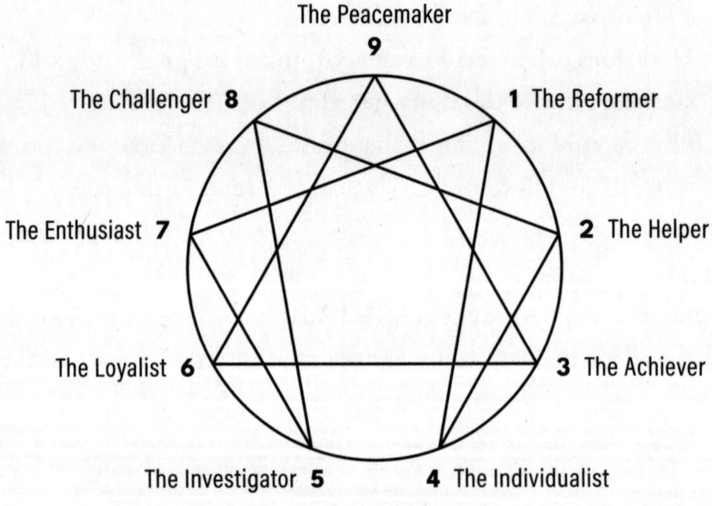

The Enneagram system was designed to give us insight into a person's deepest desires and fears. A character of a certain type is not given just a role (such as hero) to play. Instead, the Enneagram shows how our character's beliefs influence their behavior and decisions.

You can choose any Enneagram type from this list and instantly have a starter pack of desire, fear, and false belief. From there, you can build upon these personality traits and beliefs to craft a vibrant character with all the depth and complexity that only *you* can give them.

First, let's look at a breakdown of each Enneagram type.

Type One: The Reformer

Enneagram Ones are driven to be good and do the right thing, satisfying their need to feel virtuous and to avoid blame or criticism. Ones are reliable, responsible, honest, hardworking, and conscientious. They are good at analyzing situations and clarifying issues objectively, without letting emotions interfere. However, their excessive focus on virtue can lead to self-doubt and disrupt their inner peace due to extreme self-control and judgment.

Though Ones tend to be stereotyped as rule-followers, they are not afraid to challenge and question authority, especially if that authority lacks a moral compass, with no sense of right and wrong. In this way, Ones can be trailblazers and rebels, standing up for the marginalized and avenging those who can't fight for themselves.

- **Basic desire:** To be good, moral, and honorable. To set a good example for others. To make a positive difference in the world.
- **Basic fear:** Being wrong, criticized, imperfect, or falling short based on their own standards.
- **Overarching false belief:** I need to be perfect.
- **Greatest vice:** Anger. Type Ones often express their anger as a sense of frustration, self-righteousness, or resentment. They may harbor a simmering, low-grade anger when people or things aren't as they should be. At their worst, Ones can become tyrannical in their anger—holding others to impossibly high standards and administering punishment without remorse.
- **Strengths and weaknesses:** Inner critic, over-control, virtuousness, perfectionism.
- **In short, the One's driving internal conflict in all that they do is to strive for perfection in order to avoid the criticism and shame of making mistakes.**
- **Character examples:** Atticus from *To Kill a Mockingbird*, Elsa from

Frozen, Steve Rogers from *Captain America*, Thanos from *Avengers: Endgame*, and Mr. Darcy from *Pride and Prejudice*.

Type Two: The Helper

Enneagram Twos are driven to be kind, nurturing givers, satisfying their need to feel loved by showering others with affection and acts of kindness. They have a natural talent for empathy and emotional support and find their worth in being needed and valued.

Twos are amazing friends who will move mountains to support their loved ones. They're optimistic, warm, caring, friendly, reliable, and incredibly supportive. However, in their endless quest to help, they often forget about their own needs and lose touch with their true feelings. They put everyone else *first*. Underneath their cheerful and upbeat demeanor, Twos are secretly afraid they aren't worthy of the love they so freely give. At their worst, they can become manipulative and attention-seeking.

- **Basic desire:** To be kind, nurturing, helpful, and generous; to satisfy their need to feel loved by showering others with kindness.
- **Basic fear:** Being unloved, unwanted, abandoned, and alone.
- **Overarching false belief:** I'm not lovable as I am.
- **Greatest vice:** Pride. A Two's pride shows up in two ways. When they feel deflated, they're hyper-aware of their insecurities and constantly seek approval. When inflated, they take on too much responsibility, convinced they can handle everyone's needs (even when they're totally exhausted).
- **Strengths and weaknesses:** Seductiveness, generosity, martyrdom, and strategic helpfulness to make themselves indispensable.
- **In short, the Two's driving internal conflict is their desire to show love and give unconditionally, in hopes that others will love them back and meet their needs.**
- **Character examples:** Emma Woodhouse from *Emma*, Peter Pevensie from *The Chronicles of Narnia*, Samwise from *The Lord of the Rings*,

Mother Gothel from *Tangled*, and Scarlett O'Hara from *Gone with the Wind*.

Type Three: The Achiever

Enneagram Threes are success-driven achievers, constantly raising the bar, upping the ante, and striving to be the winner. They have a natural talent for dazzling crowds, making sales, building empires, and they find their worth in achieving their idea of success.

Threes are masters at crafting their image—they're all about creating success and drawing admiration through their work and appearance. While they're incredibly charming and likable, they often switch off their deeper emotions in order to maintain their carefully crafted persona. These high achievers are extremely competent and effective, getting tons of stuff done while making it look like a breeze. However, they often exhaust themselves by working too hard and lose sight of who they really are behind the mask.

- **Basic desire:** To be successful, achieve great things, and gain security or the admiration of others.
- **Basic fear:** Being a failure, unsuccessful, or losing security and stability.
- **Overarching false belief:** If I'm not a success, I'm a failure.
- **Greatest vice:** Deceit. Threes present a carefully crafted version of themselves to the world. They are masters at adapting their image, convincing themselves that they *are* the persona they've crafted. They've learned that being seen as successful and admirable is crucial for gaining acceptance and love.
- **Strengths and weaknesses:** Achievement-oriented, competitive, improvement mindset, image manipulation.
- **In short, the Three's driving internal conflict is their desire to be successful and accomplish their dreams so that they can win the admiration of others or achieve a sense of security and freedom.**
- **Character examples:** Jay Gatsby from *The Great Gatsby*, P.T. Barnum

from *The Greatest Showman*, Maverick from *Top Gun*, Tiana from *The Princess and the Frog*, and George Bailey from *It's a Wonderful Life*.

Type Four: The Individualist

Enneagram Fours are emotional seekers, driven to find their personal significance and that which they feel is missing in their lives. While they deeply desire connection and meaning, they often withhold themselves from others due to feeling vulnerable or defective. This creates a paradox: They push away the very things that could fulfill them.

Fours possess an extraordinary gift for understanding emotional depths—they're like emotional archaeologists, exploring uncomfortable feelings that others might avoid. Their natural ability to see beauty in darkness and find meaning in melancholy makes them uniquely creative and deeply empathetic. These sensitive souls have an uncanny talent for reading emotional undercurrents between people, and at their best, they express this through emotional honesty and creativity.

- **Basic desire:** To feel unique and special, to forge deep emotional connections, and to find that which they feel is missing from their life.
- **Basic fear:** Being misunderstood and emotionally exiled as the outcast, the imposter, the one who doesn't belong.
- **Overarching false belief:** If I'm not special, I'm not important.
- **Greatest vice:** Envy. The Four's core false belief is that everything they need and value lies somewhere out of reach. They desperately want love and acceptance, but at the same time feel ashamed for needing it so much. At the heart of it all is the false belief that they're fundamentally flawed or missing some crucial piece that would make them worthy of love.
- **Strengths and weaknesses:** Intense creativity; focus on suffering, emotional intelligence, and an inferior self-image.
- **In short, the Four's driving internal conflict is their desire to be**

unique and special, so they can avoid the pain of feeling defective and finally get the love and acceptance they've always longed for.

- **Character examples:** Anne Shirley from *Anne of Green Gables*, Belle from *Beauty and the Beast*, Antonio Salieri from *Amadeus*, Jo March from *Little Women*, and Loki from *The Avengers*.

Type Five: The Investigator

Enneagram Fives are driven to be competent and capable investigators, withdrawing into their minds to take refuge from the unpredictability of the world. Fives are inquisitive, clever, observant, pragmatic, and analytical. They are good at analyzing small details that most people overlook, and they have a gift for complex learning. However, the more time they spend in their minds, the less others can relate to or connect with them emotionally, which can leave the Five feeling isolated and empty.

Though Fives tend to be stereotyped as insensitive geniuses, that doesn't mean they don't have feelings—just the opposite. While Fives can appear detached and unfeeling on the outside, this trait reflects a deep, instinctive need to protect themselves from emotional pain. Because of this, Fives may have less ability to cope with complicated emotions and may even struggle to communicate their true feelings with those they care deeply about.

- **Basic desire:** To be capable, competent, and well-informed, safe in their knowledge so they can take refuge in their inner world.
- **Basic fear:** Being useless, helpless, or incapable.
- **Overarching false belief:** I don't need anyone's help or comfort.
- **Greatest vice:** Greed. Fives don't have a burning desire to collect money or possessions, but they *do* hold tightly to what they have—due to early experiences where they didn't receive enough from others. Fives have a defensive expectation that they'll always lack, which causes them to minimize their needs and withhold from others. In their minds, giving even a little means risking *everything* they have.

- **Strengths and weaknesses:** Emotional detachment, self-sufficiency, hypersensitivity.
- **In short, the Five's driving internal conflict is their desire to acquire knowledge and feel capable, cultivating a safe bubble of reality where they can withdraw from the world, protect their energy, and make sense of unpredictability.**
- **Character examples:** Scrooge from *A Christmas Carol*, Sherlock Holmes from *Sherlock*, Beth Harmon from *The Queen's Gambit*, John Nash from *A Beautiful Mind*, and Mr. Spock from *Star Trek*.

Type Six: The Loyalist

Enneagram Sixes are driven to find safety, either through the protection and support of others or through taking refuge in their own strength. Sixes are compassionate, protective, loyal, trustworthy, and resourceful. They are good at spotting danger and defending against potential threats. However, their excessive focus on safety can lead to a constant underlying sense of anxiety and suspicion toward the unknown.

Sixes make amazing friends and devoted romantic partners—but their caution and worry can sometimes border on pessimism, giving them a glass-half-empty attitude toward life. However, this doesn't come from a place of negativity; it stems from the Six's deep belief that the world is a dangerous place and you must be on your guard in order to stay safe.

- **Basic desire:** To find safety, either through the protection and support of others or through taking refuge in their own strength.
- **Basic fear:** Being without support, security, or guidance.
- **Overarching false belief:** By focusing on potential problems, I can stop them from happening.
- **Greatest vice:** Fear. Sixes often report feeling a deep sense of anxiety toward unknown experiences, causing them to often play out worst-case scenarios in their minds or suspect others' motives. Some Sixes

defend against fear by becoming strong and invincible—leveraging a sort of anti-fear defensiveness to give them a sense of safety.

- **Strengths and weaknesses:** Loyalty, hyper-vigilance, pessimism, reliance on authority.
- **In short, the Six's driving internal conflict is their desire to feel safe and secure by identifying threats, strengthening their defenses, and/or trusting in authority figures in order to avoid the anxiety of fear and to find inner peace.**
- **Character examples:** Paula from *Gaslight*, Marlin from *Finding Nemo*, Natasha Romanoff from *The Avengers*, Peter Parker from *Spider-Man*, and Rapunzel from *Tangled*.

Type Seven: The Enthusiast

Enneagram Sevens are driven to be free, uncontrolled, and spontaneous, keeping themselves excited and occupied in order to distract themselves from suffering. Sevens are optimistic, high-energy, imaginative, and not afraid to plunge headlong into new experiences. They have a good sense of humor and a knack for making the best of a bad situation. However, their excessive focus on escaping emotional pain can lead to chronic stress and fatigue as they frantically try to outrun their sadness.

Though Sevens tend to be stereotyped as happy-go-lucky and optimistic, that doesn't mean they're positive and smiling *all* the time. In fact, when sadness catches up to them, Sevens can spiral into hopelessness, suffocated by the fear that there is no light at the end of the tunnel. However, when it comes to lightening the burden of another, Sevens aren't afraid to embrace those darker, messier emotions. In this way, Sevens can be sensitive empaths who help to bring their loved ones out of the darkness and into the light.

- **Basic desire:** To be free to explore the world around them, unencumbered by structure or plans; to keep themselves excited and occupied in order to distract themselves from suffering.

- **Basic fear:** Being controlled or trapped in emotional pain.
- **Overarching false belief:** If I don't escape negative emotions, I'll be trapped by them.
- **Greatest vice:** Gluttony. This doesn't necessarily mean that Sevens are gluttons for food, drink, or overindulgence. Gluttony, for a Seven, shows up in the compulsive desire for more stimulation that distracts them from the negative feelings they're trying to avoid. If they like something, they want more of it—and enough is never enough.
- **Strengths and weaknesses:** Fun-loving, escapist, imaginative, disorganized.
- **In short, the Seven's driving internal conflict is their desire to be free and happy, enjoying new, exciting adventures in order to keep themselves stimulated and outrun the fear of being trapped in emotional pain.**
- **Character examples:** Tony Stark from *Iron Man*, Ariel from *The Little Mermaid*, Maria from *The Sound of Music*, Tristan from *All Creatures Great and Small*, and Jack Sparrow from *The Pirates of the Caribbean.*

Type Eight: The Challenger

Enneagram Eights are driven to be strong, powerful challengers, keeping themselves emotionally guarded to defend against the abuse or control of others. Eights are fearless, confrontational, rebellious, and courageous. They are good at protecting those who can't protect themselves. However, the more walls they put up to be strong and invulnerable, the more they shut people out.

Out of all the Enneagram types, Eights are the most emotionally guarded. They've learned, likely from suffering abuse or trauma in their past, that no one can be trusted—so they've become as tough, resilient, and defensive as possible to protect themselves and their loved ones from being mistreated or controlled. However, despite their tough exterior, Eights possess an incredible depth of emotion and capacity to love.

- **Basic desire:** To protect themselves and be fully in control of their life and destiny, staying emotionally guarded to defend themselves against others.
- **Basic fear:** Being vulnerable, defenseless, harmed, or controlled by others.
- **Overarching false belief:** Vulnerability is weakness.
- **Greatest vice:** Lust. Eights have an insatiable lust for intensity—they crave stimulation in all its forms, whether that be adrenaline rushes, heart-pounding adventures, fiery spices, or music that rattles your bones. They possess a relentless hunger to experience everything life has to offer and constantly push the limits with absolutely zero apologies. This primal, unapologetic quest to chase intensity can leave them feeling empty and unsatisfied.
- **Strengths and weaknesses:** Fearless, confrontational, possessive, rebellious.
- **In short, the Eight's driving internal conflict is to become strong, powerful, and invulnerable—putting up emotional walls to protect themselves from the control or abuse of others and relying solely on themselves in times of trouble.**
- **Character examples:** Ross Poldark from *Poldark*, Thor from *The Avengers*, John Thornton from *North and South*, Wicked Witch of the West from *The Wizard of Oz*, and Kaz Brekker from *Six of Crows.*

Type Nine: The Peacemaker

Enneagram Nines are driven to find peace and harmony by cultivating a conflict-free environment, satisfying their need to feel comfortable and to avoid strife. Nines are easygoing, levelheaded, agreeable, kind, and obliging. They are good at keeping the peace and being low-maintenance. However, their excessive focus on maintaining harmony can lead to suppressing their wants and neglecting their needs.

Nines tend to live by the motto "Go along to get along." They don't like confrontation or conflict and try to avoid burdening others with their preferences. This can lead them to completely check out of their own desires to the point of letting life happen to them instead of taking control of situations. If left unchecked, the Nine's passivity can lead to severe self-abandonment; they would rather go down with the ship than risk making waves by rocking the boat.

- **Basic desire:** To create harmony in their environment, to avoid conflicts and tension, to preserve things as they are by withdrawing from upsetting emotions.
- **Basic fear:** Loss, separation, conflict, or being cut off from their sources of comfort.
- **Overarching false belief:** Keeping the peace is more important than my needs.
- **Greatest vice:** Sloth. Nines have a dangerous habit of falling asleep to themselves by focusing so much on keeping the peace that they completely abandon their own needs. Sloth isn't about being physically lazy—it's a lack of motivation to take control of their own destiny. These people are often hard workers, but their laziness manifests as severe self-neglect and a stubborn refusal to face necessary discomfort. They would rather let their lives deteriorate than risk the temporary conflict required to make positive changes.
- **Strengths and weaknesses:** Indecisive, harmony-oriented, easygoing, and passive.
- **In short, the Nine's driving internal conflict is to repress their needs and wants in order to cultivate a peaceful, harmonious environment where they can feel safe and unthreatened by conflict.**
- **Character examples:** Luke Skywalker from *Star Wars*, Elinor Dashwood from *Sense and Sensibility*, James Herriot from *All Creatures Great and Small*, Beth March from *Little Women*, and Hiccup from *How to Train Your Dragon.*

Using the Enneagram in Your Writing

Now that we've made a quick study of each Enneagram type, let's see how we can apply these principles of psychology to our writing and make our characters more layered, human, and realistic.

For example, let's say your story's theme is that you are valuable and lovable just as you are. That's the ultimate realization your protagonist is going to have as a result of their journey. The flip-side *false belief* of that truth would be that no one will ever love you as you are. So then, if that's your protagonist's false belief (and their internal conflict centers around them seeking love and appreciation), what would their Enneagram type likely be?

That's right—type Two, the Helper, whose basic desire is to feel loved and appreciated, and whose basic fear is of being unloved or unwanted.

Let's try another. Suppose you're passionate about the theme of finding satisfaction right where you are instead of escaping somewhere to find it—what's your protagonist's Enneagram type? Probably a Seven, driven by an insatiable thirst for new experiences and constant stimulation.

This is not to say that every truth you can think of will have a neat-and-tidy Enneagram type to go with it. But it's a powerful way to discover the themes that are important to you.

I firmly believe that every individual is unique and too complex to fit into one specific box or label. However, personality typing systems like the Enneagram can help us to better understand ourselves and other people—which is one of the most important skills to have if you want to write relatable, flawed characters.

Taking your own Enneagram type into account, what is one powerful truth that you've learned about yourself? Was there a moment in your past when you realized the truth about something?

Consider writing *that* theme into your next story—consider giving your protagonist *your* Enneagram type and writing from your own experience and insight. (If you're not sure what your Enneagram type is, turn to page 5 of your workbook for the link to a free online test and resources for further learning.)

Don't be afraid to branch out and write Enneagram types other than your own. Stepping into the shoes of your characters is part of the fun of writing! So challenge yourself to learn more about your characters' unique inner conflicts, strengths, weaknesses, flaws, and how their perspective of the world differs from the other characters in your story.

As we've seen here, every conflicted character has a false belief unique to them. This belief is their guiding compass in every decision they make throughout the story. But . . . where did their false beliefs come from? To explore this further, we must journey to the past.

Chapter 4

BACKSTORY: THE ORIGIN OF ALL FALSE BELIEFS

By this point, you have your protagonist, their physical appearance, personality, desires, fears—but you're still not sure why they are the way they are.

Why do they believe what they believe?

Why do they want what they want?

Just because they need to?

Not a good enough reason.

Every character in your story should be there because *they* need to be there—because *they* have goals and agendas of their own. Not because the *plot* needs them to be there.

So, why exactly does your character need to be in this story? Because they have a particular goal they're trying to accomplish? Why?

If you're unsure, it's probably because you haven't figured out their core false belief—or where it came from.

OUR PAST MAKES US WHO WE ARE TODAY

Renowned author and scientist Dr. Joe Dispenza's research reveals that 95 percent of who we are is programmed by the time we reach age 35. This programming is brought about by repeated moods, attitudes, habits, and beliefs.

"A habit is a redundant set of automatic, unconscious thoughts, behaviors, and emotions acquired through repetition," according to Dr. Dispenza.[5] He suggests that every person's brain is a record of their past, which functions like a computer program, unconsciously guiding us through our daily lives according to a pattern of set emotions and behaviors.

If past experiences have caused us suffering or pain, that rush of emotion they caused is always dormant in the back of our minds. Trauma, then, could be defined as unresolved stress from a perceived threat that has long since ceased to be a threat but still elicits the same emotional response. Or, as Dr. Dispenza put it, "Every time [a person] recalls the event, they're producing the same chemistry in their brain and their body as if the event is occurring."

When confronted with a traumatic event, we respond by building emotional defenses to protect ourselves from future threats. Just like touching a hot stove will create a memory of physical pain (Ouch, that's hot!) and train our *body* to be more careful in the future, psychological pain forges a similar neural pathway, telling our *mind* to be more careful in the future.

Every individual builds up these protective walls in different ways—aggression, avoidance, denial, perfectionism, or escapism. The instinct of self-preservation extends to the emotional brain, protecting us if something like this happens to us again. Your subconscious cannot differentiate between reality and something imagined or remembered, which means that every time we relive a traumatic event from the past, the same neurons fire as if that event is happening to us now—and our coping mechanism (and false belief) is always within reach to ward off the threat.

That being said, your character is no different. Something happened in their past to make them believe this lie about themselves and the world . . . and this false belief served as a fortress to protect them from ever being hurt like that again.

You don't write a backstory for the sake of seeing what happened in your character's past. You write a backstory to make sense of who your character is in the present.

Now, I know what you're thinking:

Abbie, you keep telling me that my protagonist needs a false belief, but how do I identify it? How do I convey this false belief to the reader without coming right out and saying what it is?

Great question. To make this process easy and enjoyable, I'm going to guide you through the **10-step formula** that I use every time I create a character's false belief. It's a proven method, and you'll love how simple it is. (Flip to page 6 in your workbook to follow along with this template.)

Step 1: Find Your Story's Central Theme

You may have multiple themes for your story, but I'm referring to the central overarching theme or the big idea that excites you the most. I like to call it the story's *why*. Write it down in as few words as possible. This will be the realization your protagonist experiences at the climax of your story. (We'll dive deeper into your story's climax later on.)

If you haven't figured out your story's truth yet, grab a sheet of paper and freewrite your answers to these questions:

- **What change would you like to see in the world?**
- **What is one mindset shift that has positively impacted your life?**
- **What is a truth that's important to you? One that you want to scream from the rooftops?**

Don't strive for coherence; just be yourself. Allow your heart to overflow onto the page with the ideas that matter most to you. Take your time. The theme is the core of your story. It's what keeps you motivated to show up for your story, day after day. I speak from experience when I say: If your story doesn't matter to you . . . you're not going to stick with it for very long.

Step 2: Flip This Truth to Make It a Lie

This may feel sinister and counterproductive, but I want you to take that beautiful theme you just wrote down—the idea you're excited about, the truth you want to shout from the rooftops—and flip it upside down. What is the exact *opposite* of this truth? This will be your protagonist's false belief.

For example, let's say the theme of my story is "You are valuable and loved." My protagonist's false belief might be "I'm not valuable or loved." Or if the theme is "True success comes from nurturing relationships with your loved ones," perhaps my protagonist's lie will be "I won't be successful unless I have money and fame."

Now, let's take it one step further.

Step 3: Ask Yourself: What Could Have Happened in My Character's Past to Make Them Believe Such a Thing?

Now we're getting into the good stuff—sifting through your character's past to uncover the root of this lie. Where did it all begin? It doesn't have to be a major, catastrophic moment; it could be a small but continuous affirmation of the lie from authority figures. Remember, a persistent drip can wear a hole through a rock over time.

This isn't just a personal belief, like "My friend hurt me, so I won't have friends anymore"—it's a belief about the world. It's not that *you* can't trust people; it's that *people* can't be trusted. Do you see the difference? The false belief differs from the fear because it has become so ingrained that it has altered the way you see the world—not just how you see yourself. We make every decision (consciously or unconsciously) based on core beliefs like this one.

The younger we are when we adopt a belief, the more firmly we hold on to it. Cognitive science shows that before age seven, a child's brain is still in downloading mode, in a hypnotic brainwave state, accepting whatever they are told as truth and forming firm beliefs without the help of rational thought. (Side note: Be careful what you say to small children.)

However, this doesn't have to occur during your character's childhood. It could be at any point in their life where something significant happened and dramatically altered their worldview. Some characters—especially older ones—may have false beliefs from early- or midlife events that happened to them.

Step 4: Write That Backstory Scene for Your Character

This is the most powerful way to probe your character's inner world. In clear detail, describe the event in their past that led them to believe this lie. Yes, even from the perspective of a seven-year-old, if that's how old your character was at the time.

Write this moment from your character's perspective—showing how they went into the scene believing one thing and came out the other side believing something entirely different. This will provide insight into their inner conflict like nothing else. And, believe it or not, it will help you tremendously when it comes time to write the present-day version of this character. Who knows? You might use this scene in your novel as a flashback or to establish their false belief.

Step 5: Outline (or Write) Other Scenes from the Character's Past That Cemented This False Belief as Truth

I love writing backstories for my characters—so I take every opportunity I can to explore their complicated past. However, if you're not ready to write three or four more pivotal-moment scenes from your character's backstory—that's perfectly fine. I suggest at least going halfway and *outlining* those scenes.

Brainstorm additional moments from your character's past where something challenged their hard-won false belief, giving them the opportunity to step out and discover the truth . . . but instead, they clung to their lie. These moments of choosing the lie are crucial because they illustrate how your character's false belief grew stronger and evolved into the compass they follow today.

Step 6: Ask Yourself: How Is My Character Dissatisfied with Their Life *Today* Because They Believe This Lie So Firmly?

The real reason we can't get no satisfaction is that we believe a lie about ourselves and the world. Whether it's a lie of "I won't be happy until I'm rich and famous" or "I won't be happy until I find true love," it's all the same: dissatisfaction stemming from a belief that isn't true.

Our mindset is the only barrier between us and happiness. In the end, all your character wants is to find happiness. It's what we all want. But we each have different definitions of happiness, which brings us to . . .

Step 7: Ask Yourself: What Does My Character Think Will Make Them Happy, Based on Their False Belief?

Our definition of happiness varies and is deeply connected to our personal beliefs. This holds true for your characters as well. Long before your inciting incident pushes your character outside their comfort zone, they have a preconceived notion of what they believe will bring them true happiness and contentment. Whether it's something they've subconsciously clung to for years or something they deliberately had to puzzle out, they know—beyond the shadow of a doubt—what will make them happy.

However, *we* know it won't *truly* bring them happiness. Why? Because it's founded on a lie—the very opposite of the truth you want to shout from the rooftops.

So that's why you need to ask your character (as if they were lying on a therapist's couch next to you), "What do you want? What needs to happen for you to be happy?" Wait for their answer. It must be specific. Even if they say something like money or true love—that's still too conceptual! It doesn't provide them with an active *goal* to pursue. Keep asking your character, "What does your ideal life look like?" until they give you a concrete answer. (Yes, I talk to my characters like this. They are the best kind of imaginary friends.)

Step 8: Ask Yourself: What Steps Could My Character Now Take to Actively Pursue This Goal?

This is where the story will kick off with the inciting incident, a topic we will explore in depth in a few chapters. However, the most important part is the seven steps we just went over. We've laid the groundwork for your character's inner conflict, and this alone will make your story stronger than most books on the market right now.

I'll soon show you how all this conflict serves as the rocket fuel to launch your story off the ground. But first, ask yourself: What steps could my character now take to pursue their goal? Your answer is going to become your character's mission throughout the story. So consider the external conflict you have planned—the stuff that's going to happen *to* your protagonist—and how it matters now, in light of all this juicy internal conflict.

Step 9: Ask Yourself: How Has My Character's Fear Stopped Them from Taking This Action Already?

Going back to your character's fear will solidify their reason for not yet taking action to change their life before now. Otherwise, we won't understand the significance of the inciting incident and how it's about to shake up your protagonist's world in a new way.

The therapy session isn't over yet! Sit your character back down on that sofa and ask them, "Why don't you do what you think would make you happy? What's stopping you? What are you so afraid of? *Why* are you afraid of it?" Grill them. If they give an answer like "It's illegal," or "My parents don't want me to," or "I shouldn't," then you haven't yet dug down to their true fear.

Don't worry—if your protagonist's fear isn't yet obvious to you (fictional characters can be stubborn creatures), give it some time and thought. Keep asking yourself why. You might be surprised how quickly you uncover the specific fear lurking in your protagonist's subconscious.

Remember: We aren't born with these specific fears. When a baby takes its first breath, it only has two fears: loud noises and the danger of falling. Their lack of experience leaves them incapable of feeling any fear other than what they already know. So, how do we acquire our fears? Through life experience. When I was a small child, I stuck my fingers inside the VHS player (remember those?) and couldn't pull them out again. It hurt, and I cried. I learned: *Don't stick your fingers inside the VHS player.* These things happen throughout our lives, just on deeper, more emotional levels. For example, *my friend betrayed me by sharing my secrets with other people—I can never trust anyone again.* And that's how a fear stops your protagonist dead in their tracks.

Step 10: Clarify the Motive, the Goal, and the Plot

Here's my favorite part, because this is where the magic happens. Go back through your answers to all the previous questions and pull out **1)** the lie they started believing at a young age, **2)** what they think will bring them true happiness, and **3)** the steps they will take to make this dream a reality.

Write each one down as:

- **The Motive**
- **The Goal**
- **The Plot**

This is what I meant when I discussed plot-driven stories versus character-driven stories back in chapter 1. If the plot alone drives the story, that's all it is.

- **PLOT**

But if you begin with your character's false belief, which gives them a motive and a goal, and then allow that to drive the plot . . . suddenly, you have a much stronger and more emotionally engaging formula.

FALSE BELIEF → Drives the MOTIVE → Drives the GOAL → Drives the PLOT

This is the gold that you discover when you take the time to keep asking yourself:

Why? Why? *Why?*

Many writers don't do this. They come up with a plot and perhaps a goal for the character, but often, there's no motive or false belief *behind* the goal . . . and that's why the story falls flat. That's why it loses your interest, and you put the book down halfway through.

I don't know about you, but I want my stories to be memorable. I want them to impact my readers and spark new thoughts, ideas, and discussions. All of that starts with your character's false belief.

Turn to page 6 of your workbook to walk through this ten-step process with your protagonist.

ASK YOURSELF:

- What is my character's biggest false belief, and what is the flip-side truth they will realize in their aha moment at the end of the story?
- Was there a specific moment in my character's past when they started to believe this lie?
- What protective walls did my character build up in the wake of this event to guard themselves from emotional pain?
- How is my character dissatisfied with their life today because they believe this lie so firmly?
- What do they think will bring them satisfaction based on their false belief?

Backstory's Evil Twin: Biography

Here's a conundrum many writers struggle with: *If I write the entire backstory of my character from birth to the present moment, won't that be boring?* The answer is yes. And nobody will want to read it. So, without the help of your strict subconscious mind, how do you know which bits of information to include and which bits of information to leave out? The answer is simple: If it doesn't affect the present day, leave it in the past.

Your goal is to only write down the things that have contributed to shaping this character into who they are today and how they see the world—not to write a detailed account of everything that's ever happened to them. We don't need to know your protagonist's entire life history to make sense of the decisions they're making today. That's why biography and backstory are two very different things.

By filling in the necessary details of your character's backstory, you'll build a realistic foundation for who they are. You'll make them feel human and flawed and *real.* Remember, our beliefs are the hidden framework behind everything we say and do. All motivation—and active decisions—originate from our beliefs. They are the inner compass we all live by.

Want to see these techniques in action? In the next section, we'll return to *The Otherworld* and look at these principles in practice.

STRATEGIES IN ACTION: THEME AND FALSE BELIEF

Let's go back to building characters for my novel *The Otherworld*. Now that we've sorted out our three main characters' fatal flaws and internal conflict, it's time to develop their backstories in greater detail.

Let's look at the question prompts from the previous chapter and apply them to our protagonist, Orca Monroe.

What is Orca's biggest false belief, and what is the flip-side truth that she will realize in her aha moment?
Orca has grown up believing that she is not strong enough to face the harsh realities of the mainland—aka "the Otherworld." In the end, she will see that she has always been strong enough to overcome any challenge and to face the unknown.

Was there a specific moment in Orca's past when she started to believe this lie?
At a young age, her father instilled the idea that Orca didn't belong in the Otherworld because he wanted to protect Orca and keep her close. He always told her that the mainland was more or less a dangerous place full of unkind people. Really, he feared losing Orca in the way he had lost her mother. (Orca suspects this but doesn't know the entire story.) There wasn't so much a specific moment in Orca's past when she came to adopt this belief—more like a thousand little moments and reaffirmations.

What protective walls did Orca build up in the wake of this event to guard herself from emotional pain?
Her father's warnings couldn't dampen Orca's curiosity and longing to explore the Otherworld. Still, she built up protective walls by becoming resilient and strong. A voracious reader and quick learner, Orca learned how to live off the land, grow and preserve food, make plant medicines, and tend to injuries and illnesses, and thus became a very capable and resourceful person.

But even after all this effort, she hasn't been able to prove herself worthy in her father's eyes to go to the mainland. She thinks she needs to prove to her father that she has what it takes to handle herself out there in the world.

How is Orca dissatisfied with her life today because she believes this lie so firmly? And what does she think will bring her satisfaction, based on her false belief?

Orca's dissatisfaction with life at the lighthouse stems from feeling she's missing out, and being trapped on a remote island has afflicted her with an incurable wanderlust. All she wants is to go to the mainland and see what the "real world" is like. She sees her eighteenth birthday as the perfect opportunity to ask her father to take her to the mainland—thinking he'll give in this time, now that she's an adult.

Fantastic! We've added layers and depth to Orca's character while staying true to her internal conflict. Despite her soft flower-child appearance and sweet, optimistic personality, she also has a tough side—which will serve a purpose in this story and will serve the plot as well.

We have two other main characters in this book—Adam and Jack—so let's take a quick look at their fatal flaws and where they came from:

Jack Stevenson has spent his whole life in his older brother's shadow, which has led to his present inferiority complex. He feels like he will never measure up to Adam. On a deeper level, his desire to be his own man fuels his escapism. He has always admired Adam and wants to emulate him, but he falls short in his own estimation and feels like a disappointment.

Adam Stevenson was convinced from a young age that perfection was the only path to goodness. Being ten years older than Jack, he became a sort of third parent at a young age and learned to put his needs last to help his parents, to whom he feels he owes everything. Helping others makes him feel good about himself and reaffirms the false belief that what he wants doesn't matter.

Perfect! We've crafted a solid internal conflict for Adam and Jack and raised personal stakes. We know what's on the line for the two brothers and why it matters, and we've connected all of it back to their fatal flaws.

Now it's your turn. Take the false-belief questionnaire and use it to dig deeper into your character's backstory, uncovering their past struggles and connecting the dots to their present-day conflict.

You can repeat this process with your other characters, but don't fret too much about writing more than the one essential backstory scene for each one. Also, there's no need to give them super-complex inner conflicts. Side characters are in a unique position to add multiple layers of depth and truth to your story, but you'll want to save your most important big idea for your main character.

In the following chapter, we're going to explore side characters—how to give them complex inner conflicts and effortlessly integrate them into your story.

Chapter 5

MEET YOUR SIDE CHARACTERS

Let's discuss side characters: what they are, why they matter, and how to integrate them into your story without slowing down the momentum or losing your reader's interest.

First things first. Ask yourself: Does this side character directly engage with or impact the main character?

This is the golden rule for making your side characters meaningful (and, by extension, making your readers care about them). Remember, our brains are processing 11 million bits of information per second. Our subconscious mind handles most of that activity and allows us to recognize only the most essential information consciously, so we can take care of those need-to-know things.

Since we've used this psychological principle to help us connect to the protagonist, the same rules apply to side characters. We must see the direct connection a side character has to the protagonist in order to care about them.

Here's a good way to visualize this connection:

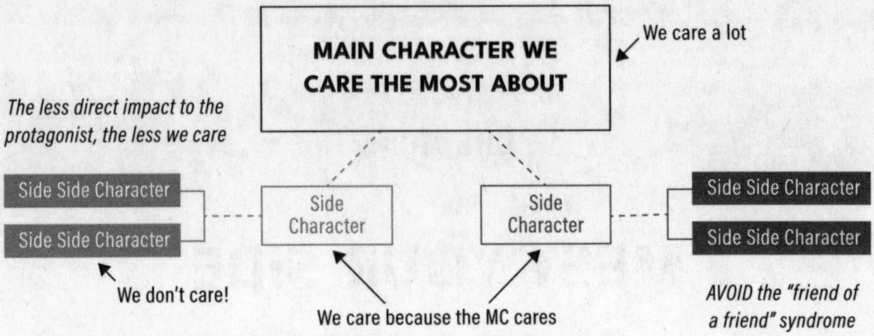

As you can see in this figure, the main character is at the center of the story—they are the one we care about the most. They have direct connections to the side characters (maybe their mom, dad, love interest, enemy, etc.). But once we drift to the side side character, we lose that direct connection. I call this the "friend of a friend" syndrome. The less direct impact on the protagonist, the less we care.

But wait, Abbie . . . what if I'm writing a story with a huge cast of characters and no one character is the main protagonist?

Don't worry—we'll address that question later in the chapter on subplots. Crafting a large cast is a whole other ball game, and different rules come into play. For now, let's concentrate on developing side characters in a story featuring one or two distinct protagonists.

Make your side characters *active heroes* in their own stories.

Remember when we talked about passive characters versus active characters? Active characters always make decisions in response to the conflict they face. They are pursuing a goal and running from a deep-seated fear. These same rules apply for your side characters.

To develop relatable side characters, we must start by figuring out their internal conflict.

THE CRAI METHOD

My favorite way to sketch my side characters and their conflicts is to use what I call the CRAI method—breaking down each subplot into four categories:

1. **Character:** Who is this character? What is their internal conflict and their reasons for appearing in the story when they do?
2. **Role:** What is the character's role in the story? How are they connected to the main character?
3. **Agenda:** What is this character's agenda? What is the goal they are actively pursuing throughout the story?
4. **Impact:** How is the character going to impact the protagonist's story? Will their actions have a direct impact on the main conflict?

The answers to these questions will help you establish the foundation for these side characters.

Another template I often use to outline my side characters' arc (or journey of change) looks like this:

Example

[Character A], [relation to protagonist], mistakenly believes [their false belief] and [takes action to accomplish their goal while avoiding their fear]. In the end, they ultimately come to realize [the truth] and impact the protagonist's story through [the consequences].

You can explore this further and outline a whole character profile for each side character, but depending on how much screen time you'll give them, a complete character profile might not be necessary.

Let's case study a classic story to see what this CRAI method looks like in action.

Side Character Case Study: Jane Bennet from *Pride and Prejudice*

As we all (hopefully) know, *Pride and Prejudice* tells the story of Elizabeth Bennet, a headstrong and independent young woman who defies social conventions and believes that only the deepest love will persuade her to marry. Elizabeth clashes with the proud and wealthy Mr. Darcy, whose snobbery leaves a bad impression on her and forces her to confront some challenging interpersonal struggles. The novel primarily revolves around Elizabeth's journey to find love and her transformation because of that journey, but many side characters support her character arc.

Jane Bennet is one of these vital side characters. As Elizabeth's closest sister and confidante, Jane is on a quest to make a good match and find true love. Her biggest flaw is that she "never thinks ill of anyone." When she falls in love with the wealthy and charming Mr. Bingley, their relationship raises red flags for Bingley's friend Mr. Darcy, who heartlessly separates the couple and disrupts his own relationship with Elizabeth. It's not until Darcy mends the rift between Jane and Bingley that he can prove he has transformed his character, which helps Jane achieve her goal and grow as she learns that some people cannot be trusted. Ultimately, she forgives Bingley for his mistake, and they both live happily ever after.

As you can see from this brief description, Jane's character significantly impacts the main character. Without the separation of Jane and Bingley, we wouldn't have the conflict between Elizabeth and Darcy—and without Darcy's choice to help reunite Jane and Bingley, we wouldn't witness the transformative journey of Darcy's character.

This story perfectly illustrates how side characters can influence the main conflict. As you're probably recognizing, a side character is not used to simply fill a role—but rather to pursue a goal, and to have a significant impact on the main character.

STRATEGIES IN ACTION: CREATING SIDE CHARACTERS

Let's revisit *The Otherworld* and look at who the side characters are and their influence on the protagonist's story. During my development process for this book, I knew I wanted to follow a small group of characters—just my protagonist, the two male leads, and their immediate family. I consider these characters to be major because they significantly affect the protagonist's decision-making and internal conflict.

- Orca's father, Lawrence
- Orca's mother, Miriam
- Adam and Jack's father, Mr. Stevenson
- Adam and Jack's mother, Mrs. Stevenson

To illustrate what this side character development process looks like, I'm going to combine the CRAI method with my character profile. Since these characters will not have as much focus and screen time as my three main characters, I won't delve as deeply into their backstories and the childhood events that shaped them into who they are today. We will develop their false beliefs, personalities, and motives, but only to the extent that it supports the protagonist's story.

Let's walk through this process with the main instigator of the story's conflict, Orca's father.

Character's name: Lawrence Monroe
Relation to protagonist: Orca's father, the only person she's ever known.
Impact on story: The main reason Orca can't visit the mainland is that her father keeps her on the island for her own "protection."
Physical description: An angular face, lean build, gray eyes, dark hair, and a scruffy salt-and-pepper beard.

Age: 50

Personality: Enneagram 6. Quiet, responsible, and loyal, he strives for order and harmony. Though he has a good heart, he's also suspicious of others and needs to feel safe. He is reliable, hardworking, and trustworthy. An excellent troubleshooter, he foresees problems and prepares for the worst as a way to protect himself against the unpredictable pain of life.

Backstory: Working as a lightkeeper on a remote island has always been the ideal situation for Lawrence, who is more of a reclusive philosopher than a corporate ladder-climber. When he was thirty years old, he married Orca's mother, the effervescent and rebellious Miriam, ten years younger than he. Opposites attract, but in Lawrence and Miriam's case, they didn't last. Once the romantic luster of life in a lighthouse on a secluded island wore off, Miriam grew bored with her life and longed for more. Two years after Orca was born, she decided she couldn't live like this anymore and divorced Lawrence, moving to Seattle to start a new life. Lawrence was heartbroken over the loss of Miriam and vowed to protect Orca from that kind of pain and to keep her close as a way of shielding himself from it, too.

What is his greatest fear? Losing Orca to the mainland, just like he lost his wife. Being left alone, abandoned, without a sense of purpose or someone to share life with.

What is his fatal flaw/false belief, and where did it come from? That isolation is the only way to have a peaceful life free of pain and loss. But what he doesn't realize is that as long as you love someone, there is no such thing as a life free of pain and loss. He needs to learn that love is worth risking everything for.

What is his agenda? To keep Orca safe from harm and free from any pain. Because of this, he has never told her the true story of what happened to Miriam. Instead, he has told her that her mother died when she was two years old. Orca has grown up without knowing who her mother is. Lawrence withheld the truth from Orca because he didn't want it to change the way she saw herself, fearing she might believe she wasn't worth staying for. But more than that, he doesn't want to lose Orca—it would be like losing Miriam all over again, and a heartbreak like that would destroy him.

How is Lawrence going to impact the protagonist's story? Because Lawrence is determined to keep Orca safe from the Otherworld, he stokes his daughter's compulsion to break free from her bubble. The tighter he holds on to her, the more she wants to escape. When Adam and Jack Stevenson disrupt her perfect world of protection, she is primed to step out of her comfort zone.

Fantastic! See how figuring out your side characters' conflicts and beliefs can help add depth and complexity to your main character's story?

With Orca and her father, he is keeping a major secret from her (that her mother is still alive) to protect her from the pain of loss. Since we are only experiencing Orca's point of view (POV), we will not know this secret until Orca discovers it much later. We can use revelations like this as wonderful plot-twist moments that change the game for the protagonist and provide us with a new perspective on everything we have seen so far.

Turn to page 10 of your companion workbook, and use this character profile to flesh out your side characters—but remember, you don't need to answer all these prompts for every character in your book. I recommend spending the most time on those characters who have a significant supporting presence in your story. If they only appear for a scene or two, you won't have much time to explore their internal conflict, so there's no need to build their backstory, beliefs, and goals. Every character should have a reason for appearing in your story, but we don't need to know all their motivations for being the way they are.

Once you have your cast of characters and their conflicts sorted out, we'll move on to one last crucial aspect of writing relatable characters: relationship dynamics (the magic ingredient that makes your characters feel like they've been here all along, and the reader is just now joining in on their lives).

RELATIONSHIP DYNAMICS

To create realistic characters, it is imperative to go beyond their internal conflicts and explore the relationships they have with one another.

For instance, if I'm writing two characters who are sisters, I need to understand more than their individual internal conflicts—I need to know how they feel about each other. Perhaps one sister is protective of the other, or perhaps one sister is jealous of the other. Those are two very different conflicts that would completely change the way I'd write the story.

Relationships between your characters take your story to the next level. They make your reader feel like they've just stepped into a world of real people who have been coexisting for a long time and have a complicated history of emotional struggles.

Relationships and Conflicts

Ask yourself the following about each character with whom the protagonist has a direct relationship. The character could be a friend, family member, love interest, mentor, or enemy.

> **In a few words, describe the protagonist's relationship with this other character.** Use your favorite story examples as references. I often use example stories because they help me better understand the complexities of a relationship.

> **What are the points of conflict in their relationship?** These could include conflicts of beliefs, perspectives, standards, or something more obvious, like class differences or age gaps.

What do they agree on? What do they disagree on? Beliefs! Beliefs! I cannot stop talking about beliefs! These make your characters feel like real people. Defining these agreements and disagreements early on helps fuel the fire of future conflicts and arguments.

Do they keep any secrets from each other? If so, what and why? If I need to make a character more layered and interesting, I give them a secret.

How did they meet, and how long have they known each other? This question might not apply if they meet during the story.

How will their relationship change throughout the story? Remember, the journey of change is what satisfies the reader and makes them feel like they've been on an emotional journey with these characters, watching them struggle, face challenges, and transform. That's what makes a story memorable.

You don't need to fill out this questionnaire for every relationship in your book—only use it for the characters who receive the most attention and whose relationships will change significantly throughout the story. Alternatively, you can write a brief paragraph describing the relationship dynamic between two characters and how their conflicts with each other lead to inner change.

STRATEGIES IN ACTION: RELATIONSHIP DYNAMICS

Let's examine some relationships in my novel *The Otherworld*, to see how these dynamics unfold when we toss all our conflicted characters into the same world.

Family Relationships

Orca and Papa:

On a beautiful, remote island, Orca and her father share a unique bond, relying solely on one another. Their love runs deep, but Papa's protectiveness sometimes feels overwhelming. This comes from a place of caring, as he fears losing Orca just as he lost his wife. This overprotection leads to a strained relationship as Orca matures and yearns for freedom.

Adam and Jack:

With a ten-year age gap between them, Adam has always been like a second father to his younger brother, Jack, who is more reckless and restless. Although the two brothers share a close bond and Jack looks up to Adam, he also sees Adam as the perfect goal he aspires to become. When Orca enters the picture, Jack perceives it as a competition between him and Adam—a rivalry to win her heart. Adam and Jack are very close and would do anything for each other, but Orca introduces a new conflict into their relationship, complicating matters and causing a rift between them.

Romantic Relationships

Orca and Adam:

Orca nurses Adam back to health after his plane crashes near her island. Having never met a young man before, she finds herself falling head over heels for him almost instantly. Adam feels an unexplainable connection to Orca, but he wrestles with doubts, thinking Orca might only be infatuated with him. He worries their whirlwind romance is only possible while stranded on the island, and when the time comes to part, he tries to accept it. Yet, Orca is determined to be with Adam, no matter the challenges.

Jack and Orca:

This story unfolds like a classic love triangle, but Jack's feelings are unrequited. Orca treasures him as a close friend, and Jack misinterprets some of her affectionate behavior as a sign that she shares his feelings. Meanwhile, Adam tries to maintain his distance, allowing Orca to experience being with Jack to see how strong their bond is. However, Jack can't help but turn it into a competition, which causes tension and results in disastrous outcomes.

Relationships = Conflict . . . and Conflict = Story

As we explore the dynamics of these relationships in greater depth, can you see how the lines between character and plot are starting to blur? Characters' beliefs shape their decisions, and their decisions guide the story.

Life doesn't create conflict—people do. So, as you craft these complex relationships between your characters, notice how their relationships and inner conflict lead to choices that spark external conflict (the plot).

We're on our way to crafting a captivating story featuring a cast of conflicted and wonderfully flawed characters. Now that we clearly understand who each character is, what they desire, what they fear, and how they will impact the protagonist's journey, we can move on to crafting the external conflict (the plot) that will send them all on a transformative adventure together.

Turn to page 12 of your workbook to craft the relationship dynamics between your characters.

KEY TAKEAWAYS

- Your side characters aren't here because the plot needs them to be. They're here because *they* need to be. Give each side character a role, an agenda, and an impact on the story.
- Avoid the "friend of a friend" syndrome by giving each character unique significance to the protagonist and showing us how their direct connection impacts the overarching conflict of the story.
- Life doesn't create conflict—people do. Craft complex relationships between your characters, and notice how their relationships lead to choices that spark external conflict.

ASK YOURSELF:

- **Who is this side character?** What is their internal conflict and their reason for appearing in the story when they do?
- **What is this character's role in the story?** How are they connected to the main character?
- **What is this character's agenda?** What is the goal they are actively pursuing throughout the story?
- **How is this character going to impact the protagonist's story?** Will their actions have a direct impact on the main conflict?

Part 2

BUILDING A BRILLIANT PLOT

"Give me six hours to chop down a tree and I will spend the first four sharpening the axe."
—Abraham Lincoln

Chapter 6

STORY STRUCTURE (AND WHY IT MATTERS)

I can hear that little voice in your head right now: *Oh no. She's going to say I need to use story structure to write a good book!* But don't fret; I promise I won't turn this process into a boring drudgery of mapping out 3x5 cards or using geometric calculations or phases of the moon to dictate how your story should unfold.

However, story structure is crucial for a reason. Regardless of whether you're a plotter, pantser, or something in between, it's essential to have a clear sense of direction to understand where your characters are going on this journey and how they will transform.

Remember, impactful stories revolve around character change. That's why I'm going to share a character-based three-act story structure with you. Unlike other story structures, this storytelling method is grounded in psychologically proven principles, ensuring our primary focus remains on the characters and why what's happening matters to them. Step by step, we'll walk through each story beat, and I'll show you, with examples, why this method aligns with brain science.

What Is a Story Beat?

The easiest way to think of story beats is like pins on a map. The journey is the whole road map, but the story beats are those big, pivotal moments along the route—places where something significant happens to your characters and they have to make an active decision that could alter the direction the plot takes next.

Outlining your story *before* you write it will not only strengthen your characters, plot, and themes, it will also assist you during the editing process—because you won't need to majorly rework the story's structure. I know that plotting and outlining can feel quite overwhelming—especially if you're used to flying by the seat of your pants. I'm a hardcore plotter myself, but every writer is different and must discover their own unique process. Here's the best part: You can plot as little or as much as you desire.

Your outline should serve you, not the other way around

This is why many writers hate outlining or adhering to a story structure; they feel trapped by their plot, unable to color outside the lines.

I've been there. When I first started writing, I was a pantser. I didn't outline or use story structure; I just let my imagination run wild and take me wherever it wanted to go. But then I realized I was looking at story structure all wrong.

I viewed story structure as a box I couldn't escape once I trapped myself inside. This is a common misconception. Your story's outline should not restrict you; it should empower you to explore new ideas because you can see your entire story from a thousand-foot view.

So don't worry; this story structure won't trap you or limit your creativity. Instead, it will free you and give you a road map to make your characters' journeys shine. And the best part? You'll fly through your first draft with ease and clarity, knowing your story's framework is solid. This means you'll never have to do major rewrites to the plot structure itself. As Abraham Lincoln allegedly once said, "Give me six hours to chop down a tree and I will spend the first four sharpening the axe." Think of story structure like sharpening your axe. It might seem like extra work now, but it's going to save you a tremendous amount of time later.

There are five reasons why I love this story structure and use it for all my books:

1. **It's tried and true.** Thousands of successful, bestselling, history-making stories have used this story structure, including timeless classics such as *Pride and Prejudice*, *A Christmas Carol*, *Star Wars*, *Romeo and Juliet*, *The Lion King*, *To Kill a Mockingbird*, *The Wizard of Oz*, and many others.
2. **It's all about the protagonist's internal journey.** Most story structures focus too much on the external events (the plot) without delving into why these events matter to the characters. This is the primary reason I love this story structure—because it flows seamlessly with the external conflict, and at every story beat, we are unearthing the reason why everything that happens *matters* to the characters.
3. **It's flexible.** Once you understand the science behind each story beat, you can tailor this structure to suit your story's specific needs. You don't need the inciting incident to occur precisely 15 pages in, or the plot twist to unfold at the 50 percent mark. You can adjust this structure to serve your unique story, and it will hold up.
4. **It's supported by brain science.** At each story beat, we'll test these techniques against established psychological principles to ensure we stimulate our readers' curiosity and keep them turning pages late into the night.
5. **It works for every genre.** Whether you're crafting a cozy small-town rom-com or an epic space opera, this structure transcends the limitations of genre and brings your story to life in a way that resonates with the human heart—no matter how big or small the scope of your fictional world.

THE CHARACTER-DRIVEN THREE-ACT STORY STRUCTURE AT A GLANCE

As I keep emphasizing, story structure is all about character transformation—also known as a character arc. Every compelling character arc follows a journey of change. Usually, the flow goes something like this:

> The main character is plagued by internal conflict; they desire something, but their fear is standing in their way. An event occurs that pushes them outside their comfort zone and sets them on the path of their journey, where they will encounter obstacles and plot twists while pursuing their false belief-based goal. Eventually, a disaster strikes, leaving them hopeless and confronting their greatest fear. They must overcome this fear and crush their false belief to continue to the climax and face their biggest challenge yet, thus proving their transformation.

Now, if you're thinking, *Abbie, did you just read my notes when I wasn't looking? How did you know how my story was going to unfold?* Don't worry. I didn't sneak into your computer and read your notes. But if the above paragraph feels familiar, that's a promising sign! It means you have a character-driven, conflict-ridden story simmering to life in your imagination, and all you need now is the method to deliver that story to your readers.

Here's how the story structure breaks down:

Act 1: The Setup
Act 2: The Conflict
Act 3: The Resolution

Within each act, we have story beats—fourteen in total.

In Act 1, we have . . .

- The hook
- The inciting incident
- The impossible choice
- First pinch point

In Act 2, we raise the stakes with . . .

- The pre-midpoint reactionary protagonist
- Game-changing midpoint
- Post-midpoint action protagonist
- Second pinch point

In Act 3, we wrap up with . . .

- The supposed victory
- Disaster
- Dark moment (or temptation)
- The aha moment
- Climactic confrontation
- Victory/resolution

If you feel overwhelmed by this whole outline, don't worry. I'm going to break this down step by step, story beat by story beat. We'll explore how our characters' conflicts and decisions weave effortlessly into this structure. Because they are the agents of change (not punching bags for the plot), the story will practically write itself through the momentum of their every choice.

I know you're excited to dive in, so let's get right into it with Act 1, beat one: the hook.

WRITING A POWERFUL OPENING ACT

Chapter 7

WRITING A STRONG OPENING HOOK

Let's start from the beginning: Act 1, beat one, known as the hook.

The hook is exactly what it sounds like: the first thing that's going to capture a total stranger's attention and pull them into the first pages or first chapter of your book. It could be something exciting, mysterious, funny, embarrassing, or unexpected—anything that makes us sit up and pay attention.

Every story needs a hook—whether it's a novel, a movie, a TV series, or a short story. The question isn't "Do I need a hook?" The question is "How the heck do I write a hook that grabs my readers by the throat and pulls them into my story?"

The first few pages of a story are the scariest and most difficult pages you will ever write. If you're intimidated by writing that first chapter . . . you're not alone. Every single writer on Earth is right here with you.

But just because it's scary doesn't mean it's impossible. You are more than capable of writing a captivating opening hook for your story. I believe that your story's hook is lying dormant just beneath the surface, and all you need to do is ask yourself the right questions to uncover it.

THE SCIENCE OF CAPTURING YOUR READER'S ATTENTION

Here's another reason why the hook is so important. Scientific research shows that the average adult attention span is now only five minutes, down from twelve minutes just a decade ago. As we discussed in chapter 1, your brain processes 11 million bits of information every second. However, the subconscious mind filters out most of this and allows you to focus on only forty bits of information that are important enough to warrant your attention.

Conclusion? Something must *matter* to us for our brains to pay attention to it.

So this becomes our mission: Make the reader empathize with the protagonist ASAP by showing what matters most to them.

But, Abbie! My book is good! My characters are well-developed! They have strong internal conflicts, false beliefs, and goals to pursue throughout the story. I love this story, and I know my readers will, too, if they give it a chance!

Yes, all of that is true. However, if you don't make your readers care within the first five minutes—if you don't pull them in with that crucial hook—they won't experience how awesome this story is (because they won't make it past the first few pages).

Remember how we talked about character and plot, and how you must find a balance between them to make your story unputdownable? That's what you need to remember when crafting your story's hook. It doesn't matter how much action, peril, or exciting stuff you include in the first chapter. Your only goal with the hook is to *make them care.*

THE HOOK

Introduce Your Protagonist's Internal Conflict

The hook is rooted in internal conflict—a tug-of-war between desire and fear. Contrary to popular belief, the internal conflict begins long before the plot shows up to disrupt your protagonist's life. In fact, that conflict has been simmering just beneath the surface all along—otherwise, your plot wouldn't matter. See, external conflict (the plot) is all about what happens, but internal conflict (the story) is about why it matters.

BRAINSTORM PROMPT:

How does the protagonist's fear stand in the way of what they believe will bring them happiness?

When your story begins, your protagonist is a disaster waiting to happen. Why? Because they harbor a deeply rooted fear and false belief that has been hiding in their psyche for a long time—and it will only take a spark to make them act upon their fear and false belief and turn their life upside down.

When a story first opens, your reader is unfamiliar with your protagonist's inner conflict. That's why it's so vital to introduce them to this secret struggle as quickly as possible. But how exactly do we *show* our character's inner conflict without coming right out and explaining it?

The Five-Minute Rule

What if I told you there's a secret ingredient at the beginning of every classic Disney movie that tugs at your heartstrings and makes you empathize with the characters within just five minutes of the film?

Want to guess what that secret ingredient is?

That's right: internal conflict.

For example, imagine *Frozen* without the musical number "Do You Want to Build a Snowman?" We would have no backstory to understand why Anna feels lonely and isolated, why her sister, Elsa, shuts her out, and the false beliefs that hinder them both. Without their backstory, we wouldn't grasp why anything matters to these characters, which provides insight into their unique internal conflict. Other classic Disney films follow this same fundamental structure of a character-establisher song; think "Reflection" from *Mulan* or "Part of

Your World" from *The Little Mermaid*. This is a strategic storytelling mechanism Disney writers use to reveal the protagonist's innermost conflict (desires versus fears), thus setting the stage for the external conflict they'll face as the plot unfolds.

If you've already completed your protagonist profile, you should now have a good grasp of their internal conflicts and the challenges they will face throughout the story. You might also identify ways to reveal their desires and fears within the first five minutes of your story.

The Power of a Story Question and Micro-Goal

If you want to capture your reader's interest on page 1, that doesn't mean you have to get their attention with something loud and flashy.

A dramatic explosion, a character running for their life, or waking up from a traumatic nightmare *can* work in some cases—but most of the time, these devices feel like gimmicks designed to make the reader look. It's like shouting, "Hey! Pay attention! This is important!" But if you don't show us *why* it's important to the characters, we have no reason to care about it.

A cliché hook shouts; a powerful hook *whispers*. Simply put, a hook can be intriguing and juicy and captivating without being a life-or-death scenario. So instead of falling back on melodrama, lead with a clear story question.

Establishing a story question is infinitely more powerful than kicking things off with an overly dramatic hook. A story question shows us immediately that something is at stake for the main character, and it matters to them because they have a personal involvement in what's going on.

For example, let's look at two story hooks—one that leads with a flashy, dramatic plot-driven event, and one that leads with a story question.

Overly Dramatic:

The bomb went off at precisely 6:03 AM, ripping through the quiet street and sending a fireball into the sky. Sarah jolted awake in her bed three blocks away, heart pounding. She stumbled to the window, the sky already glowing orange. Somewhere, sirens began to wail.

Why It Doesn't Work:
Sure, it's loud and dramatic—but . . . who's Sarah? Why should we care that she woke up? Is this a normal Tuesday in her life or a life-altering event? Without context or emotional connection, the explosion is just noise. There's no character motivation, no stakes, and no reason for the reader to care what happens next. It's spectacle without substance.

Story Question:
At 6:03 AM, the letter slid under Sarah's door. No signature, no return address—just five words in stark black ink: *I know what you did.* Sarah read it five times, her heart lodged in her throat as dark spots crowded her vision. Downstairs, a door thudded shut. The messenger had vanished without a trace, but someone knew. And they wanted Sarah to *know* they knew.

Why It Works:
There's an immediate *story question*: What did Sarah do? Who sent the letter? What's at stake for her if someone finds out? It's subtle but loaded with tension. It matters to *Sarah,* and therefore it matters to *us.* No explosions, no cheap thrills—just juicy personal stakes that make the reader lean in and ask, *Why?*

You can build upon this sense of urgency by giving your protagonist a very clear micro-goal. Even something simple like "I just need to catch this bus" makes us feel like this character is actively moving toward something that matters to them. When we understand the importance of accomplishing this micro-goal, we want to read on to see if they're actually going to pull it off.

We're playing with suspense here—giving the reader a sense that *something* is about to disrupt the protagonist's normal life. By introducing a micro-goal on page 1, we get a glimpse of what this character cares about and why they need to accomplish this goal.

Study Your Favorite Stories

As I mentioned before, I love studying stories. It's one of my favorite things to do: hunker down with a cup of tea, a notebook, and one of my favorite movies or TV shows—then psychoanalyze it minute by minute, figuring out why this story is so darn good. I would highly recommend this to any writer. Compile a list of your favorite stories, and then watch or read the first five minutes to analyze what hooks your attention.

One of my favorite stories—and a great example of a strong opening hook—is the BBC drama *Poldark,* based on the novels by Winston Graham. Here are my notes on what happens in the first five minutes of *Poldark,* season one, episode one:

> Virginia, 1780. Ross Poldark, a British soldier, is in the woods with his comrades when they are ambushed by American soldiers. The attack kills many, injuring Ross and rendering him unconscious. He dreams about his love, Elizabeth, back home in England; the two are very close. Fast-forward two years later, and Ross returns home to Cornwall. On the carriage ride home, he learns his father died while he was away, and his estate is in ruins and debt. The news hits Ross hard, but he keeps his cool and goes to see his uncle. At his uncle's house, he is thrilled to see Elizabeth but heartbroken to discover that she is engaged to his cousin Francis—assuming he had died in the war. Ross's entire life has flipped upside down.

What a strong opening! When I first started this show, I knew nothing about it, but those first few minutes grabbed my attention, and to this day, *Poldark* is one of those TV series I go back to watch again and again.

STORY CASE STUDIES: THE OPENING HOOK

Let's look at a few more story examples of what these strategies look like in action:

- ***A Christmas Carol***: Our main character, Scrooge, is a tightfisted old miser who loves money and hates Christmas—but his struggle within is even more complex than it appears. It's clear that he was once a good-hearted person, but time has worn him down into a jaded version of himself. We see him turning his back on the world around him—but most importantly, on the kindness and goodness in the world.

- ***Pride and Prejudice***: Our main character, Elizabeth Bennet, is one of five sisters facing financial ruin if they don't marry well before their father dies. The stakes are high, but Elizabeth is free-spirited and before her time. Only the deepest love will persuade her into matrimony. On page 1, we see Elizabeth's mother, Mrs. Bennet, thrilled by the prospect of marrying off one of her daughters to the wealthy young man who has just moved into town.

- ***The Chronicles of Narnia: The Lion, the Witch, and the Wardrobe***: During the London bombings of 1941, the Pevensie siblings—Peter, Susan, Edmund, and Lucy—evacuate to the countryside to stay with the mysterious Professor Kirk. The move challenges each sibling in different ways, as they struggle to get along with each other in this new and unfamiliar setting.

KEY TAKEAWAYS

- The hook makes internal conflict clear and compelling. If we can get a glimpse of the protagonist's internal struggle on page 1, we immediately connect with them.
- Your hook can be an external event, but you must quickly show the reader why it matters to the characters. (Remember: Plot is the fist; internal conflict is the punch.)
- Lead with a story question rather than a flashy, dramatic hook. You want to spark your reader's curiosity, not trick them with an attention-grabbing gimmick.
- Avoid world building in the hook. Save it for when it *matters* to the characters. Nobody cares about a world, however unique, until we know why this world matters to the characters.

ASK YOURSELF:

- How can I show my audience in the first five minutes why what's happening matters to my protagonist, given their desire, fear, and false belief?
- How can I give a sense of suspense so the reader is aware that something is about to disrupt my protagonist's normal life?

Now it's your turn. Turn to page 14 of your companion workbook and fill out the Hook section for your story outline.

Chapter 8

THE INCITING INCIDENT

Ah, one of the most familiar literary terms: the inciting incident. In this chapter, we will explore what the inciting incident is, what many people mistakenly think it is, and how to write an inciting incident that draws readers into your story and guarantees their attention for the rest of the story.

First, let's determine what an inciting incident is *not.* If you do a quick internet search for "What is an inciting incident?," you might encounter results like this one:

> *Definition: interrupts the peace and balance of the situation; and one or more of the characters come into conflict with an outside force, himself, or another character. Questions to ask yourself: What is the first important thing that pulls me into the story?*

What is important? Who is it important to? Me? The character? The world? The government? And why is it important? This question is too vague and detached from any emotional root to help us craft an inciting incident that matters.

Here's another:

The inciting incident is how you get characters to do something. It's the doorway through which they can't return.

Why do we need to get the characters to do something? Do what? Why does it matter to them? Why does it matter to me? Why should I care about what they do?

One more:

Inciting incident: When the conflict is introduced. The inciting incident sets the plot in motion. Example: Justin injures himself.

Why should I care about Justin injuring himself? Was Justin about to do something important? Does being injured mean he can't achieve what he wants? Or does it allow him to avoid something he was fearful of? Why does it matter?

The inciting incident must do more than simply set the plot in motion. It's the driving force that triggers your protagonist's whole roller-coaster ride (also known as their character arc). The inciting incident is a plot point that forces the protagonist out of their comfort zone and into action. That's why it's often referred to as the call to adventure.

This character arc is based on inner transformation—and that's what gives the plot meaning. Here's a diagram that shows the different phases of this character arc, which we will explore in more depth throughout this book.

The line graph on the next page illustrates what a positive character arc looks like, aligned with the three-act story structure. By positive character arc, I mean the arc for a protagonist who shines as a positive role model—someone readers can root for and admire.

Now, I'm not suggesting that you make your protagonist a flawless angel from start to finish. Of course not! Not only would that be absurdly unrealistic (and not relatable), but it would defeat the entire purpose of transformation. A perfect character doesn't face internal conflicts or moral dilemmas. An enlightened character cannot experience an aha moment—and cannot deliver a

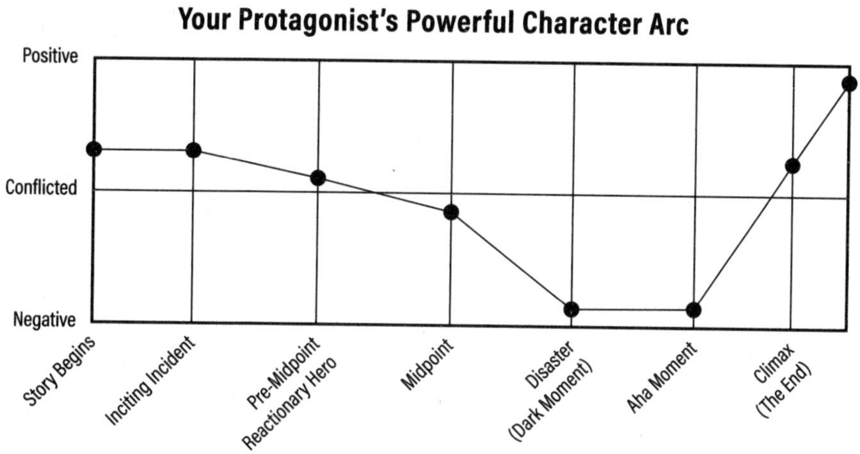

powerful message to your reader. That's why it's vital to give your protagonist a character arc that includes ups and downs.

Let's take a moment to analyze this line graph. The spectrum from positive to negative represents how *okay* or *not okay* your protagonist is at a given moment in the story. If things are positive, they're fine; if things are negative, they're in trouble. The middle ground indicates a conflicted state—where your character makes tough decisions and struggles with their false belief.

On page 1, your protagonist is a conflicted person. That's why I placed their starting point on the line graph just north of the conflicted state. They're probably a good person at heart, but they have some serious issues and false beliefs that are making their lives complicated. When your inciting incident shows up to push them outside their comfort zone, they're primed to make a fear-based decision.

When you see this line slowly declining within the timeline of your story, it doesn't mean your protagonist is becoming a bad person. It simply means that, as the story progresses, they're getting themselves in more trouble.

Why? Because they harbor a deep-seated fear and false belief that has been hidden in their psyche for a long time—and until they experience their aha moment, they will make all their decisions based on this misconception. It serves as their guiding compass. It influences their every decision—and, incidentally, lands them in more conflict than they know what to do with.

At the very start of your story, your protagonist hasn't stepped outside their comfort zone. As brain studies have shown again and again, our subconscious wants to keep us comfortable *far* more than it wants us to be happy—especially when happiness appears to be outside the comfort zone we're used to. In other words, we remain in this bubble because we're afraid of what lies beyond it. Within our comfort zone, we feel safe, but outside the zone, we feel vulnerable.

That's why you need the inciting incident to push your protagonist outside their comfort zone. This gets the ball rolling and sets the story in motion.

The inciting incident typically appears around the 10–15 percent mark of a story. However, to be frank, I prefer to cut that number in half and make the inciting incident happen as soon as possible. (Let's be real. We live in the age of microwaves, elevators, and the internet . . . goldfish have longer attention spans than most people.)

Let's study the description of the inciting incident, as seen in my three-act story structure template (available in your companion workbook on page 15).

INCITING INCIDENT

Protagonist Is Pushed Outside Their Comfort Zone

Your inciting incident doesn't have to be a grand, epic call to adventure; it just needs to push your protagonist outside their comfort zone and force them to face their fears. A conflict arises—something the protagonist must face head-on. It's that simple. Don't overcomplicate it, as many writers do. If you understand why the inciting incident matters to the protagonist and you allow them to react as any normal person would (running for cover because of fear), then congratulations. You nailed it.

Right away, you've raised the stakes. By pushing your character outside their comfort zone, you're forcing them into a direct confrontation with fear and the possibility of pain. All humans instinctively try to avoid fear and pain, and this makes our brains hungry to engage with stories where a fictional character experiences them. Why? Because not only can we escape our reality and go on an adventure without ever leaving our couch (and without actually enduring

BRAINSTORM PROMPT:

Why does this inciting incident matter to my protagonist? How does it push them outside their comfort zone? What internal conflict will arise for my protagonist in the wake of the inciting incident?

that pain ourselves), but we can also learn from this character's experience and navigate our own world with greater emotional intelligence.

Our brain is designed to avoid pain. When confronted with a choice between two different kinds of pain, we will always opt for the less painful option. We will explore this further when we analyze the first plot point in the next chapter. But for now, let's look at a few pitfalls to avoid with the inciting incident.

Why Do or Die Is Not Strong Enough

You might think that the highest stakes a person could face would be do or die—aka survival. If the character doesn't respond to the inciting incident, they risk losing their life. However, as we discussed in part 1, you need to go beyond a character's basic survival mode reaction when confronting perilous external circumstances. The reader needs to know why this dangerous situation is uniquely challenging to your protagonist because of their desires, fears, and false beliefs.

The adrenaline of survival mode may fire our mirror neurons for a while, but it quickly loses its luster when no internal conflict is present. Yes, survival is an entire genre in itself. But what separates good survival stories from mediocre ones is a unique and compelling *internal conflict*—getting to know the characters *apart* from the disastrous situation they find themselves in.

Let's say you want to write a survival story about a character trapped on an island with man-eating sloths. While the sloths might technically serve as antagonists, they lack a specific motive or internal conflict. Therefore, the challenge of surviving the sloth attacks must compel your character to confront their deeper fears and misconceptions. Their fear can't be simply "I'm afraid of getting eaten by a sloth"; likewise, their desire can't simply be "survive the sloths." Internal conflict must go deeper than the immediate threat.

It must be based on something your protagonist dealt with long before they arrived at Sloth Island. The sloth problem merely forces them into the ring to confront this deep-seated fear.

Of course, your protagonist has the primal instinct of self-preservation. They want to survive. But what would survival mean to them? What will they do *if* they survive? Why is it so important that they survive?

In other words, *Why does it matter?*

If you don't know the answer to that question, your reader won't know the answer, either.

STORY CASE STUDIES: INCITING INCIDENTS THAT WORK

- **In *A Christmas Carol*,** Scrooge is visited by the ghost of Jacob Marley, his deceased business partner, who warns him to change his selfish ways and tells him about the three ghosts of Christmas that are coming to pay him a visit. Shaken, yet still his cynical old self, Scrooge reacts to this inciting incident by staying up for the foretold ghost—just to prove the whole thing wrong.

- **In *Pride and Prejudice*,** the Bennet family attends the Meryton ball, where they meet the charming Mr. Bingley and his rather aloof friend, Mr. Darcy, who proves himself to be proud and uncivil. While Mrs. Bennet is keen to set Bingley up with one of her daughters, Lizzy overhears Darcy making an insulting remark about her. Hurt by his scathing criticism and put off by his arrogance, she vows to loathe Darcy for all eternity.

- **In *The Chronicles of Narnia: The Lion, the Witch, and the Wardrobe*,** Lucy stumbles upon a wardrobe in Professor Kirk's house that opens to a magical land called Narnia. She explores the magical winter wood, where she meets a faun named Tumnus, who introduces her to the conflict of the world. He explains that the evil White Witch has cast a shadow over Narnia, plunging the land into an endless winter. Meanwhile, Edmund enters Narnia and meets the White Witch, who tries to lure him into a trap by promising him the throne of a king (and Turkish delight) in exchange for bringing his siblings to her.

KEY TAKEAWAYS

- The inciting incident isn't merely the first big thing that happens; it is the external event that pushes your protagonist out of their comfort zone. Knowing the protagonist and grasping their comfort zone is the only thing that makes us see the significance of the inciting incident.
- Since you've already introduced us to the protagonist's inner conflict in the hook, the reader can now understand how particularly painful this situation will be for them to navigate.
- Remember that your protagonist's false belief has been quietly growing stronger for a long time, meaning that when something pushes them outside their comfort zone, they're primed to make a decision based on that belief.

ASK YOURSELF:

- Why does this inciting incident matter to my protagonist? How does it push them outside their comfort zone?
- What internal conflict will arise for my protagonist in the wake of the inciting incident?

Now it's your turn. Flip to page 15 of your companion workbook and fill out the Inciting Incident section for your story outline.

STRATEGIES IN ACTION: THE HOOK AND INCITING INCIDENT

To illustrate what these principles look like in action, let's dissect the three-act story structure of *The Otherworld*. It's time to delve into the actual plot, starting with the first two beats: the hook and the inciting incident.

The Hook

As we explored in the previous chapter, the most important thing the hook must do is connect us with the protagonist's internal conflict—what they want and what they're afraid of. In *The Otherworld*, we have three main characters, but we only meet Orca and Jack at the beginning of the story, so we'll craft separate hooks for these two characters.

How can we open the story in such a way that will make the reader instantly empathize with the characters and relate to their struggle? Let's begin with our protagonist, Orca Monroe.

How can we show the audience in the first five minutes why what's happening matters to Orca, given her desire, fear, and false belief? How can we create suspense so the reader knows something big is about to disrupt Orca's everyday life?

We first meet Orca in a prologue, which unveils some of her backstory—how she grew up at the lighthouse and has known nothing but her small island and her devoted father. The hook shows us how Orca has always longed to visit the mainland, which she affectionately calls the "Otherworld," but her father won't allow it.

In chapter 1, we meet Orca on the morning of her eighteenth birthday, bursting with excitement because she thinks this is the day her father will finally say yes to her adventure in the Otherworld. Instead, he dashes Orca's hopes when he tells her he must travel to the mainland to meet the Coast Guard and that she won't be coming with him.

Orca is deeply disappointed and complains to her dog, Lucius, her only friend in the world. Through a one-sided conversation with Lucius, we see how desperately Orca longs for the Otherworld and just how lonely her life is.

Inciting Incident

Later that day, as Orca strolls along the beach, she stumbles upon a mysterious backpack that has washed ashore. Curiosity piqued, she opens it and discovers some personal items, including a ringing cell phone she can't answer in time. Realizing that this backpack has come from the Otherworld, Orca keeps it a secret from her father. Excited and nervous, she figures out how to call back the number and meets Jack, the younger brother of a pilot who crashed his plane near her island a few days earlier. Frantic with worry and desperation, Jack pleads with Orca to help him search for his missing brother. Pushed outside her comfort zone but also thrilled by the prospect of a new adventure, Orca eagerly agrees to help Jack in his search, all while keeping it a secret from her overprotective father.

Perfect! The stakes are set. We've crafted the setup for Orca's story to be set in motion—and ensured that each external event matters to her, considering her internal conflict. It's even better that we've added a ticking clock (three days until Orca's father returns) to up the ante even more and give a sense of urgency.

Let's leave Orca and Jack there for now. After being pushed outside her comfort zone and thrust into the main conflict, it's time for her to make an impossible choice.

Chapter 9

THE IMPOSSIBLE CHOICE

Many writers may refer to this moment in the three-act story structure as the first plot point, but I prefer to call it the impossible choice. This will be the first significant decision your protagonist makes in response to the inciting incident, which then determines what will happen next in your story.

Let's take a closer look at this plot point from the three-act story structure template.

IMPOSSIBLE CHOICE

Protagonist Makes a Decision Which Determines What Happens Next

Your protagonist is a conflicted individual, torn between desire and fear. When the inciting incident steps in and shoves them outside their comfort zone, their fear takes over, and they respond based on their false belief, which sets up more obstacles that will unfold over the rest of the book. The human brain makes decisions by avoiding the most pain—so what will be the least painful choice in the long run for your protagonist? Most likely, to venture into the unknown and take risks as they try to accomplish what they have always wanted.

BRAINSTORM PROMPT:

How will my protagonist react to the inciting incident, given their fear and false belief about the world? What decision will they make now to avoid the most pain (and achieve their desires while steering clear of the thing they're afraid of)?

If the hook was the setup for the inciting incident, the inciting incident is the setup for the impossible choice.

Here's what happens in your brain when you're forced to step outside your comfort zone. Your internal defense mechanisms go on autopilot, sending a very clear SOS to your conscious mind:

Something pushed me outside my comfort zone! I'm scared! I can either venture into unknown territory and try to accomplish my goal, or I can retreat to the shadows and endure the pain of not getting the thing I desire.

That, in essence, is the impossible choice. It needs to be a choice; otherwise, your protagonist becomes a passive character, and the plot starts making decisions *for* them. In order to create intrigue and suspense for the reader, we need to see how the protagonist agonizes over their options and ultimately makes their *own* decision.

Before we explore what this means for your characters, we first need to understand the psychology behind how people make decisions—big ones, like "What should I do with my life?" and small ones, such as "What time do I need to get out of bed tomorrow?"

Pain vs. Pain

What if I told you that every choice you've ever made was with the intention of avoiding the most pain? I know it's hard to believe—you've faced some tough challenges in life. But even when you thought you were choosing the more difficult or painful path, you actually weren't. You were merely rewriting the definition of pain in your mind.

Let's use an example we're all familiar with: waking up in the morning. Imagine you have to get up super early because you need to catch a flight leaving at 7:00 AM. It takes you an hour to get ready, thirty minutes to drive to the airport, and you like to be through security at least an hour before your plane takes off. So, you set your alarm for 4:30. This gives you two and a half hours—all the time you need, right?

Well. When that alarm rings at 4:30 . . . you don't want to get up. Your bed feels so soft, warm, and comfortable. It's still dark outside, and you're *so tired.* The thought of getting up is painful. So you hit the snooze button.

You don't need an hour to get ready anyway, right? The pain of giving yourself less time to get ready is not as painful as the idea of getting out of bed right now. So, you sleep longer. And then . . . the alarm rings again.

You *still* don't want to get up because it's *still* dark outside and you're tired. So, you hit the snooze button again. You don't need that much time to reach your gate anyway, right? Last time, the flight was delayed, and you sat there for like twenty extra minutes! You can sleep some more.

So you do. Because the pain of rushing through the airport to find your gate is still less painful than the pain of getting out of bed right now. But then . . . the alarm rings again. It's 5:00 AM.

You now have only two hours to get ready, drive to the airport, go through security, find your gate, and board your plane. Thirty minutes less than you needed. Which means you're running late, and you could miss your flight.

This time, you shut off your alarm and leap out of bed, hurrying to get ready. Why? Because the pain of missing your flight is greater than the pain of getting out of bed.

But here's the thing: The feeling of getting out of bed didn't change. Only your *perception* of it did.

You started comparing it to the pain of something *more* significant: missing your flight. Whether you were aware of it or not, you were comparing the pain of getting out of bed with the pain of other unpleasant situations, such as hurrying to get ready and sprinting through the airport terminal to find your gate. Finally, a tipping point arrived when you recognized that the pain of not getting out of bed outweighed the pain of getting out of bed. So, you got out of bed.

Most of this comparison decision-making happens backstage in the subconscious mind. We usually don't even notice it.

Your Brain Is Wired to Avoid Pain

It seems like a simple formula: If we avoid pain, we avoid danger and we live longer. This primal self-preservation instinct often works in our favor. However, it doesn't *always* do so because each time we give in to this instinct, it reinforces the brain's default path-of-least-resistance program—which makes it harder to switch gears when we need to. For example, to conquer procrastination, you must take the steering wheel and say, *I will do the harder thing, because I know it's the right thing to do.*

But here's the unsettling part: Your survivalist brain literally won't allow you to choose the more painful thing. So instead, using your conscious mind, you rewrite the definition of pain so you can override your subconscious survival instinct.

As psychology researchers Dr. Sirois and Dr. Pychyl explain, "Procrastination may function as an emotion-regulation strategy . . . tasks are avoided in order to manage the short-term discomfort they produce, despite the long-term negative consequences."[6] In other words, your brain perceives the hard thing as a threat and redirects you toward comfort. But if you rewrite the definition of pain, you can override this response.

For example, let's look at the most rigorous military training program in the world: the path to becoming a United States Navy SEAL. When you consider the punishing physical and mental challenges that a person must undergo to become a Navy SEAL, it doesn't seem humanly possible.

The most infamous part of SEAL training is called Hell Week—it's designed to push a person beyond their limits and test their endurance under extreme physical pain and exhaustion. Forget about getting out of bed at 4:30 to catch your flight—recruits are only allowed *four hours of sleep* for the entire week. (It's called hell for a reason.)

This raises an important question: Why would anyone want to put themselves through actual hell to become a Navy SEAL?

Aha! The answer lies within the question: Why? Everyone who completes

Navy SEAL training knows the answer before entering the program. They must understand why they are motivated to become a SEAL. If they don't know and embrace their personal reasons for taking on the challenge, they won't make it through the first phase of training.

If you consciously intend to put yourself through hell, you must have a clear reason why the outcome matters so much. You must have a desire so motivating, it becomes *more painful* to ring the bell and quit the training than it is to go through Hell Week.

So yes, you *can* choose to do the harder thing, if you redefine pain on your own terms. You have to make the harder thing less painful by anticipating the grim outcome of *not* doing the harder thing.

So What Does This Mean for Your Story?

As your story unfolds, your characters will encounter one choice after another, and each one will be more difficult. They will have opportunities to pursue their desires, but they will also confront their fears and risk losing what is most precious to them. If you want your characters to seem real, they must confront this relatable struggle of pain versus pain. When the inciting incident pushes them outside their comfort zone, they are presented with options:

> **Option #1: Stay inside my comfort zone and risk *never* achieving what I desire.**
>
> **OR:**
>
> **Option #2: Venture into the unknown and accomplish my goal while still avoiding my fear.**

As your protagonist weighs their options, they realize that the least painful option in the long run is to venture into the unknown and risk some danger . . . if they want to achieve what they have always desired. Even though this option might seem uncomfortable, or even terrifying, it's more rewarding in the long run.

So, with the impossible choice, they make a tough decision and move forward. Because we, the readers, understand the significance of this choice, our curiosity is instantly engaged. We're interested, even desperate, to find out *what's going to happen next.*

Curiosity Is an Addictive Drug

Brain studies show that curiosity activates the part of the brain that processes pleasure and rewards, prompting the release of dopamine, the feel-good hormone. Taking certain addictive drugs also has this effect, which means that forcing a character to make an impossible choice will hook your readers. They'll become addicted to your story, unable to turn the pages fast enough. This is because the human brain gets high on watching other people make decisions. Don't believe me? Just think of all the television shows that force participants to make choices, from game shows like *Jeopardy* and *The Price is Right* to real estate programs like *Love It or List It.* This principle of psychology proves itself true again and again, as audiences enjoy the suspense of observing how someone else will make a decision.

Neurons that fire together wire together, which means that your reader's brain is engaged in an endless cycle of question, curiosity, answer, reward, dopamine—rinse and repeat. This chemical reaction tells your reader, *Hey, you're enjoying this! You should keep reading this book! You should stay up all night and finish it because you need to know how it ends!*

It all starts with giving your characters tough choices.

STORY CASE STUDIES: THE IMPOSSIBLE CHOICE

- **In *A Christmas Carol*,** Scrooge is visited by the first spirit (the Ghost of Christmas Past), who brings him back to his childhood and young adult life. Scrooge is shown several pivotal moments from his past, such as the Christmas when his fiancée, Belle, releases him from their engagement, feeling she has been replaced by his growing obsession with wealth. This impossible choice isn't a decision Scrooge makes at the present moment, but rather a series of decisions he made throughout his life, which the spirit forces him to revisit. The choice, in retrospect, still seems impossible: continue pursuing wealth, knowing it will lead to loneliness and regret, or choose to value relationships over riches.

- **In *Pride and Prejudice*,** Elizabeth Bennet faces an impossible choice when her dreadful cousin Mr. Collins proposes marriage. While his offer promises financial security for her and her family, marrying him would mean a life tethered to a man she neither respects nor loves. Elizabeth's decision to reject Mr. Collins proves her commitment to her inner compass over societal expectations.

- **In *The Chronicles of Narnia: The Lion, the Witch, and the Wardrobe*,** the Pevensie siblings learn they have a special destiny to fulfill by ending the White Witch's reign. The choice between returning to the safety of their own world or fighting to save Narnia becomes even more challenging when Edmund secretly betrays his siblings by sneaking off to the White Witch's castle. This turn of events not only draws Peter, Susan, and Lucy deeper into the conflict but also forces them to take on the responsibility of rescuing Edmund and fulfilling the prophecy.

You're probably thinking of a hundred other fantastic examples of this impossible choice right now. As I always say, "Story is the best teacher of story." So try this exercise! Write down the impossible choices from some of *your* favorite stories, and study the many ways this story beat can unfold.

KEY TAKEAWAYS

- The first plot point is the moment your protagonist makes the impossible choice, which determines what happens next. Remember to show your reader why this impossible choice is so challenging for *your* protagonist to face, because of their desire, fear, and false belief.
- The human brain makes decisions based on avoiding pain. Even when you think you're doing the harder thing, you are actually just rewriting the definition of pain in your mind. There comes a tipping point when inaction is more painful than action (even if the action is extremely painful).
- That being said, your protagonist is primed to make a decision based on their false belief. They can stay inside their comfort zone and risk *never* getting what they desire, *or* they can venture into the unknown and accomplish their goal while still avoiding their fear. Upon consideration and redefining pain in their mind, your protagonist will realize that the second option is more rewarding in the long run.

ASK YOURSELF:

- How is my protagonist going to react to the inciting incident, given their fear and false belief about the world?
- What decision are they going to make now to avoid the most pain (and get what they want while steering clear of the thing they're afraid of)?

Now it's your turn. Flip to page 16 of your companion workbook and fill out the Impossible Choice section for your story outline.

STRATEGIES IN ACTION: IMPOSSIBLE CHOICE

Let's return to *The Otherworld* and explore the impossible choice our protagonist, Orca, is left facing after she experiences the inciting incident.

How will Orca react to the inciting incident, given her fear and false belief about the world? What decision will Orca make now to avoid the most pain (and take a step toward achieving her desires while steering clear of the thing she's afraid of)?

Orca's Impossible Choice

Orca is driven by her dream of exploring the Otherworld, and to achieve this, she must prove to her father she is strong and capable enough to handle its "dangers and darkness." She believes that her mission to rescue Adam is the perfect opportunity to fulfill her desire. She hopes that if she can shoulder the responsibility of helping this missing pilot, her determination and resilience will impress her father, and he'll let her visit the mainland. This active goal is what sets the plot in motion for Orca and drives her every decision going forward.

See what we just did there? By outlining the possibilities (comfort zone versus danger zone) and connecting them to the characters' deepest desires and fears, we can show how these characters make *active* decisions and inadvertently set up the conflict for the rest of the story.

This is what I mean when I say that your characters need to be the agents of change, rather than mere punching bags that get knocked around by the plot. While Orca will take some hits from external conflict, it is essential for her to make choices in response to the challenges thrown at her, just as she is doing here. That makes her an active, not passive, protagonist.

Now that we've sorted out the first few story beats of *The Otherworld*, it's time to move into Act 2. However, before we transition, let's conclude Act 1 by discussing one final story beat: the first pinch point.

Chapter 10

THE FIRST PINCH POINT

We're getting very close to wrapping up our discussion of Act 1. However, before we move on to Act 2, there's one last plot point to explore: the pinch point. This is where we have the opportunity to use foreshadowing and suspense to give the reader a sense that something is going to disrupt the protagonist's plan.

This disruptive force might be another character, like a villain or antagonist, or it might be something less tangible, like the protagonist's greatest false belief.

What's an Antagonist?

An antagonist is any character in your story who acts as a force of opposition to the protagonist. Not all antagonists are villains—sometimes they can be good characters, just morally confused or doing bad things for seemingly good reasons. Many stories also leverage nonhuman antagonistic forces such as nature, society, animals, monsters, aliens, and plagues.

What is a pinch point? Essentially, it's our first clear opportunity to hint at the opposition looming on the horizon. There are two pinch points in the three-act story structure. One appears at the very end of Act 1 (where we are now), and the other appears at the end of Act 2, before the big climax.

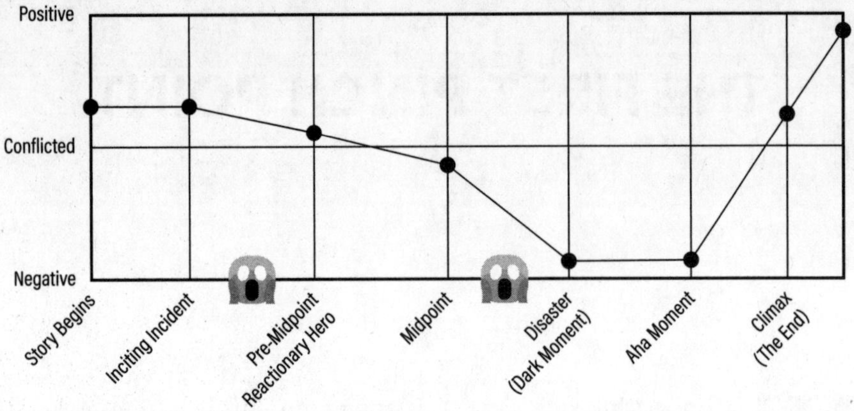

FIRST PINCH POINT

Opposition or Antagonistic Force Looms in the Distance

You can have a pinch point even if you don't have an antagonist in your story. It doesn't have to be a villain, or even a person—it just needs to be something that will come back to cause trouble later. Perhaps your protagonist's greatest opposition is a dark, magical force; a natural disaster; society; or even the protagonist's own false belief.

BRAINSTORM PROMPT:

What opposition or antagonistic force will my protagonist have to confront later? How can I convey to the reader that it is already looming in the distance?

The Three Types of Suspense

In storytelling, it is universally recognized that there are three types of suspense:

1. **Vicarious suspense:** The audience is in on what's about to happen, but the character has no idea.
2. **Shared suspense:** The audience and the character are both in on it.
3. **Direct suspense:** The audience is worried about something unrelated to a character—such as a visual jump scare in a movie.

Vicarious suspense and shared suspense are the most relevant options for us now. Both forms of suspense are excellent, gut-gripping choices—and there is a time and place for each. In fact, I recommend using both: vicarious suspense for the first pinch point and shared suspense for the second pinch point.

Studies in media psychology have proven that vicarious suspense in film elicits the strongest emotional reaction from viewers.[7] The reason for this is simple: Audiences enjoy feeling smart. We derive a lot of satisfaction from knowing something that a character does not, moderate satisfaction from knowing something alongside the character, and dissatisfaction (or detachment) when the character knows something we do not or seems smarter than we are.

Remember the last time you played a trivia game with friends? You know that *one* person who got almost all the answers right? After the game, they gloated over their victory, smug in their superior knowledge, while you silently wished you could wring their neck.

So it goes for characters in a story. When you know things the character doesn't, it's like being the person winning at trivia with their eyes closed. Dopamine fires all over your brain because you feel smarter than everyone else. But when the *character* knows things you don't, *they* become that know-it-all person—and their omnipotence can be downright frustrating. That's why the reader's brain responds best to vicarious suspense.

As Alfred Hitchcock once famously explained in his interview with François Truffaut, suspense comes not from a jump scare of surprise, but from the audience's dread of impending doom: "The audience is longing to warn the characters on the screen: 'You shouldn't be talking about such trivial matters. There is a bomb beneath you, and it is about to explode!'"[8]

Surprise doesn't last long, but suspense can make your story unputdownable. Knowing what will happen, or at least what *might* happen, is far more emotionally engaging than being clueless alongside the character. And guess what—it doesn't make your story predictable!

Consider the movies you've seen about a tragic historical event—like *Titanic* or *Pearl Harbor*. Chances are you knew, before watching these films, what they were about. You weren't surprised when the *Titanic* sank or when Pearl Harbor was attacked. There was a lack of surprise, and yet, there was suspense—fueling the audience's curiosity about the choices the characters had to make in response to terrifying events. This just goes to show that what makes a story memorable is not so much what happens, but how what happens affects characters and spurs them into action.

There is no one-size-fits-all recipe for a good pinch point, but here are some of your options:

- **Full Vicarious:** where the reader sees something the protagonist can't see (i.e., a villain scheming behind closed doors).
- **Subtle Clues:** where you sprinkle in clues to the future conflict hidden in plain sight (i.e., the protagonist can see the clues but has no idea what they mean).
- **Shared Suspense:** where the protagonist learns about the conflict they're going to face head-on later (and they already feel intimidated).

There are more styles of pinch points, but these three are the most common. The first two are my personal favorites, so let's explore them further by looking at story examples that feature these pinch points.

STORY CASE STUDIES: PINCH POINTS

- **In *A Christmas Carol*,** the first pinch point appears between the visitation of the Ghost of Christmas Past and the Ghost of Christmas Present. This interlude is filled with Scrooge's contemplation and growing unease. He is visibly shaken by the revelations of his past—his isolation, the end of his engagement to Belle, and his increasing cold-heartedness. Scrooge is beginning to realize the full extent of what his greed has cost him, not just in personal relationships but also in his happiness and humanity. Because there is no exterior antagonistic force, Scrooge faces the conflict of the protagonist versus himself.

- **In *Pride and Prejudice*,** the first pinch point arrives with Mr. Wickham, a suave and manipulative officer who quickly charms Elizabeth Bennet. This encounter has a major impact on the story, as it adds layers to Elizabeth's prejudice against Mr. Darcy. Mr. Wickham shares the story of his past with Darcy, portraying himself as a wronged man who lost his inheritance because of Darcy's supposed cruelty. This adds to Elizabeth's internal conflict as she wrestles with her initial impressions of Darcy's character, now seemingly validated by Wickham's version of the story.

- **In *The Chronicles of Narnia: The Lion, the Witch, and the Wardrobe*,** the first pinch point occurs shortly after the Pevensie siblings decide to stay in Narnia to find Aslan and fulfill the prophecy. Meanwhile, at the White Witch's palace, Edmund has already betrayed his siblings' location. The White Witch, determined to maintain her grip on power, sends her secret police to tear apart Beaversdam in search of the prophesied kings and queens of Narnia. The discovery that the Witch is aware of their presence and is actively hunting them highlights the urgency and peril of their quest. This scene works as the first pinch point because it raises the stakes and shows the antagonistic force closing in.

KEY TAKEAWAYS

- The purpose of a pinch point is to hint at the future conflict that the protagonist will confront later. This hint can manifest as vicarious suspense, shared suspense, or subtle clues—you decide how much or how little you want to reveal.
- Remember, suspense beats surprise. There is a time and place for surprise, such as during a plot twist, but now is the moment to offer your reader a glimpse of the conflict and danger ahead, perhaps without fully disclosing what that threat may be.
- Even if you give away what will happen or might happen, your story does not become predictable. If that were the case, there would be no stories based on famous historical events. What makes a story interesting is not just what happens, but how those events affect the characters.

ASK YOURSELF:

- What opposition or antagonistic force will my protagonist have to confront later? How can I show the reader that it is already looming in the distance?
- How can I balance suspense and surprise, reserving some revelations for a shocking plot twist while still conveying a sense of dread for the characters?

Now it's your turn. Flip to page 17 of your companion workbook and fill out the First Pinch Point section for your story outline.

WRITING AN UNPUTDOWNABLE MIDDLE ACT

Chapter 11

THE PRE-MIDPOINT REACTIONARY PROTAGONIST

Now that we've crafted a compelling opening act that will grab your readers' attention and draw them into the story, it's time to explore the next section of your book: Act 2.

The flow of this act is pretty simple:

Reaction → Plot Twist → Action

Act 2 consists of four story beats:

- Pre-midpoint reactionary protagonist
- Game-changing midpoint
- Post-midpoint action protagonist
- Second pinch point

In this section of the book, your character will pursue their goal while striving to avoid what they fear. At the midpoint, they will encounter a game-changing plot twist that complicates matters and makes their life more difficult. In light of this twist, they will need to change their approach. As Act 2 builds toward Act 3, we want to raise the stakes for our characters and present them with obstacles that challenge their false beliefs and weaknesses, forcing them to grow, change, and become stronger.

For this reason, I like to call Act 2 the journey. While the entire story represents your character's journey, this midsection (everything between the impossible choice and the climactic ending) is where most of your characters' challenges arise. Think of it like a road filled with obstacles they must face and conquer to reach the destination of their ultimate goal.

To start, let's focus on the first story beat of Act 2.

PRE-MIDPOINT REACTIONARY PROTAGONIST

Protagonist Pursues Their Fear-Based Goal

Thanks to the decision your protagonist made at the end of Act 1, they now have a plan—a clear goal that they are pursuing. Essentially, they're chasing the thing they believe will bring them happiness while still steering clear of the thing they're afraid of. Whether they're running away from or moving toward something, their motivation is the same: Avoid as much pain as possible and reach the finish line where their idea of happiness awaits.

BRAINSTORM PROMPTS:

- How is my protagonist going to execute their plan (i.e., achieve goal; avoid fear)?
- What is their step-by-step plan for making this happen (even if they don't know every step themselves)?
- How can I show the reasoning behind my protagonist's actions (aka: how their every decision is fundamentally based on their false belief)?

Remember how we explored the science of how our brains make decisions? How even when you think you're doing the harder thing, you're actually just redefining pain in your mind? There comes a tipping point when inaction becomes more painful than action (even if the action is really painful).

That being said, your protagonist made a decision based on their false belief at the end of Act 1. They weighed their options and saw that they could either remain in their comfort zone and risk never achieving what they desire, or they could venture into the unknown and pursue their goal while still trying to avoid their fear. After some reflection and redefining pain, your protagonist realized that the second option would be more rewarding in the long run. They faced an impossible choice. And what follows any choice? That's right: a plan.

Here's the Plan

If your protagonist doesn't have a plan going forward, there will be no incentive for your reader to stay engaged with the story. Without this plan, the story becomes a random assortment of events bumping into the protagonist. That's why it's so important for your characters to be agents of change, actively making choices rather than merely absorbing whatever life throws at them.

That's why I emphasized the concept of the impossible choice so strongly in Act 1—because when you present your protagonist with an impossible choice and force them to make a difficult decision, then reveal their reasoning behind this decision . . . the second act practically writes itself.

You know exactly what your protagonist will do next to pursue their goal while avoiding what they fear. Let's call this the pre-plot-twist fear-based plan. Or simply, the stupid plan.

It's a stupid plan because it's based on your protagonist's false belief. They are doomed from the start because, to truly achieve happiness, they need to let go of their false belief and transform from the inside out. However, right now, they are in the throes of internal conflict, which means they don't think it's a stupid plan—they think it sounds like an excellent idea.

I mean, come on. It's a way to get what they desire while steering clear of what they're afraid of! Brilliant, right? Unbeknownst to them, this plan is going to lead to a disaster.

But wait, Abbie—won't that just make my story predictable?

Absolutely not. First, because you're about to write a game-changing midpoint very soon, which will turn everything upside down. Second, because we can only look forward to the future if we can *anticipate* what lies ahead.

Remember when we talked about vicarious suspense at the end of Act 1? How showing your audience the bomb under the table holds their attention longer than a bomb randomly exploding for no reason? The same rules apply to Act 2 of your story.

If we have a sense of where this story is going and we're in on the protagonist's plan, it actually intensifies our anticipation. This sparks our curiosity, which lights up the pleasure-and-reward center in our brain, which stimulates the release of dopamine, which makes us literally addicted to reading what happens next. We know one thing for sure: This plan will not turn out the way the protagonist *thinks* it's going to turn out.

STORY CASE STUDIES: PRE-MIDPOINT REACTIONARY PROTAGONIST

- **In *A Christmas Carol,*** following his encounters with the Ghost of Christmas Past and the Ghost of Christmas Present, Scrooge faces a deep internal struggle. He has always believed that money is essential, but he starts to realize that it can't bring you love or shield you from loneliness. Slowly but surely, Scrooge begins to see the significant effects of his actions. However, he's still trapped by his false beliefs and tries to justify his actions.

- **In *Pride and Prejudice,*** Elizabeth's complicated relationship with Darcy reaches a boiling point. Initially swayed by Wickham's account of Darcy's injustices, her bad opinion of him is further cemented when she learns that he influenced Bingley to move on from Jane, believing the match imprudent. This revelation not only heightens Elizabeth's disdain (she sees it as interference that caused her sister great unhappiness) but also challenges her to grapple with the complexities of Darcy's character.

- **In *The Chronicles of Narnia: The Lion, The Witch, and the Wardrobe,*** the Pevensie siblings are on a quest to find Aslan, fulfill the ancient prophecy, and rescue their brother Edmund from the White Witch's clutches. As they navigate the perilous landscape of Narnia, each sibling grapples with their fears and doubts. Peter, in particular, struggles with the weight of his role as a leader. As they stave off attacks from the White Witch's wolves, the siblings must overcome their differences and band together to reverse the curse on Narnia.

KEY TAKEAWAYS

- After your protagonist makes their impossible choice at the end of Act 1, it's time to make a plan. If your protagonist has no plan moving forward, the reader can't anticipate what might happen—which eliminates curiosity or dread for the characters. Your protagonist doesn't need to know every step of the plan, but one action should lead to another through a natural flow of cause and effect.
- Your protagonist's plan is flawed, even though they think it sounds like a brilliant idea. After all, it's a way to get what they desire while avoiding what they fear! Little do they realize, this will ultimately lead to disaster.
- Every decision your protagonist makes should stem from their fatal flaw. If your protagonist's reason for doing what they do is the same reason all the other characters have for doing what they do, your story will become plot-driven and forgettable. Develop the protagonist's internal conflict *before* you throw them into the ring with the external conflict.

ASK YOURSELF:

- How is my protagonist going to execute their plan (i.e., achieve goal; avoid fear)?
- What is their step-by-step plan for making this happen (even if they don't know every step themselves)?
- How can I show the reasoning behind my protagonist's actions (aka: how their every decision is fundamentally based on their false belief)?

Now it's your turn. Flip to page 18 of your companion workbook and fill out the Pre-Midpoint Reactionary Protagonist section for your story outline.

STRATEGIES IN ACTION: THE PRE-MIDPOINT REACTIONARY PROTAGONIST

Before we explore the pre-midpoint reactionary protagonist story beat of *The Otherworld*, I want to highlight an important point about story structure. Every story has its own unique structure. Depending on the genre you're writing, the journey you're taking your characters on, and the tropes you're incorporating, the structure of Act 2 can take many forms.

For example, an enemies-to-lovers romance might have its own structure within Act 2 that looks something like this:

- Resentful allies in a time of crisis
- Overcoming differences and false beliefs
- Midpoint friendship
- Unexpected romantic feelings

if you're writing a heist novel, you might structure the plot around the steps of the plan for the heist. Or if you're writing a story centered on a tournament, you could organize the midsection around the series of challenges and competitions your characters must overcome to reach the climax (Act 3) of your book.

You have complete creative freedom here. Now that you understand the rules, you can confidently bend them. As long as your character's journey adheres to this natural cause-and-effect flow of reaction, plot twist, and action, you can make this midsection of the story unique to your characters and their goals.

It's also important to note that each act of your story may differ in length. In *The Otherworld*, Act 1 is significantly shorter than Act 2. However, since each event flows seamlessly into the next, there are no distinct beginnings or endings to the acts that a reader would notice.

So, going into Act 2, we begin with the pre-midpoint reactionary protagonist. Let's pick up where we left off with Orca, who is on a mission to find the missing pilot, Adam.

The Pre-Midpoint Reactionary Protagonist in *The Otherworld*

Driven by her desire to show her father just how strong she can be, Orca embarks on a daring quest to find Adam. After two unsuccessful days of searching the island, her confidence begins to waver—but she holds out hope for Jack's sake. Meanwhile, on the mainland, Jack struggles to believe that his brother is still alive, battling the growing fear that Adam may not return.

One stormy night, Adam Stevenson shows up at the lighthouse, and Orca finds him collapsed on the doorstep. Jack is overjoyed when he hears that Adam is alive. Because of the intense storm, Adam and Orca find themselves stranded on the island together for several days. As Orca nurses Adam back to health, she finds herself spellbound by his inquiring mind and rugged good looks. Simultaneously, Adam is captivated by her wild beauty and kind heart. Orca and Adam enjoy long conversations, opening up to each other about their vulnerabilities, fears, and desires. However, because of the ten-year age gap between them—and her father's determination to protect Orca from outsiders—Adam knows they can never be together. He plans on returning to the mainland as soon as the storm passes.

When the weather permits, Jack flies to the island to pick up Adam and meets Orca in person for the first time. He instantly feels drawn to her, but there's no opportunity for them to get to know each other. Adam gives a love letter to Orca, which leaves her feeling more heartbroken and lonelier than before. When Orca's father returns and discovers the budding romance between Orca and the charming young pilot, he is furious and forbids her to see Adam again. Back on the mainland, Adam decides to keep his distance. But there's just one hiccup: Jack has developed feelings for Orca, too, and—having no idea how his brother feels about her—he's determined to help her break free from her unhappy situation.

It may sound like a lot, but all of this occurs between the end of Act 1 and the game-changing midpoint at the novel's halfway mark. As you can see from this example, it's perfectly fine to add twists and extra layers of conflict to your story's pre-midpoint reactionary protagonist moment. It's a golden opportunity to immerse your reader in the thick of the action while making them deeply invested in the emotional stakes.

Remember, as long as we continue to force our characters to make active, fear-based decisions—thus determining their own fate—we can throw almost any conflict at them. Make this section of the book uniquely yours, leveraging the stakes you established in Act 1.

Chapter 12

THE GAME-CHANGING MIDPOINT

If you Google the question "What is a plot twist?," you would probably find something like this:

A plot twist is a radical change in the expected direction or outcome of a story's plot. It is a common practice in narration, used to keep the audience's interest, usually by surprising them with a revelation.

While this definition is valid, it lacks an important element: internal conflict. How does this plot twist affect the characters? Why does it matter?

By this definition, a plot twist is "used to keep the audience's interest," but this is where many writers go wrong. As I've said before, they focus too heavily on the plot and not enough on the characters—constantly striving to keep the audience entertained with exciting, high-stakes events. In contrast, here's the description of the plot twist from my character-driven three-act story structure template.

THE GAME-CHANGING MIDPOINT

Plot Twist!

A game-changing midpoint doesn't have to be an epic or crazy twist of fate. In fact, all a game-changing midpoint must do is surprise the protagonist and shift their goal. Bonus points if you can surprise the reader at the same time! It can be as dramatic as "Everything the protagonist believes is actually a lie," or as simple as "The protagonist realizes they are falling in love with their nemesis."

BRAINSTORM PROMPTS:

- What unexpected thing will upend my protagonist's plan (and entire life)?
- Why does it matter to my protagonist, given their desire and fear?
- How is it going to change the game for my protagonist?

All Game-Changing Midpoints Are Plot Twists, but Not All Plot Twists Are Game-Changing Midpoints

The game-changing midpoint story beat occurs in the middle of your story's timeline. It doesn't have to be a dramatic, big reveal, like the surprise twist that audiences expect at the end of an episode of *The Twilight Zone.* It should be surprising, but the surprise isn't the main point.

As cognitive scientist Vera Tobin explains in her article *The Science of the Plot Twist,* "A major part of the pleasure of plot twists . . . comes not from the shock of surprise, but from looking back at the early bits of the narrative in light of the twist. The most satisfying surprises get their power from giving us a fresh, better way of making sense of the material that came before."[9] This insight can help you craft a powerful midpoint for your story.

Yes, you do want to surprise your audience and then give them the satisfaction of rediscovering the clues they may have missed before. But I invite you to go beyond the shock factor and make this plot twist deeply significant to your characters.

A game-changing midpoint is more than just a surprising twist of fate; it's a crucial turning point for your protagonist. In short, it changes the game.

When crafting a game-changing midpoint, leverage your character's internal conflict and throw a monkey wrench into their plans. What is the most unexpected thing that could happen to this character? What would turn their world upside down and compel them to confront their fears in an entirely new way?

STORY CASE STUDIES: GAME-CHANGING MIDPOINT

- **In *A Christmas Carol*,** the plot twist occurs when Scrooge encounters the Ghost of Christmas Present. This spirit reveals the joys and struggles of the current Christmas Day in various households, specifically the Cratchit family. Scrooge witnesses the effects of his miserliness, particularly on Tiny Tim, who suffers from illness due to poverty—a situation Scrooge has the power to alleviate. This revelation contrasts starkly with Scrooge's prior indifference, prompting a shift in his perspective.

- **In *Pride and Prejudice*,** shortly after Elizabeth learns about Mr. Darcy's interference in her sister Jane's romance with Mr. Bingley, Darcy unexpectedly proposes to her. His confession of love, accompanied by an admission that he fell for her against his better judgment, shocks and offends Elizabeth. She declares that he is the last man in the world she could ever marry, explaining her scruples—both his interference with Jane and his mistreatment of Mr. Wickham. Darcy exits, stunned by her rejection. This twist transforms their relationship and turns Elizabeth's world upside down in a new and unexpected way.

- **In *The Chronicles of Narnia: The Lion, the Witch, and the Wardrobe*,** the game-changing midpoint appears when the Pevensie siblings meet Aslan, the true king of Narnia. His presence and the Narnian forces around him inspire hope and courage, marking a turning point in their journey. This moment signifies their commitment to the Narnian cause, transforming them from frightened runaways to proactive leaders in the fight against the White Witch. Aslan's introduction deepens the mystical elements and underscores the prophecy at the heart of the story, setting the stage for the ultimate battle in Act 3.

KEY TAKEAWAYS

- A great plot twist is more than just a radical change in the anticipated direction of the plot. It changes the game for your protagonist—which then affects the plot in a meaningful way because it impacts their goal.
- Don't let your plot twist be merely an unexpected thing happening; it should directly influence the character's internal conflict. A plot twist can fall flat if it doesn't accomplish this goal.
- Remember, a game-changing midpoint doesn't have to be an epic or crazy twist of fate. It can be as dramatic as "Everything the protagonist believes is actually a lie," or as simple as "The protagonist realizes they are falling in love with their nemesis."

ASK YOURSELF:

- What unexpected thing will upend my protagonist's plan (and entire life)?
- Why does it matter to my protagonist, given their desire and fear?
- How is it going to change the game for my protagonist?

Now it's your turn. Flip to page 19 of your companion workbook and fill out the Game-Changing Midpoint section for your story outline.

STRATEGIES IN ACTION: GAME-CHANGING MIDPOINT

Let's return to outlining *The Otherworld*. While plotting this book, I knew exactly what would upend all three of my main characters' lives in an unexpected plot twist: Orca's decision to leave her island for the mainland. However, like all character decisions, this choice could not be made lightly. It had to involve another pain-versus-pain moment, leveraging the inner conflict of my characters to build up to another impossible choice.

Game-Changing Midpoint in *The Otherworld*

Heartbroken in the wake of Adam's departure, Orca struggles to readjust to life—and the new conflict with her father makes her feel more isolated than ever before. Meanwhile, on the mainland, Adam tries to get over Orca, which is a silent burden he must bear alone. Believing there is no future for them, he chooses to keep everything to himself, even leaving Jack in the dark about what happened on the island.

However, Jack knows how restless and frustrated Orca feels, and he's determined to set her free and show her the world she's never known. One day, while Adam is away, Jack secretly flies out to Orca's island and confronts her father, triggering a heated argument. Now, Orca is left facing an impossible choice: She can either stay at the lighthouse to keep her father happy or take a leap of faith into the unknown and risk everything for love. Inspired by the hope of reuniting with Adam, she chooses to embark on this adventure with Jack into the Otherworld.

When Adam sees Orca again, he realizes just how much conflict Jack has caused by bringing her to the mainland. He tries to convince Orca to return home and reconcile with her father. However, Orca feels rejected and hurt by Adam's response and refuses to go back to the island, saying that Jack is the only one who truly understands her.

The whole situation creates more tension for all three characters. Orca had hoped her reunion with Adam would be a joyful occasion, but now she fears that Adam might not love her as he once did. Adam is left to face the consequences of their relationship, which has created friction not only between him and Jack but also between Orca and her father. Meanwhile, Jack remains blissfully unaware of the troubles his actions have caused, but he's determined to help Orca fulfill her dream of seeing the Otherworld, and he's convinced that he can win her heart.

See what just happened? Through the twist of the midpoint, a character takes an action, one that inadvertently creates more conflict and drama for everyone. Now they are all forced to make *new* choices and revisit their goals as they move through Act 2 of the story.

Can Your Characters' Motivations Change?

Absolutely. Your characters' personalities and beliefs should stay consistent, but their motivations and goals will likely change as the story progresses, and external conflicts challenge them in new ways. It's good to give your characters new (or refreshed) motivations for each act of your story, because this keeps the momentum strong and helps to hold your reader's attention. If the motivation isn't strong enough, the reader won't be on the edge of their seat, wondering if this character is going to overcome the next hurdle to get what they want.

At every major turning point in the plot, I like to check in with my characters' motivations and see how they may have shifted since the beginning of the story. While they are likely still struggling with their fatal flaw and false belief, their plans and goals can shift and evolve.

As you can see from this example of *The Otherworld*, Orca's desire (to see the mainland) has now shifted to make Adam love her again. Jack's desire (find Adam and bring him home) has now shifted to make Orca's dream come true and start a relationship with her. Adam's desire (don't disrupt Orca's life) has now shifted to heal the discord between Orca and her father, as well as preserving his relationship with Jack.

These three interwoven and conflicting goals will add momentum to the conflict as we transition into the second half of the story.

BRAINSTORM PROMPTS:

- How have my protagonist's motivations shifted since Act 1?
- Do they have a different idea of what will bring them happiness?
- Is this altered goal still rooted in their ultimate belief system?
- How can I show the reasoning behind my protagonist's decision-making process and how it connects to their desires?

Chapter 13

THE POST-MIDPOINT ACTION PROTAGONIST

After the game-changing midpoint, your protagonist must shift their focus. At the beginning of Act 2, they were a *reactionary* protagonist; now they have become an *action* protagonist. In other words, the plot twist has changed the game and raised the stakes. If it doesn't, you'll need to revise your plot twist until it matters to the characters. A shocking turn of events is not powerful enough on its own; it must mean something.

Go beyond the shock factor and give your midpoint profound implications for your protagonist, shifting their perspective and complicating matters in a deeply personal way. In response to this plot twist, your protagonist will be faced with the next crossroads.

POST-MIDPOINT ACTION PROTAGONIST

Protagonist Approaches Their Goal from a Different Angle

Figure out how your protagonist is going to respond to the plot twist. It acts almost like another inciting incident, pushing them further out of their comfort zone and introducing a new, unexpected challenge. As the main character responds to the game-changing midpoint, consider their internal and external journey thus far. Then equip them with a plan for the future—and a sense of direction.

BRAINSTORM PROMPTS:

- What will my protagonist's new and improved plan be, based on the game-changing midpoint and its implications?
- How does my protagonist think their new plan is going to actually work and lead them to their goal while still avoiding their fear?

Cause and Effect

Similar to the inciting incident, the game-changing midpoint pushes your protagonist further outside their comfort zone and forces them to make another impossible choice. And this choice, in most cases, will lead them into deeper trouble. Remember, the story is building up to a major disaster moment in Act 3.

However, your protagonist is completely oblivious to the trouble they're getting into. Their false belief is still influencing their every decision, and we know this will lead them into dangerous territory. But the protagonist doesn't know this. In fact, they believe they're making a wise decision (and the reader may think so, too!).

If you've been developing your story based on the characters' internal conflicts, you know exactly what to expect now. Their fear and false belief will continue to take precedence in every decision they make. Let their beliefs guide this journey and dictate how they respond to the game-changing midpoint.

Similar to the inciting incident, your plot twist presents an impossible choice—only this time, the stakes are higher. They have even more to lose than they did at the beginning of the story. They're still facing the choice of *pain* versus *pain*, but it's a little more complicated now because of all the external conflict that's shaken up their world.

Your protagonist *could* confront their internal conflict by simply recognizing the truth—the opposite of their false belief—and spare themselves a lot of trouble. But unfortunately for them, it's going to take a dark moment for them to see the light. For now, the protagonist proceeds with a new, seemingly brilliant plan. But little do they know . . . it's going to backfire.

Follow this natural flow of cause and effect. Then ask yourself: What will be my character's next logical decision in light of the game-changing midpoint? How are things now more complicated than they were at the beginning of the story?

STORY CASE STUDIES: POST-MIDPOINT ACTION PROTAGONIST

- **In *A Christmas Carol,*** Scrooge reacts to the game-changing midpoint when the Ghost of Christmas Present reveals the grim reality of Tiny Tim's deteriorating health and the struggles of the Cratchit family. Moved by these revelations, Scrooge exhibits signs of emotional transformation, inquiring of the spirit whether Tiny Tim will survive. This indicates his growing concern for others, which sharply contrasts with his earlier indifference. Scrooge's motivations have shifted since the beginning of the story.

- **In *Pride and Prejudice,*** Elizabeth Bennet is left reeling after Mr. Darcy's marriage proposal. He writes her a letter revealing the true character of Mr. Wickham, who turns out to be a manipulative gold-digger who seduced Darcy's younger sister and left her heartbroken. This revelation is a lot for Elizabeth to come to terms with, leading her to feel that some of her judgments may not have been as sound as she previously believed. Initially, she tries to avoid another awkward encounter with Mr. Darcy, but their paths cross again, and he begins to challenge her preconceived notions by revealing a more amicable side of himself. As a result, Elizabeth's opinion of Mr. Darcy gradually improves.

- **In *The Chronicles of Narnia: The Lion, the Witch, and the Wardrobe,*** the momentum escalates as Edmund is rescued and reunited with his siblings. Shortly after, a tense confrontation unfolds between Aslan and the White Witch, where she demands Edmund's life as a traitor's sacrifice according to the Deep Magic from the dawn of time. Aslan negotiates privately with the Witch, ultimately offering himself instead of Edmund. This selfless act serves as a pivotal turning point in the narrative, showcasing Aslan's heroism and setting the stage for the ultimate demonstration of his power.

KEY TAKEAWAYS

- After your plot twist changes the game for the protagonist, they face another impossible choice. The protagonist must shift their plans to meet the new challenges that the plot twist has introduced.
- Remember that curiosity triggers dopamine in the reader's brain and keeps them engaged. Maintain your readers' curiosity by presenting your protagonist with a new and unavoidable conflict that affects their mission moving forward.
- The choice your protagonist makes here will eventually lead them to a disaster. However, they are unaware of this—in fact, they think this is a very good decision! After all, it's a way to continue pursuing their false belief-based goal while *still* avoiding their fear.

ASK YOURSELF:

- In what ways has this plot twist changed things for my protagonist and had an impact on the pursuit of their goal? How are things more complex now than they were at the start of the story?
- What will my protagonist's new and improved plan be?
- How does my protagonist believe that their new plan is going to actually work and lead them to their goal while *still* avoiding their fear?

Now it's your turn. Flip to page 20 of your companion workbook and fill out the Post-Midpoint Action Protagonist section for your story outline.

Chapter 14

THE SECOND PINCH POINT

It's not quite time for the disaster moment, so don't get too excited! Here, at the end of Act 2, we can use another pinch point to build suspense for the impending disaster.

SECOND PINCH POINT

The Opposition or Antagonistic Force Gets Closer

Remember, the opposition or antagonistic force doesn't have to be a villain, or even a character; it can be the protagonist's false belief looming in the background, ready to strike during Act 3. Whatever the major opposition your protagonist will face at the climax of your story, that's what you want to hint at during this story beat.

> **BRAINSTORM PROMPT:**
>
> How can I reveal the opposition or antagonistic force that is getting closer to disrupting the protagonist's life?

Just as we saw at the first pinch point, this moment provides an opportunity to weave suspense into your story, giving us a feeling of dread for what may happen to the characters. Remember, a sense of what will happen—or at least what *might* happen—is far more emotionally engaging than being clueless about it. And it doesn't make your story predictable!

Whether you're using shared suspense or vicarious suspense at the second pinch point, the goal remains the same: to make the reader eagerly anticipate the clash between the protagonist and the opposition that will unfold in the third act. The only difference between the first and second pinch points is that the opposition has gained considerable ground since the beginning of the story. In other words, the disaster is getting closer to disrupting your protagonist's plan—and their entire life.

I've written second pinch points that shift to a villain's point of view to see the revenge they are plotting for the protagonist. I've also written second pinch points where the protagonist notices a clue that hints at the looming disaster but doesn't think anything of it.

In my opinion, there is no one-size-fits-all method for pinch points. You have complete creative freedom to make them as revealing or as cryptic as you wish. Just make sure it matters to your characters, and you're good to go.

KEY TAKEAWAYS

- All the second pinch point must do is show the opposition getting closer to disrupting the protagonist's plan—and their entire life. You can utilize vicarious suspense or shared suspense here. Choose what best suits your story, and find a creative way to show your antagonist or opposition closing in.
- As you wrap up Act 2 of your story, keep in mind how the characters' goals and perspectives have shifted over the course of their journey so far. They might be facing a completely different struggle now than they were at the beginning of your book, and that's okay. As long as they are still filled with

internal conflict and making decisions based on their false beliefs, you're on the right track.

Now it's your turn. Flip to page 21 of your companion workbook and fill out the Second Pinch Point section for your story outline.

STRATEGIES IN ACTION: THE POST-MIDPOINT ACTION PROTAGONIST AND SECOND PINCH POINT

Let's round out Act 2 of *The Otherworld* by clarifying the characters' new plan and hinting at what's coming next: the impending disaster, ushered in by the second pinch point.

In the wake of the game-changing midpoint, Orca feels rejected and hurt by Adam's reaction. He hopes she'll return to her island to make amends with her father, but Orca refuses to go back—insisting that Jack is the only one who truly understands her. With this misunderstanding hanging between them, Orca turns her attention to fulfilling her original dream of exploring the Otherworld. As Jack takes her on a whirlwind tour of the mainland, he falls more in love with her each day. Meanwhile, Adam wrestles with his own feelings for Orca, caught between desire and self-doubt.

After reconciling with Adam, Orca promises to return home and mend things with her father, but only after she learns more about her mother. All her life, Orca has been eager to learn about her mother, yet her father refuses to talk about it. Sympathizing with her struggle, Adam agrees to help Orca track down her mother's relatives. This gesture stirs feelings of jealousy and frustration in Jack, who remains unaware of the deep love his brother has for Orca.

At this point, the two brothers are on parallel quests—Jack is wholeheartedly committed to showering Orca with joyful, thrilling experiences that will make life memorable and fun. Meanwhile, Adam is trying to give Orca something she can hold on to—a strong sense of identity, connecting her to her roots and helping her understand where she belongs. Both Adam and Jack have their own motives for this, since they are both in love with Orca.

At last, Orca and Adam discover a long-lost aunt, leading to a world-shattering revelation: Orca's mother is still alive and currently living in Seattle with her husband. Shocked and bewildered by this realization, Orca grapples with feelings of betrayal, realizing her father has deceived her all these years.

See how things have shifted since the first half of Act 1? Each of the main characters has moved beyond mere reaction and into the realm of action. In light of new events, they are pursuing different paths to achieve their goals—unaware that their misguided decisions will inevitably lead to disaster.

WRITING A GUT-GRIPPING CLIMAX

Chapter 15

THE FALSE VICTORY

Act 3. The home stretch. This is where your protagonist's character arc comes full circle as they confront their greatest challenge at the climax of the story.

Act 3 is an emotional roller-coaster ride. This is where we push your protagonist to their breaking point and force them into the ring with their greatest fear—only this time, instead of making false belief-based decisions, they will have an aha moment, realize that their false belief is in fact false, and transform as a character to continue to the climax and overcome their greatest challenge yet.

The third act is comprised of five (potentially six) power-packed story beats:

1. False victory (optional)
2. Disaster (or temptation)
3. Dark moment
4. Aha moment
5. Climactic confrontation
6. Resolution and end

Let's begin with the first optional plot point for this final act.

FALSE VICTORY

Protagonist Believes They Have Overcome Every Obstacle

Making progress with their new and improved plan, the protagonist feels confident of victory. Perhaps they have overcome the smallest of challenges, which makes them feel good about their strategy. Little do they know, disaster is on the way. (Note: This plot point is optional, but powerful when executed well.)

BRAINSTORM PROMPTS:

- Why does my protagonist think they will be victorious?
- What's happening to make them feel so close to achieving their goal and finding happiness?

Depending on your story, you may have room for this plot point, or you may not. Sometimes it simply doesn't fit into the narrative you've crafted—and that's perfectly fine. But if you have room in your story to create this sense of confidence in a character—fooling them into believing that they've already overcome any opposition and that their ultimate plan will be a success—your disaster moment will be twice as devastating and impactful.

What you're leveraging here is what I like to call emotional dynamic change. It's the way that emotions rise and fall as characters interact with each other. Think about it—if your characters are constantly feeling and projecting the same emotion (suspense, anger, sadness, happiness, excitement, fear), then the story is going to feel predictable. In order to make big, emotional moments stand out, we need the up-and-down contrast of emotional dynamic change.

This term originates from orchestral composing. Dynamic change is a tool composers use to add depth and complexity to their music. It refers to variation in volume, intensity, and tempo throughout each movement of the music. These changes allow a composer to convey a wide range of emotions and build up to climactic moments.

It's one of those things you don't even notice with a well-composed film score. You're so absorbed in the emotion of the music, you don't even notice how the composer has leveraged different sounds, tempos, and moods to create an atmosphere. In other words, we *need* that roller-coaster ride of emotions—that rise and fall of intensity—to be moved emotionally.

When we take our protagonist from a high moment at the false victory story beat and plunge them into the devastating moment that comes next, it creates an emotional roller-coaster ride for our reader, which keeps their brain engaged.

Here's where the false victory (if used) fits into the whole movement of the third act:

Dynamic Change in Act 3

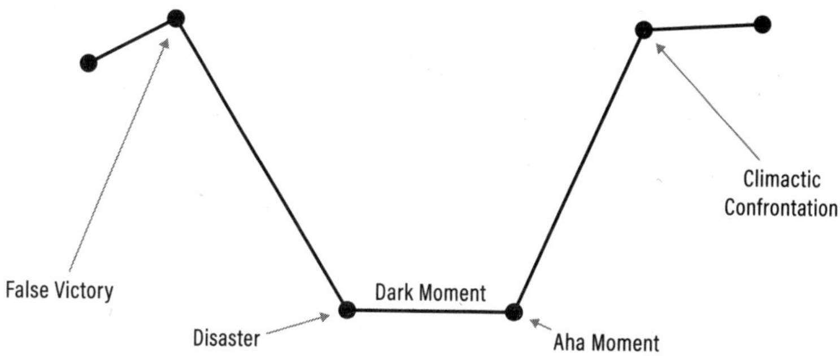

By positioning the false victory story beat right before the disaster, we're leveraging a powerful technique I call *expectation versus reality.*

Expectation vs. Reality

Readers are always trying to figure out what will happen next based on how the story seems to be unfolding. As we watch the characters navigate their conflicts and obstacles, we try to predict the most likely outcome. But then, just when we form a reliable expectation, reality comes charging in like a wrecking ball to ruin the protagonist's plan.

Here's how this dynamic works:

Expectation: I'm going to get in my car and drive to the grocery store to buy waffles.

Reality: I break down on the side of the road halfway there.

Now, it sucks to break down on the side of the road, no matter what you were going to do . . . but what if the stakes were higher than just buying waffles? What if I were on my way to an interview for my dream job, an interview that I've worked for months to secure?

Suddenly, this event becomes a crisis. Suddenly, you, the reader, care a whole lot more—because there was something that I desired more deeply than waffles. I had expected to achieve my idea of happiness . . . but now an obstacle has risen in my path and messed everything up.

If you want your characters to feel like real people, they have to face this universal struggle of expectation versus reality. Your job as the author is to show us this struggle. That's why I love the false victory story beat and try to include it in all my stories, if I can. By contrasting a disaster with the expectation of victory, you can make it even more heart-wrenching for the protagonist and more emotional for the reader.

STORY CASE STUDIES: THE FALSE VICTORY

- **In *A Christmas Carol,*** the false victory occurs after Scrooge meets the Ghost of Christmas Present and begins to show a shift in character. The ghost's revelations about Tiny Tim's health and the Cratchit family's struggles affect Scrooge, evoking newfound empathy and concern. Scrooge's worry for Tiny Tim's fate suggests a growing desire to affect positive change. This moment is a turning point, where we see a glimpse of hope for Scrooge's redemption.

- **In *Pride and Prejudice*,** the false victory moment appears when Elizabeth, touring the countryside with her aunt and uncle, visits Mr. Darcy's estate. At this point, Elizabeth begins to see Darcy in a new light, impressed by the beauty of his home and the favorable accounts of his character from his servants. This moment serves as a temporary triumph in Elizabeth's emotional journey as she starts to entertain the possibility of a relationship with Darcy, unaware of the impending scandal that will ruin her prospects. This moment in the story marks Elizabeth's shift in perspective—but she's not out of the woods yet.

- **In *The Chronicles of Narnia: The Lion, The Witch, and The Wardrobe,*** the false victory shows up when the Pevensie siblings believe Aslan has successfully negotiated with the White Witch, securing peace and safety for Narnia. They are relieved and joyful, thinking that Aslan's diplomatic efforts have saved the day. However, unbeknownst to them, Aslan has made a secret, self-sacrificial deal with the evil queen, offering his own life in exchange for Edmund's. This moment of temporary triumph is laced with an underlying tragedy that the siblings are yet to discover.

KEY TAKEAWAYS

- The false victory story beat isn't essential for a compelling climax, but it can deliver a powerful impact at the beginning of your third act by contrasting expectation with reality.
- Emotional dynamic change is a wonderful way to make your reader feel more for your character by showing a wide range of emotions as they prepare for victory, face off with their fears, and get ready for the big showdown of your final climax.
- Whether your supposed victory involves a romantic relationship reaching a point of safety and mutual trust, a competition that your character is

fully prepared to win, or a business decision they believe will bring them wealth and stability, there are many ways to leverage this moment and give your character a taste of what they've always wanted.

Now it's your turn. Flip to page 22 of your companion workbook and fill out the False Victory section for your story outline.

STRATEGIES IN ACTION: THE FALSE VICTORY

Let's return to *The Otherworld* and study how the false victory moment raises the stakes and impacts the characters.

When Orca discovers that her mother is still alive, she is shocked—viewing her past in a completely new light. It's heartbreaking for her to realize that her father has held on to this secret for so long. Although Orca truly wants to connect with her mother and see what she's like, Orca is hesitant, worried about the possibility of rejection from someone who, it seems, didn't love her enough to stay.

While she grapples with what to do next, Jack makes it his mission to distract her from the situation, recognizing her distress and blaming Adam for interfering. He takes her on a date to the arcade, encouraging her to embrace her playful side. As the night draws to a close, he takes her dancing aboard a luxurious yacht, experiencing his own moment of false victory as he tries to convince himself that Orca is falling in love with him.

The next morning, Orca decides to take a brave step and face her mother. Accompanied by Adam, she travels to Seattle to meet her, uncertain of what to expect. Ever the optimist, she hopes for the best outcome; however, her mother proves to be a coldhearted and selfish person who never attempted to visit her daughter all these years. Orca begins to see the situation—and her conflict with her father—in a new light. Feeling betrayed and heartbroken once again, she decides to return home.

Throughout this portion of the story, I played with emotional dynamic change to raise my characters' hopes, only to dash them in various ways. Jack believes he is on the verge of winning Orca's heart. Adam thinks that his involvement in Orca's search for her family will lead to a positive outcome. Orca holds on to the hope that her mother may have a reasonable explanation for her absence and will show her the love she longs for. However, all these hopes are clearly false, soon to be shattered by the impending disaster.

Perfect! Now that we've crafted a false victory moment for Orca, the reader is left hanging in suspense, wondering what the outcome will be. The stakes are set, but the reality is still unknown, which is an ideal position to put your protagonist in as we build up to the disaster plot point.

Next, we'll explore the best way to bring your protagonist to their knees—by rooting their disaster in their greatest fear and false belief.

Chapter 16

THE DISASTER

As you probably know by now, authors are wicked creatures. We love to torture our characters and throw them into painful, challenging, traumatic situations to make them change and grow. Nothing is more satisfying than making your character suffer—and while they've been struggling through a harrowing journey, you've hunkered in the shadows behind your keyboard, plotting the worst ways to destroy them and dash their dreams to dust.

I know you're eager to dive into this story beat and make something terrible happen to your protagonist—something that will compel them to realize the truth and undergo a transformation—but there's a common pitfall that many writers encounter at this stage . . . and I want to help you avoid it.

IF A DISASTER ISN'T PERSONAL, WE DON'T CARE ABOUT IT

As we discussed in the chapters on inciting incidents and game-changing midpoints, your story becomes boring when the stakes are the same for every character. This means that if the disaster you envision carries the same weight for any of your characters, you need to think of a different disaster. It has to hit the protagonist hard, on a personal level.

This moment isn't just another obstacle or setback; it's the pivot point that forces your protagonist to confront their fears and false beliefs at the deepest level. It's a crisis so personal, so uniquely tailored to your protagonist, that for them, it feels as if the world has ended. Without an impactful rock-bottom moment like this, your character's arc will collapse, and the climax will feel lackluster.

Let's look at the description from my three-act story structure template, and then we'll unpack the brain science behind this powerful story beat.

DISASTER

Everything Goes Wrong

Bring your protagonist to their knees by rooting the disaster in their greatest fear and false belief. It might be something that's terrible for anyone to experience, but take it a step further by ensuring it's especially devastating for your protagonist because of their specific fear and false belief. Every choice they have made throughout the story has led them to this moment . . . which means they are to blame for their own ruin.

BRAINSTORM PROMPTS:

- What does this disaster specifically mean to my protagonist?
- How does it force them to realize that they're the one to blame for this crisis?
- How does it completely disarm them and make them face off with their fear and false belief?

There's a lot to unpack in this brief description, but I don't want to overwhelm you. We'll stay focused on just one thing: rooting the disaster in your character's greatest fear. That's it! Throughout the process of creating your story, you've been building your protagonist's unique internal conflict, showing us how they make every choice based on this struggle. Here's why you've been doing this: to completely destroy them.

Because nothing else will. I mean, think about it. Some things may hurt them, cause them pain, or make them suffer. Anyone could crack under the pressure of a personal crisis—but this isn't a story about just anyone. This is a story about your unique protagonist. So, what would completely destroy them? Hmm, maybe the thing they've always been afraid of? Maybe the thing that's so deeply rooted in the core of their being that they would do anything to prevent it from happening? The thing they've spent most of this story running from like it's the plague?

The Trap Most Writers Fall Into

Many writers become absorbed in the disaster itself, asking themselves, *What bad thing will happen to my character?* They forget to make the disaster matter specifically to their character in a way that it wouldn't matter to anyone else. Just like we explored with the inciting incident, the definition of your character's comfort zone is what makes the disaster so disastrous. Without this personal significance, your reader won't be able to step into the character's shoes and feel their unique desires and fears. They just feel their own biochemical reactions to the peril happening on the page—a direct result of stimulating the reader's mirror neurons, not their empathy.

Don't let your character be a punching bag for the plot, remember?

But wait, Abbie . . . If the disaster is going to destroy my character, doesn't that make my character a punching bag?

Yes and no. Recall this line from the definition of the disaster moment: **Every choice they have made throughout the story has led them to this moment . . . which means they are to blame for their own ruin.**

This is what truly makes the reader shake their fists at the character and scream, "I told you so!" Perhaps they saw it coming from a mile away. Remember, the reader has had a front-row seat to this character's journey the whole time. They've watched, page by page, moment by moment, as your protagonist made one fear-based decision after another. By leveraging expectation versus reality, we give the character a moment of surprise when the disaster strikes—because they didn't see this coming—but the reader most likely anticipated that it wasn't going to be all sunshine and rainbows.

Because you've been stoking your reader's empathy throughout this whole story, they should now feel a deep emotional connection to the protagonist. That's why, when disaster finally strikes, this moment can be incredibly heart-wrenching—but only if it's rooted in your protagonist's deeper fears and false belief.

STORY CASE STUDIES: THE DISASTER

- **In *A Christmas Carol*,** the Ghost of Christmas Yet to Come reveals a haunting glimpse of Scrooge's future. He witnesses scenes of his own death, where it seems the world has forgotten him. There is no one to mourn his passing; instead, people steal his belongings and rejoice in his demise. The pivotal moment unfolds when Scrooge finds his neglected grave, symbolizing a lonely and meaningless end if he doesn't change his ways. This vision fills him with fear and desperation, making him realize the serious impact of his choices.

- **In *Pride and Prejudice*,** a dramatic turn occurs when Elizabeth's youngest sister, Lydia, elopes with the charming yet unscrupulous Mr. Wickham. This reckless act threatens to destroy the reputation of the Bennet family, casting a shadow over future marriage prospects for Elizabeth and her sisters. Amid the turmoil, Elizabeth feels that the possibility of a relationship with Mr. Darcy is all but lost due to the scandal that surrounds her family and their reduced social standing.

- **In *The Chronicles of Narnia: The Lion, the Witch, and the Wardrobe*,** the disaster moment appears when Aslan sacrifices his own life on the

Stone Table. This selfless act appears to hand victory to the White Witch, casting a shadow of despair over Narnia. The Pevensie siblings, especially Edmund, are deeply affected by this turn of events. Having been rescued from the Witch's clutches by Aslan's intervention, Edmund is moved by the profound display of mercy embodied in the lion's sacrifice. Aslan's death marks a critical point in the story, seemingly dooming Narnia to the Witch's rule, and forces each sibling to confront their own limiting beliefs to uncover their inner strength.

KEY TAKEAWAYS

- Bring your protagonist to their knees by rooting the disaster in their greatest fear and false belief.
- Remember to make this disaster especially meaningful to your protagonist because of who they are. If any of your characters would face the same stakes in the face of this disaster, you need to make it more personal.
- A disaster doesn't have to be earth-shattering or epic to be devastating for your protagonist. It can be as simple as a breakup, losing an important competition, or encountering an insurmountable obstacle that prevents them from completing an important quest or mission. Make it personal to the protagonist, and show us the uniquely devastating consequences that will follow.

ASK YOURSELF:

- What does this disaster specifically mean to my protagonist?
- How does it force them to realize that they're the one to blame for this crisis?

- How does it completely disarm them and make them face off with their fear and false belief?

Now it's your turn. Flip to page 23 of your companion workbook and fill out the Disaster section for your story outline.

STRATEGIES IN ACTION: THE DISASTER

To illustrate what these principles look like behind the scenes, let's continue unpacking the three-act story structure of my novel *The Otherworld*. I want to show you how I utilized these techniques to create a compelling disaster moment.

After meeting her estranged mother, Orca feels let down, realizing that her mother never wanted a relationship with her. Back at the Stevensons' house, she locks herself in her room, refusing to come out. Jack, furious at the sight of Orca's heartbreak, confronts Adam and blames him for the whole disaster. Adam struggles with guilt, knowing he was the one who incited and enabled the search for Orca's long-lost relatives. He's stirred up secrets that should have remained buried and forgotten, and he feels terrible about it.

That night, Jack takes off in anger to drown his sorrows while Adam stays behind to comfort Orca. She confesses that she now views her family situation in a new light, and she understands why her father kept this secret from her all these years. With renewed love for her father, Orca decides to return home the next morning. Adam still struggles with self-doubt, wondering if he is good enough for Orca, but a conversation with his mother the following morning helps him realize that they are perfect for each other. Mrs. Stevenson encourages Adam to speak to Jack and clear the air between them, as well as to admit his feelings for Orca. Adam agrees to do just that when he returns from bringing Orca home.

But before Adam can fly Orca back to the lighthouse, Jack catches them passionately kissing in Adam's airplane hangar and realizes the true nature of their relationship. Feeling shocked and betrayed, Jack storms in to confront his brother and finally loses his temper—punching Adam in the face and triggering a heated fistfight. Orca is heartbroken to see the two brothers at each other's throats, feeling responsible for the misunderstanding and unwittingly leading Jack on when she only ever saw him as a friend.

See how we've woven together multiple disasters for each character, yet made them all uniquely relevant because of what each character is struggling with? For Jack, who is in love with Orca and believed that she loved him, it's devastating to learn that she has been in a relationship with his brother this whole time. For Adam, who always strives to keep the peace and set a good example for his brother, it's disastrous to see how his own lack of communication has caused strife between him and Jack. And for Orca, who loves both Stevenson brothers in different ways, it's heartbreaking to see them at odds with each other—over a conflict that she feels is entirely her fault.

This moment sets the stage for what each character needs to learn in their personal aha moments. In the next chapter, we'll explore how this disaster leads to a dark moment and how the dark moment sets the stage for the ultimate aha moment that will transform our characters.

Chapter 17

THE DARK MOMENT (OR THE TEMPTATION)

After the disaster, we arrive at the dark moment. You might have heard this moment referred to as "the dark night of the soul." This is a vital moment in your story because it's within this darkness that your protagonist will finally see the light.

DARK MOMENT

Protagonist Feels Hopeless in the Wake of the Disaster

It's always darkest before dawn. Your protagonist needs a rock-bottom moment to experience an aha moment—and that's what makes the revelation so satisfying. However, in the aftermath of the disaster, your protagonist feels utterly broken, confused, lost, and disappointed.

BRAINSTORM PROMPT:

How is my protagonist facing their worst nightmare in the wake of the disaster?

Again, we'll leverage our character's unique internal conflict in their dark moment. Reviewing your character profile can be especially helpful here, as you can reflect upon their personality and inner motivation to uncover the thing that would crush their soul.

As I've emphasized from the very beginning, this story structure can be reshaped and customized to fit your specific narrative needs. Don't become too obsessed with aligning your story with every aspect of the structure; it's okay if you need to make some adjustments. If your climax doesn't unfold in the same flow as these story beats, that's perfectly fine! This isn't about adhering to a specific structure down to the last page number. Don't stifle your creativity by confining yourself to a mold! It's just important to grasp the principles that lie *behind* the structure and ensure that your story always prioritizes the characters' internal journey. Yes, you can bend the rules (and even break them sometimes!) to create a story that is truly unique and like nothing anyone has read before.

The purpose of the dark moment is to bring your protagonist to rock bottom. Your deeply conflicted protagonist has made a series of fear-based decisions that have led them to this moment. Now there's nowhere to run, nowhere to hide. Facing the ugliness of every mistake they've made, they realize how much they've been controlled by fear. They see how wrong their decisions have been . . . Yet here at the bottom, they see a light at the end of the tunnel: a hopeful future that could be theirs if they let go of their false belief, overcome their fear, and change from the inside out.

Why Do We Need a Dark Moment in Order to See the Light?

Hard-won beliefs are nearly impossible to let go of. Why? Because we adopt them over time and nurture them with affirmations of truth. When this false belief first took root in your character, it was like a little sapling. With the right influence, your character could have uprooted this lie and embraced the truth instead. However, left to the passage of time and circumstance, the sapling eventually grew into a strong and powerful tree. Now it's going to take something major—a disaster or a dark moment—to fell this tree and show your character the truth.

However, there's more than one way to reveal this profound inner transformation. Despite what I've already said, you don't need to destroy your protagonist to lead them to the aha moment. Instead, you could do the opposite by giving them everything they've ever wanted. I call this the temptation.

TEMPTATION

Alternative to the Disaster and Dark Moment

With this option, instead of everything going wrong for your protagonist, everything goes right. They are given the opportunity to finally have the thing they've always wanted—the false belief-based goal they've been pursuing all along. But now, they choose to turn it down. After undergoing this transformative journey, they realize they no longer desire it. They have discovered something far better: the source of true happiness.

BRAINSTORM PROMPTS:

- What is the specific false belief-based goal that my protagonist has been chasing this whole time?
- How is my protagonist offered the chance to finally have this thing they've always wanted?
- How will my protagonist prove their transformation by turning down this offer?

You often see the temptation story beat in more lighthearted or comedic narratives, but it can certainly work just as effectively in a story with a more serious tone. I love the temptation-to-aha-moment plot device just as much as the disaster-to-aha-moment, because both can be profoundly impactful if executed properly—that's why it's up to *you* to choose which is best for your story.

Having options keeps your story fresh and engaging—unpredictable, yet still following a clear path of cause and effect. Sometimes, it can be more satisfying to give your character a moment of temptation rather than a disaster that shatters them. Since we, the readers, have been inside this character's mind, feeling their desires and conflicts at every turn, we know exactly what this character desperately wants. And now, when it's finally within their grasp, we think, *Oh my goodness, the moment has come at last! They're on the cusp of having everything they've ever wanted! What will they do?*

But we, like the protagonist, feel differently about this goal now that it's being offered on a silver platter. After watching the protagonist go on their transformative journey, we can see it won't bring them true happiness. And *that's* when the aha moment shows up. At last, their eyes are opened, and they realize: *I don't want this thing anymore.* Why? Because they've changed from the inside out.

The temptation story beat is a perfect way to showcase your protagonist's transformation, because we all *think* we know how the protagonist will react when offered the thing they've always wanted. The old version of them would seize the opportunity with both hands. However, somewhere along their journey, they have exchanged their old self for a new self—a person with different values, beliefs, and desires.

That's what makes the temptation so satisfying. In fact, it would be majorly dissatisfying if the protagonist were to say, "Oh, hey, awesome! That's what I always wanted! *Now* . . . I can be happy." We'd slam the book shut and throw it across the room in frustration because the character didn't change.

Inner transformation is the heart and soul of your story. When we look back and compare the protagonist at the beginning with the protagonist at the end, we should be able to spot some significant differences. If you've ever undergone a paradigm shift in your own life, you know what this feels like.

You might look back at the person you were ten or twenty years ago and catch yourself saying, "I feel like I was a different person then." That's the same life-altering transformation you can give your protagonist through the temptation moment.

STORY CASE STUDIES: THE TEMPTATION

- ***Roman Holiday* (1953 film):**
  Roman Holiday tells the story of European princess Ann, who is fed up with her tightly scheduled life and longs for freedom. When Ann escapes from her country's embassy and finds herself lost on the streets of Rome, she meets Joe Bradley, an ambitious journalist who offers her a place to spend the night, not realizing who she is—until the following morning, when he discovers that she is the missing Princess Ann.

  It's a once-in-a-lifetime opportunity, and Joe quickly seizes it, betting $500 that he can secure an exclusive story about Ann. We observe him working to accomplish this throughout the film, all while allowing Ann to believe he's simply being a nice guy, spending the day with her as she makes a fool of herself.

  But throughout that day, Joe's character changes—he begins to fall for Ann, and by the time they part ways, he feels deeply conflicted about exploiting her for his own benefit. This is the moment of temptation—Joe has the opportunity to sell his $5,000 story and win the $500 bet with his boss, but after getting to know Ann, he just can't bring himself to do it. That idea of success no longer seems so attractive. He has gone on a journey—and transformed because of it. When he shows up at the royal press conference the next day, Ann is shocked; she realizes he's a reporter and has been aware of her identity all along. But Joe makes it clear to the princess that he won't exploit her in the press. Although the story doesn't have your typical fairy-tale ending, it's satisfying because of Joe's character transformation.

- ***Baby Boom* (1987 film):**
  J. C. Wiatt—also known as "the Tiger Lady"—is an ambitious businesswoman from Manhattan whose career plans are upended when a distant relative passes away and leaves her a highly complicated inheritance: a baby. This inciting incident pushes J. C. far outside her comfort zone. For a time, she tries to juggle being a mom and a career woman, but eventually, her life falls apart, and her hopes of becoming a partner in the company are shattered. That's when J. C. decides to leave the rat race, pack up everything, and move to Vermont . . . which introduces a whole host of other problems.

  Despite the odds, J. C. manages to get back on her feet by starting her own business selling baby food. Eventually, word of her success reaches her former boss in New York, who invites J. C. back and offers to buy her company for millions. This is the moment of temptation—J. C. has the opportunity to secure the job she has spent years fighting for and make a lot of money in the process. However, after experiencing a very different kind of life, she just can't bring herself to accept the offer. J. C. loves her adopted daughter and her new life in Vermont more than she ever thought she would. She surprises herself as much as everyone else when she turns down the offer and decides to maintain her business—and her lifestyle—just as it is. She has discovered what truly matters to her.

KEY TAKEAWAYS

- You don't need a disaster for your character to come to their senses! In fact, it could be just the opposite: Your character might be presented with the very thing they've always desired . . . but they realize they no longer want it. They have found true happiness and have transformed as a result of their journey.

- Make it clear to your audience why your protagonist no longer finds this goal appealing. Throughout the story, their goal has shifted from a misguided definition of happiness to a clear understanding of what happiness truly looks like. Their character arc comes full circle as they finally see the truth that you intended to convey through this story.

ASK YOURSELF:

- What is the false belief-based goal that my protagonist has been chasing this whole time?
- How can I offer my protagonist the chance to finally have this thing they've always wanted?
- Why will my protagonist turn down this offer, and therefore prove their transformation?

Now it's your turn. Flip to pages 24–25 of your companion workbook and fill out the Dark Moment/Temptation section for your story outline.

STRATEGIES IN ACTION: THE DARK MOMENT

Let's return to *The Otherworld* and look at what's happening during this dark-moment portion of the story.

At this point in the story, Adam and Jack have just experienced a major fallout. Jack is feeling hurt and betrayed, while Adam grapples with feelings of regret. Orca, caught in the middle, feels guilty about the rift between the two brothers. Orca returns to the lighthouse, reuniting with her father, making peace with the past, all while looking forward to a brighter future with Adam. Meanwhile, on the mainland, Adam is trying to rebuild his relationship with Jack, but it's proving to be quite challenging. Despite Adam's heartfelt apology for not being more open about his relationship with Orca, Jack can't shake the feeling that he's always been second best, struggling with the belief that he'll never truly measure up to Adam.

Frustrated with his life and yearning for a drastic change, Jack decides to join the military so he can find himself. He still doesn't fully understand who he is, but he's determined to find out. Meanwhile, Adam moves out to give Jack some space. That night, after contemplating a life without his brother, Jack has an epiphany: He realizes that he's the one pushing Adam away. Remembering how much the thought of losing his brother nearly destroyed him, Jack feels compelled to make things right with Adam. The two brothers reconcile and resolve their conflicts.

Here's a question I frequently receive from writers: *If I'm writing a story with multiple main characters, should they all have their aha moments at the same time?* The answer is: Not necessarily. As you can see from this example from *The Otherworld*, I've staggered my characters' individual aha moments to align with their biggest internal challenges. Depending on your unique story, the timing of each dark moment and aha moment will play out differently. In *The Otherworld*, I wanted each of my main characters' transformations to truly shine on their own, so I spaced them apart and gave them each a specific challenge to lead them to that pivotal moment.

In the next chapter, we'll look at Orca's and Adam's aha moments and see how they play off each other's internal conflicts.

Chapter 18

THE AHA MOMENT

At last, we've arrived at my favorite story beat: the aha moment (the most vital and pivotal moment in your entire story).

Remember how we began this journey by highlighting the importance of character arcs? The long and short of it is this: Without character arcs for the protagonist and other main characters, you really don't have a story. You just have a random assortment of stuff happening to a random assortment of individuals.

But if you've been following this book chapter by chapter and crafting your story with deeply conflicted characters, here's the good news: You have a masterpiece in the works. Now it's time to bring your protagonist's character arc full circle with the aha moment.

AHA MOMENT

Protagonist Has a Transformative Realization

After your protagonist has been brought to their knees by the disaster—or offered the thing they always wanted—they experience a revelation moment. They can suddenly see how their fear and false belief have led them to make the wrong decision about everything. They realize their mistakes—but most importantly, they see that they'll have to overcome their fear and false belief and make the *right* decision to achieve their goal: true happiness.

BRAINSTORM PROMPTS:

- What aha moment will naturally arise for my protagonist in the wake of all these events? How does this moment connect to their fear and false belief, so it isn't just a random revelation?
- What lesson are they learning (and simultaneously teaching the audience)?

Why Does This Aha Moment Matter to You?

The aha moment is truly your moment—yes, you, the author! It must encapsulate the truth you want to shout from the rooftops, the big idea that motivated you to write this story in the first place. To be honest, you've probably had this aha moment yourself at some point in your life, and now you want to share it with others.

Imagine that the entire world has stopped to listen to you. What will you say? If thinking about the whole world feels too overwhelming, focus on just one person instead. Think of the one person out there who is just like your protagonist—with the same desires and the same fears and the same false beliefs holding them back. Imagine you could sit down across from that person and give them hope. Give them truth. Give them purpose. What would you say?

That's what you're doing in this pivotal moment of your story. You are giving your character the aha moment that you wish you could give the world. And, through this fictional story, you're actually giving it to the world. This is just one of the many reasons why I love writing so much! This is why I've written this book: I genuinely want you to write a story that matters to you, your characters, and the world.

Only after your protagonist experiences their aha moment can they continue to the climax of the story. Without this revelation, they will lack the courage to confront their biggest challenge yet. However, with this insight, the protagonist can finally overcome their fear, shatter their false belief, and show the reader how much they have grown and developed since the beginning of the book.

STORY CASE STUDIES: THE AHA MOMENT

- **In *A Christmas Carol,*** Scrooge discovers that his fate is not set in stone and that he has the power to transform both his own life and the lives of those around him. Confronted with the stark reality of potentially dying alone and unloved, Scrooge experiences a change of heart. He earnestly pleads with the Ghost of Christmas Yet to Come for a chance to change his ways and find redemption, promising to embrace the spirit of Christmas with all his heart. Scrooge's character arc feels earned because we have watched him confront his past, present, and future—ultimately coming to a transformative moment as a result of this metaphysical journey.

- **In *Pride and Prejudice,*** Elizabeth's aha moment shows up shortly after Lydia runs away with Mr. Wickham. News arrives that her uncle somehow managed to persuade Mr. Wickham to marry Lydia—which ultimately saves the Bennet family from disgrace. However, when Elizabeth discovers that it was Mr. Darcy who convinced Wickham to marry Lydia and financed the entire arrangement, everything changes. Elizabeth is astonished—her disgraceful family saved from disgrace by the man who called them disgraceful? She realizes that while she was busy calling Darcy out for his pride and prejudice, she was being quite prideful herself. She had resolved to loathe Darcy for all eternity, but now, she sees the truth: Darcy is actually admirable, courageous, and willing to prove his love for her. And just like that, "the last man in the world she could ever be prevailed upon to marry" becomes the only man in the world she would marry.

- **In *The Chronicles of Narnia: The Lion, the Witch, and the Wardrobe*,** the aha moment occurs when the Pevensie siblings each experience realizations before the climactic battle against the White Witch. Peter recognizes the need to become a strong and decisive leader and prepare the Narnian forces for battle. This new identity contrasts with the hesitant boy who first entered Narnia, as he embraces his destiny as a king. Meanwhile, Susan and Lucy come to understand that they must rely on their own strengths, stepping out of Aslan's protective shadow. They realize that their power and roles are crucial to the success of their cause, embodying the leadership and resilience they previously lacked. Edmund, redeemed by Aslan's sacrifice, supports Peter, showcasing his growth from a self-serving traitor to a loyal and brave brother. Together, these aha moments empower the siblings, preparing them for the challenges ahead in the final showdown with the White Witch.

KEY TAKEAWAYS

- Only after your protagonist experiences their aha moment can they continue to the climax. Without this revelation, they lack the courage to confront their greatest challenge yet. However, with this insight, the protagonist can finally conquer their fear, crush their false belief, and show the reader how much they have transformed since the start of the book.
- Remember, if you don't have a character arc, you don't have a story. You just have a random assortment of stuff happening to a random assortment of people. Your character arcs make your story engaging, satisfying, and memorable.

- Why does the aha moment matter to you? This is the reason you wanted to write this story in the first place. This is the truth you want to shout from the rooftops! If the whole world stopped to listen, what would you say? Bring your passion into the aha moment, and you will leave a lasting impression on your audience.

ASK YOURSELF:

- How will my protagonist overcome their fear and continue to the climax, therefore developing as a character?
- What lesson will they learn (and simultaneously teach the audience)?

Now it's your turn. Flip to page 26 of your companion workbook and fill out the Aha Moment section for your story outline.

STRATEGIES IN ACTION: THE AHA MOMENT

Let's return to *The Otherworld* and look at the aha moments for Adam and Orca.

At the lighthouse, Orca talks to her father about her love for Adam and their hopes for a future together. He's open to the idea and now realizes that while attempting to shelter Orca from the harsh realities of the world, he deprived her of essential life experiences. Orca's aha moment appears in her newfound ability to see her own inner strength. At the start of the book, she believed that her father wanted to keep her from the mainland because he didn't consider her strong enough. Now, in light of her transformative journey, she sees that she's always possessed the strength and independence she longed for—and her father was merely trying to protect Orca from heartbreak by keeping her away from the Otherworld.

Just when things start to look up for Orca, and she feels hopeful about the future, her father suddenly collapses from a cardiac episode. In a panic and unsure of what to do, Orca calls Adam and Jack to fly out in the midst of a violent storm and take him to the hospital. Though the three of them come together in this moment of crisis and succeed in saving Mr. Monroe's life, Orca blames herself, knowing that her selfish behavior has broken her father's heart. Terrified that another episode could be fatal, Orca resolves to give Adam up, aiming to protect her father from facing any further drastic changes.

At first, Adam is stunned and disappointed that Orca is pushing him away, so in an effort to do the right thing, he takes a step back. Jack has a heart-to-heart talk with him, helping him realize that he needs to fight for Orca, despite the obstacles that may stand in their way. Adam feels more motivated than ever to prove his love for Orca and secretly asks her father for permission to marry her. Mr. Monroe is somewhat reluctant at first, but he understands that Orca will never be truly happy without Adam, so he grants his blessing—on the condition that Adam proves his commitment for one year before they marry. Adam is overjoyed with this arrangement and is determined to show Orca how much he loves her and to remain loyal to her.

In this portion of the book, Adam realizes that he is good enough for Orca and that he doesn't need to be perfect to deserve the life he wants. Reconciling his past mistakes and striving to do better sets him on a path toward a brighter future.

For Orca, her fear of losing her father and her guilt for weakening his heart with stress and grief drive her decision to return to the lighthouse. Although she desperately wants to be with Adam, she has gained a new perspective on what truly matters. We see how she has grown and matured emotionally since the start of the story by being willing to give up what she wants for her father's well-being.

Looking back at Orca's character at the beginning of the story, we can see how much she has changed—which is an ideal position to put your protagonist in after the aha moment. They can't continue down the same path they've always taken, which means they must take a new path as they face their greatest challenge of all: the climactic confrontation.

Chapter 19

THE CLIMAX AND RESOLUTION

We have three story beats to cover in this chapter, because they all flow together as part of the ending climax sequence—so get ready for a wild ride to the finish line:

1. Climactic confrontation
2. Victory
3. Resolution

First, I want to debunk some common myths that writers have about the climax and then explore the brain science behind what makes a climax genuinely exciting and unputdownable.

The Biggest Mistake Writers Make with the Climax

Do you know the main reason why most writers struggle to create a gripping, riveting, and memorable climax that keeps readers on the edge of their seats? It's because many writers are overly focused on making the climax exciting. They think that to truly engage the reader, they must fill the story with thrilling, perilous, and scary external conflicts. They believe that adrenaline is the cause, not the effect, of the reader's interest. All of this is simply not true.

Remember our motto? Say it with me: **Story is not about what happens—it's about how what happens affects and transforms the characters.**

If external conflict and high-stakes action were the secret essential ingredients of a successful story, then all writers would be prioritizing these nail-biting life-or-death situations. But they aren't. Why? Because all external conflict does is trigger your mirror neurons to fire as if these events are happening to you.

I'm sure you've encountered numerous science fiction adventures filled with action and exploding spaceships that lack a real story. You've probably also experienced many slower-paced, character-driven stories that were so compelling and emotional, you will never forget them.

YOU CAN'T RAISE THE STAKES UNLESS YOU KNOW WHAT THEY ARE AND WHY THEY MATTER TO EACH MAJOR CHARACTER

The stakes cannot be the same for every character. If they are, you end up with a plot-driven story with a protagonist who could easily be swapped out for any side character. The stakes also cannot be *merely* do or die, because, once again, you're falling back on those mirror neurons! You want to trigger your reader's empathy, not just their fight-or-flight response.

Okay, Abbie, but how can I raise the stakes if there's no life-or-death situation?

Oh, there *could* certainly be a life-or-death situation. But I encourage you to go beyond that and let your protagonist's internal conflict take center stage. A story *without* a life-or-death scenario can be every bit as exciting, climactic, and suspenseful as a story with perilous do-or-die stakes. But before we dive deeper into the climax, let's take a look at the definition of this crucial story beat.

CLIMACTIC CONFRONTATION

Protagonist Faces Their Biggest Challenge Yet

This is the moment everyone has been waiting for. It's a true test of the protagonist's character, and how they respond to this confrontation will prove their transformation. Your protagonist has already won the internal battle (in their aha moment), but now it's time for them to win the external battle, which will force them to face their greatest fears.

BRAINSTORM PROMPT:

How does my protagonist prove their transformation by crushing their false belief and facing their greatest fear with courage?

Crafting an Irresistible Climax for Your Story

So, what does this look like in a story? Well, it depends on the genre. If you're writing in one of the more action-packed genres—like sci-fi, fantasy, or thriller—your climax might center on a dangerous showdown between the protagonist and the antagonist, or a battle between two armies.

However, keep in mind that the climax isn't solely about surface events; it's fundamentally about why this confrontation matters to the protagonist. That's what can make a cozy, contemporary rom-com just as suspenseful and climactic as an epic fantasy.

I primarily write contemporary stories, and one of my favorite things to do is build tension within a very small, ordinary premise—raising the stakes to the point where I have my reader on the edge of their seat. It's a challenge at times, but it's a worthwhile one because it improves your skills as a writer.

So if you write contemporary fiction, don't worry. Your climax can still be nail-biting and suspenseful! Your protagonist can still confront an intimidating challenge that forces them to prove their transformation. Only *you* know what that challenge will be.

If you can make your reader care about your character—if you can get them emotionally invested—they will be interested in reading about *anything* that happens to this character, whether they are fighting an intergalactic battle with a formidable villain or professing their love for their worst enemy in a romantic meadow at sunrise. Because, at the end of the day, we don't care the most about *what* happened. We care the most about *who* it happened to.

VICTORY

Protagonist Overcomes

Following the climactic confrontation, we enter the moment your character has been waiting for. This doesn't necessarily mean the protagonist wins the external battle or that things turn out exactly as they hoped. However, the protagonist does experience a personal victory—overcoming their fear and destroying their false belief. Here's my rule of thumb: If your reader doesn't understand how the character has transformed as a result of their journey, you need to rewrite your book until they do.

BRAINSTORM PROMPT:

How has my protagonist changed as a result of their journey?

No, your protagonist doesn't have to live happily ever after. However, they should come to the realization that their false belief has been dead wrong. The protagonist *must* experience inner change as a result of their journey. That's what makes a character arc powerful and a story memorable.

I love happy endings—because I personally believe the world needs more happiness. However, not all stories can have happy endings. Sometimes it's just too late to make things right, but that can be a profoundly thought-provoking theme in itself, one that might even change the way your reader thinks about their own life.

Regardless of the tone you choose at the end of the story, you must show the reader how the protagonist has changed. Otherwise, why does anything matter?

RESOLUTION

Wrapping Up Loose Ends

At this point, the reader should be left with no missing information or unanswered questions. If the book has an open ending, consider what specific ideas and questions you intentionally want to leave the reader contemplating. If the book is part of a series, consider ending on a cliffhanger by replacing the victory story beat with another plot twist. If the book is a standalone, ensure that the readers' questions are addressed by the time they reach the final page.

> **BRAINSTORM PROMPT:**
>
> Where will my protagonist go from here? What does their life look like now that they have overcome their false belief?

This story beat is optional and depends on the style of your book. Some readers enjoy abrupt endings that allow them to imagine the rest of the story themselves. Other readers appreciate when the author alludes to the characters' future or wraps things up with a satisfying epilogue that answers all their questions and leaves them feeling like the story is truly complete. The only downside to an epilogue is that it can limit your options. What if you decide to write a sequel? Sometimes, an epilogue paints you into a corner because you've already told the rest of the story and didn't leave extra room for future conflicts.

I recommend finding a balance between satisfying your reader and leaving them hungry for more. It's never a bad thing to have your readers clamoring for another story! That's the best feeling in the world—to receive letters and comments from readers who loved your book so much that they can't wait for you to release another.

STORY CASE STUDIES: THE CLIMACTIC CONFRONTATION

- **In *A Christmas Carol*,** Scrooge awakens on Christmas morning, overjoyed to discover that he has a chance to change his ways. He starts by sending a large turkey to the Cratchit family and then ventures into the streets, greeting everyone with newfound kindness. Scrooge also makes a generous donation to the charity he had previously scorned and joins his nephew Fred for a delightful Christmas dinner, surprising everyone with his transformed demeanor. The story concludes with Scrooge embracing the spirit of Christmas and becoming a loving, caring, and generous figure, beloved by all.

- **In *Pride and Prejudice*,** Lady Catherine de Bourgh (Darcy's aristocratic aunt) confronts Elizabeth, demanding that she renounce any engagement with Darcy. Elizabeth refuses to make such a promise, asserting her right to make her own choices. Mr. Bingley returns, confessing his love for Jane and offering his hand in marriage. Jane happily accepts. Elizabeth realizes that Darcy is responsible for bringing her sister back together with her one true love. Darcy proposes to Elizabeth again, and this time she accepts, having overcome her prejudice against him and realizing just how much she truly loves him.

- **In *The Chronicles of Narnia: The Lion, the Witch, and the Wardrobe*,** the Pevensie siblings confront their greatest challenge in the final battle against the White Witch. Each sibling plays a pivotal role in the fierce fight for Narnia's freedom. Aslan's return with reinforcements turns the tide against the Witch, culminating in her defeat and the victory of good over evil. The Pevensies are crowned kings and queens, fulfilling the prophecy and ushering in the Golden Age of Narnia. They rule with wisdom and kindness, drawing on the lessons learned in their adventures, ensuring Narnia's peace and prosperity, and bringing a satisfying conclusion to their journey from ordinary children to extraordinary leaders. In the end, Peter, Susan, Edmund, and Lucy return to the professor's house through the wardrobe, only to find that no time has passed in their world. They are saddened to leave Narnia behind, but they are comforted by the knowledge that they can return to the magical land whenever they wish.

KEY TAKEAWAYS

- Most writers fail to craft a dramatic climax because they focus too much on making it "exciting." However, external conflict (the plot) means nothing without internal conflict (the transformation). If a dramatic life-or-death situation were the key to a good climax, everyone would be writing one! But that's not the case. Internal conflict is the secret ingredient that keeps the audience emotionally invested.
- Raise the stakes by clearly defining what this climax means to your protagonist. Identify the internal conflict and allow that to take center stage in your climax. Remember, this is the ultimate challenge your protagonist must overcome—and how they confront it will demonstrate their transformation.
- No antagonist to defeat? No problem. Contemporaries can be just as nerve-wracking as thrillers. If you make your readers care deeply about your protagonist, they will be eager to see how they will overcome their own false belief and transform from the inside out.

- If your readers don't understand how the protagonist has transformed as a result of their journey, you need to rewrite your book until they do. Your protagonist doesn't have to win the battle and live happily ever after, but they must change as a result of their journey. How they overcome their biggest challenge (the climax) proves that they have crushed their false belief once and for all.

ASK YOURSELF:

- How does my protagonist prove their transformation by overcoming their false belief and confronting their greatest fear with courage?
- How has my protagonist changed as a result of their journey?
- Where will my protagonist go from here?
- What does their life look like now that they have overcome their false belief?

Now it's your turn. Flip to pages 27–29 of your companion workbook and fill out the Climactic Confrontation section for your story outline.

STRATEGIES IN ACTION: THE CLIMAX AND RESOLUTION

Let's return to *The Otherworld* one final time to look at the ending scene, which resolves the story.

Orca returns to the lighthouse with her father, determined to be more emotionally mature from now on. Her growth shines through as she learns to put her desires aside for the sake of her father's well-being. However, Orca's father sees how much she misses Adam and helps to bring him back into her life. He shares the news that a man is going to fly out to the island every week to help with chores, but Orca has no idea who the man is until Adam shows up one day. Orca realizes that it was her father's decision to invite Adam to come to the island, proving his growth as well, as he lets go of his overprotective habits and learns to release control. Overcome with joy, Orca runs to greet Adam on the beach, and they share a heartfelt embrace. Adam proposes to her, and her heart swells with happiness as she says yes. The novel concludes with a triumphant final scene as Adam carries Orca back to the lighthouse, ready to start their new life together.

Through this climax and resolution, we've tied up all the loose ends of the story and alluded to a hopeful future for Orca and Adam, as well as the supporting characters. They have all changed drastically since the beginning of the story. Orca has learned about sacrifice and the complexities of love. Adam has learned to forgive his own mistakes and stop putting himself last. Jack has learned to stop comparing himself to Adam and to heal conflicts instead of escaping them. And Orca's father has learned to loosen his protective hold and set his daughter free to live her own life.

There are many different ideas that readers will take away from this book, and that's the beautiful thing about storytelling. Everyone gets something different out of a story—something they need to see, reflected in the struggles and triumphs of the characters. In *The Otherworld,* I set out to tell a story that felt like fairy-tale love captured within the brokenness of the real world. I aimed to write a story that embodies hurt, healing, and the feeling of coming home. Now, looking back at this finished novel, I feel I accomplished exactly that.

So don't get too caught up in the intricacies of themes and key takeaways at your story's ending. If you reach the final page with a satisfied smile and feel that you have conveyed the story you set out to tell . . . Congratulations! You made your story matter.

Before we wrap things up here, let's take a closer look at a few powerful ways to end your story and leave a lasting impact on your reader.

Chapter 20

WRITING THE FINAL CHAPTER

Writing the final chapter of a novel can be just as challenging as writing the first one. With so many possible ways to end a story, it can feel overwhelming to choose just one.

Do you need to tie up all the loose ends, or is it better to leave room for the reader to imagine what happens next? Should you conclude with a shocking twist, or perhaps an epilogue? Should it be a happily-ever-after, or should you make everyone die?

I've seen many negative book reviews in which readers enjoyed the story but felt that the ending fell flat . . . and it ruined the whole book for them. You don't want to get reviews like this when you send your book out into the world! You want your readers to be satisfied with an unforgettable ending that leaves them hungry to read more of your work as soon as possible.

Which leads us to the big question: *How do you write the final chapter?*

To find the answer to that question, I'm going to walk you through a series of interactive questions that will help you write a powerful and satisfying ending for your story. We're going to explore the many possibilities for your story's final scene—whether you're writing a sweet rom-com, a spine-chilling thriller, or an epic fantasy adventure. I'll share ideas, valuable prompts, and story examples to help you visualize your book's impactful ending.

QUESTIONS TO ASK YOURSELF WHEN WRITING THE FINAL CHAPTER

Is This Book Absolutely a Standalone, or Is It Part of a Series?

Even if you originally planned on this book being a standalone, I urge you to consider whether there is series potential. Sometimes you don't know until you're deep into the drafting process and realize you have more stories in you for these characters.

The final chapter will differ greatly depending on whether you're writing a standalone or a series. For example:

The ending of a standalone should:

- wrap up all loose threads (or intentionally leave the ending open).
- show us how the characters have changed as a result of their journeys.
- leave no questions unanswered.
- maybe allude to the future or give closure with an epilogue.

The ending of a book in a series should:

- set up the next book with an irresistible cliffhanger.
- wrap up loose threads for plotlines that won't be returning.
- resolve conflicts for the current book while setting up new conflicts for the next book.
- raise the stakes and make the reader want the next book ASAP.

Take a few minutes to explore the possibilities your book offers. If you're torn between the two options and you're not sure what the future may hold for this story, consider leaving the standalone somewhat open-ended to allow for a potential sequel if you choose to write one—and if your readers beg you for it.

How Have the Characters Changed as a Result of Their Journey?

You've heard me say this a lot, but I'll say it again: If your readers don't understand how the protagonist has transformed as a result of their journey, you need to revise your book until they do.

Your protagonist doesn't have to win the battle and live happily ever after, but they must change. How they overcome their greatest challenge (the climax) serves as proof that they have conquered their false belief and faced their fear, once and for all.

If you don't have a clear idea of how your protagonist has transformed, I recommend creating two lists for your own reference that compare the protagonist at the beginning versus at the end. Write down a few bullet points on each side—highlighting their character traits, behaviors, and beliefs. Some traits may simply reflect their personality, which might not change throughout the story, and that's fine. However, their perspectives on their life and values should evolve, even in subtle ways, because that's what storytelling is all about. That's why it matters.

Once you have your two lists written out, you can compare them side by side and see the contrast. This will help you highlight your character's transformations at the end of your book and show the reader how much they have changed—even in small ways. Small changes still count!

How Do You Want Your Reader to Feel When They Close the Book?

This is one of my favorite questions to ask myself, because the answer will be very different for every author and every book. I recommend starting by making a list of all the emotions you want your reader to feel when they reach the final page. Is it love, joy, surprise, amazement, sadness, triumph, or some combination of all those feelings? Get super specific with your answer to this question.

Then, once you have your list of emotions, consider what type of scene would make you feel this way as a reader. If you want to experience joy, love, and forgiveness, perhaps you should conclude with a heartfelt reconciliation between two characters who have been at odds throughout the story. Or, if you want to feel shock and surprise, you might need to finish with a shocking revelation of a secret that has been concealed until this moment—some hidden truth that alters everything.

Trust your instincts on this. Sometimes the ending scene you initially envisioned doesn't evoke the emotions you want your reader to experience at the end of the book, and that means it's time to go back to the drawing board and imagine a new scene.

On a more practical note: The emotion you leave your reader with on the final page is the emotion they carry with them when writing a review of your book. Keep this in mind as you develop the last chapter.

What Themes or Other Ideas Do You Want Your Reader to Think About Long After They Finish the Book?

Like the emotions your reader is left with, the big ideas you convey are part of the legacy of your book. The themes should resurface at the end, as the character arcs become complete and the reader has the opportunity to step back and look at the big picture.

Imagine a group of friends all read your book and decided to sit down and discuss it. What questions and observations would come up? Make a list of these questions and ideas, then draw inspiration from them as you craft your final chapter. Pro tip: You can use this list to generate prompts for book club discussions!

If Writing a Series, How Can You Make the Ending of This Book Work as the Inciting Incident for the Next Book?

We all want to write a juicy cliffhanger that leaves readers eager for the next installment . . . but be careful with cliffhangers. It's easy to throw your characters into a life-or-death scenario, let the curtain fall, and say, "Ha! Now you have to wait to see if they make it out alive!"

Sometimes nail-biting cliffhanger endings *do* work . . . but I would urge you to focus less on *How can I make this exciting?* and more on *How can I make this final moment the springboard, or inciting incident, for the next book?*

A good cliffhanger introduces a new conflict and raises the stakes, setting up an even bigger problem the characters will face head-on in the next book. That's what makes us eager to read more as soon as possible. We want to see how they navigate this new conflict and overcome the next impossible challenge.

Now, if you're thinking, *This all sounds great, but I still don't know how my story should end . . . I need ideas!* Don't worry; I've got you covered. Let's explore ten unforgettable ways to conclude your story, from the surprise twist to the cliffhanger, from the tragedy to the happily-ever-after.

01. THE TWIST

Ending your story with a surprise twist is a surefire way to leave a lasting impression on the reader. Just make sure the reveal is well planned and fits the story's plot and character journeys. Foreshadowing the twist throughout the story will make the surprise reveal more believable and satisfying. Rather than a convenient *deus ex machina*, make your twist a well-crafted secret that has been hidden up until now.

STORY CASE STUDY: *GASLIGHT*, A 1944 FILM BY GEORGE CUKOR

A great example of a surprise twist ending can be found in the 1944 psychological thriller film *Gaslight*. The story revolves around Paula, who marries a pianist named Gregory and moves into her deceased aunt's house in London. Soon after, strange things begin to happen in the house, and Paula starts to doubt her sanity. Gregory convinces her that she is losing her mind and makes her believe that she is responsible for the strange occurrences. As the story unfolds, it becomes clear that Gregory is manipulating Paula as part of a larger plan. He is searching for a valuable treasure that he believes is hidden somewhere in the house, and he will stop at nothing to find it. In the end, Gregory is exposed as the murderer who killed Paula's aunt years ago and has been hoping to lock his wife up in an asylum in order to search for the missing jewels he failed to steal at the time of the murder.

BRAINSTORM PROMPTS FOR THE TWIST:

- What is the twist, and how will it change the reader's understanding of the story as a whole?
- What clues or foreshadowing can you plant throughout the story to make the twist more believable?
- How does it fit with the story's themes and character development?
- What impact will the twist have on the characters? Will it be satisfying or frustrating?
- Does the twist make sense within the logic of the story's world?
- What red herrings (misdirections) can you plant throughout the story to make the twist more satisfying?

02. THE EPILOGUE

An epilogue can provide closure to the story by showing what happens to the characters after the main events of the novel. Epilogues can take us through the next few months, the next year, or even decades—giving us a clear vision of what happens to these characters in the future. Note that with a far future epilogue, you leave little to no room for a sequel, as you are essentially giving the reader a summary of what happens next instead of writing a book about it.

STORY CASE STUDY: *PERSUASION* BY JANE AUSTEN

The novel ends with the main character, Anne Elliot, and Captain Wentworth, her one true love, finally confessing their feelings for each other and reuniting after years of separation. The novel concludes with an epilogue about their engagement and the promise of a happy future together, despite the obstacles they faced along the way. It also provides satisfying closure to subplots, such as the fate of the scheming Mr. Elliot and how Captain Wentworth helps Anne's best friend improve her living situation. The epilogue gives us a sense of perspective on the work as a whole because we can look back and see how far the characters have come.

BRAINSTORM PROMPTS FOR THE EPILOGUE:

- What happens to the characters after the curtain falls? How much of their future do you want to show the reader?
- What emotions do you want your reader to feel while reading the epilogue, and what events can you show them to inspire that feeling?
- Should the epilogue be told from the perspective of one of the characters or from a more omniscient point of view?
- What new information or insights should the reader gain from the epilogue?
- How does the epilogue reflect upon and emphasize the overarching themes of the story?

03. THE OPEN ENDING

Leaving the ending open can be a great way to allow readers to use their imagination and create their own interpretation of the story. This can also leave the door open for a sequel or a series. Open endings can also challenge the reader to think about the story's themes and messages and to draw their own conclusions as to how events turn out. However, it is vital to ensure that the open ending still feels satisfying and complete, even if some questions are intentionally left unanswered.

STORY CASE STUDY: *THE GIVER* BY LOIS LOWRY

In a utopian society, protagonist Jonas is chosen to be the Receiver of Memory, a role that requires him to receive and keep all the memories from the past, including the painful ones. As Jonas begins to experience the memories, he realizes that his society's way of life is flawed and that they have sacrificed important aspects of human emotion and experience for the sake of stability and conformity. With the help of his mentor, the Giver, Jonas decides to escape from his society and share the memories with others, hoping to bring about change. The novel ends with Jonas leaving his community and heading toward an unknown future, leaving us to imagine what will happen to him. The open ending allows the reader to interpret the story in their own way and imagine various outcomes for Jonas.

BRAINSTORM PROMPTS FOR THE OPEN ENDING:

- What questions or conflicts would you like to leave unresolved at the end of the story?
- What themes or big ideas should linger with the reader?
- How can you leave the ending open while still giving some closure to the story and some allusion to the future?
- What are some possible interpretations of this open ending? Do they align with your mission for this story, or are you leaving too much open to interpretation?
- How do you want your open ending to make the reader feel?

04. THE FULL CIRCLE

Ending the novel where it began can be a satisfying way to bring the story to a close. This method not only ties up loose ends but also gives the reader a sense of closure. For example, maybe we discover on the final page that this whole narrative has been told by one of the characters who lived the events and is now telling someone else about it. Or maybe the first page of the book started with a flash-forward to the final scene, and we have that full-circle moment where we finally understand the context of the mysterious ending that was hinted at in the beginning.

STORY CASE STUDY: *THE CHRONICLES OF NARNIA: THE LION, THE WITCH, AND THE WARDROBE* BY C. S. LEWIS

The story follows four siblings, Peter, Susan, Edmund, and Lucy, as they are sent to live with a professor in the English countryside during World War II. While exploring the professor's house, Lucy discovers a magical wardrobe that transports her to a snowy, enchanted land called Narnia. Together, with the help of a talking lion named Aslan, the Pevensie siblings must defeat the White Witch and break her curse over Narnia. After winning the final battle, the siblings return to the professor's house through the wardrobe, only to find that no time has passed in their world. Although they have lived an entire lifetime as kings and queens of Narnia, they now find themselves back to being children in the real world. They are saddened to leave Narnia behind, but they are comforted by the knowledge that they can return to the magical land whenever they wish.

BRAINSTORM PROMPTS FOR THE FULL CIRCLE:

- What themes or motifs can be repeated in the beginning and end of the story?
- Are there any objects, locations, or characters that can be reintroduced at the end of the story to bring it full circle?
- Can the ending offer additional insights or new interpretations of the beginning of the story?
- What is the significance of the story coming full circle? How does this reinforce the story's themes or messages?

05. THE CLIFFHANGER

Ending your novel on a cliffhanger can be a risky but effective way to keep readers invested in your story. Make sure the cliffhanger is high-stakes enough to keep the reader wanting more, but not so high that they feel unsatisfied with the ending. Remember, you want to make your reader hungry for more, but not angry enough to throw the book across the room. Find the balance between keeping your reader on the edge of their seat and satisfying them enough to hold their attention until the next installment.

STORY CASE STUDY: *THE BLOOD RACE* BY K. A. EMMONS

My favorite example of a cliffhanger ending is in my sister's novel, *The Blood Race*, which literally ends with the protagonist falling off a cliff. College student Ion Jacobs's life flips upside down when Hawk, the mysterious girl next door, unearths his darkest secret: that he possesses extraordinary superpowers. Hawk renames him Icarus and inducts him into the Dimension, a whole world of anomalies just like him, destined to use their powers to save future Earth. Icarus struggles to control his powers as he commutes between realms. But when he starts a disastrous fight with his nemesis, Icarus inadvertently seals the fate of the Anomalies—cutting them off from the real world forever. Now a traitor, Icarus is exiled to the Worlds Beneath, the mysterious ravine where nobody knows what lies at the bottom.

BRAINSTORM PROMPTS FOR THE CLIFFHANGER:

- How does this cliffhanger raise the stakes and change the game going forward?
- How can you make this cliffhanger moment serve as the springboard or inciting incident for the next book?
- Can you wrap up other conflicts that won't be returning in the next book in order to satisfy the reader and spotlight your grand finale cliffhanger?
- Imagine you are the reader experiencing this cliffhanger . . . are you excited for the next installment or frustrated with the story's ending?
- How can you use the cliffhanger to reinforce or highlight the story's themes or messages?

06. THE TRAGIC END

A tragic ending involves a sad, unfortunate, or disastrous outcome for the protagonist. Tragic endings often involve the death of the protagonist or other key characters, but they can also present other types of negative outcomes, such as the loss of a crucial opportunity or the end of a relationship. If you're writing a negative character arc for your protagonist, the story will likely end in tragedy. All in all, the tragic ending is a powerful device that can leave a lasting impression on the reader and add depth and complexity to your story.

STORY CASE STUDY: *HAMLET* BY WILLIAM SHAKESPEARE

One of the most famous tragic endings can be found in Shakespeare's play, which tells the story of Prince Hamlet, who is visited by the ghost of his father and learns that his uncle, Claudius, has murdered his father, married his mother, and taken the throne. Hamlet contemplates avenging his father's death while navigating the complex political landscape of the Danish court, then finally he moves forward with a plan to do so. At the end of the play, nearly all the main characters die, including Hamlet himself. The tragic ending teaches the audience about the destructive power of revenge and the consequences of inaction.

BRAINSTORM PROMPTS FOR THE TRAGIC END:

- What is the disastrous final outcome of the characters' decisions?
- How are you going to make the tragic ending emotionally impactful and make the reader think?
- How does the tragedy reinforce the story's themes or messages?
- Which characters will be affected by the tragic ending? How will they react and cope with the outcome?
- What questions and ideas will your reader ponder after reading the tragic end?

- How can you ensure that the ending feels satisfying and complete, even if it doesn't end on a positive note?

07. THE HAPPILY-EVER-AFTER

The happily-ever-after ending is just what it sounds like: a story that ends with a tidy resolution of conflicts, and the characters live happily ever after. This type of ending is often associated with fairy tales and romance novels, but it can be used in any genre. The happily-ever-after ending gives the reader a sense of satisfaction and closure, knowing that the characters they have grown to love have found happiness.

STORY CASE STUDY: *YOU'VE GOT MAIL*, A 1998 FILM BY NORA EPHRON

This classic romantic comedy follows Joe Fox and Kathleen Kelly, business rivals who unwittingly fall in love over the internet, each unaware of the other's true identity. Their journey from rivals to soulmates unfolds against the backdrop of a bustling New York City, as they challenge each other's beliefs and values, forcing each other to change from the inside out. The climax reveals Joe's true identity, leading to a heartwarming finale in a sun-dappled park where Kathleen, realizing that her virtual love is actually Joe, responds by saying, "I wanted it to be you so badly." And, of course, they live happily ever after.

BRAINSTORM PROMPTS FOR THE HAPPILY-EVER-AFTER:

- What conflicts need to be resolved for the characters to live happily ever after?
- How can you make this ending feel satisfying but not overly predictable or convenient?
- What imperfections and little conflicts still remain between the characters?
- How does the happily-ever-after underline the story's themes or messages?
- Will this ending be believable and realistic, given the characters and the world of the story?

08. THE HOPEFUL TRAGEDY

Let's say you tackle some tragic and heavy topics in your story, but you don't want to leave your reader depressed for days. Maybe you need to end with what I call the hopeful tragedy. It can be a thought-provoking way to end your story if you want to be true to life and show both the good and bad that we all encounter throughout our lives. Nothing is ever perfect, but through the darkness, we can find light. If your story aligns with this idea, you might want to conclude with a bittersweet ending.

STORY CASE STUDY: *TO KILL A MOCKINGBIRD* BY HARPER LEE

An example of the tragic-but-hopeful ending can be found in the novel *To Kill a Mockingbird*, where the main character, Scout, reflects on the events of the past few years, including the trial and tragic death of Tom Robinson, whom her father fought to defend in the face of their hateful and prejudiced community. The tragic events of the story eventually lead to Scout befriending her neighbor, Boo Radley, who saves her brother from certain death. Scout comes to the realization that she has been naïve and judgmental, and that true courage means standing up for what is right even when it is difficult. The novel ends with Scout looking out into the neighborhood and feeling hopeful for the future.

BRAINSTORM PROMPTS FOR THE HOPEFUL TRAGEDY:

- What is the tragedy or disaster that your story centers around?
- How can you make the ending feel hopeful or uplifting despite the tragic outcome?
- How does the tragedy shift the perspectives of the characters and provide a sense of hope?
- How can you use the tragic ending to reinforce the story's themes or messages?
- Does the hopeful element of the ending feel earned and believable within the world of the story?
- What questions and ideas will your reader ponder after reading the hopeful tragedy?

09. THE HAPPY-FOR-NOW ENDING

Like the happily-ever-after, the happy-for-now ending is uplifting and hopeful, but not as fairy-tale perfect as the classic happily-ever-after. There are still conflicts for the characters to resolve, and we can sense this is just the beginning of a longer journey they must embark on . . . but it leaves us with a sense of optimism and perhaps shifts the way we look at our own lives. (This is my personal favorite!)

STORY CASE STUDY: *100 DAYS OF SUNLIGHT* BY YOURS TRULY

My debut novel, *100 Days of Sunlight,* follows temporarily blind Tessa, who learns how to love and embrace life again with the help of Weston, an optimistic boy who (unbeknownst to her) is an amputee. The whole story builds up to the moment of truth where Tessa regains her sight, and Weston's secret is revealed. The ending scene is bittersweet as Tessa realizes she has been selfish and unfeeling toward Weston, who has faced much greater difficulties than she has. Weston assures her that she has helped him just as much as he has helped her, and we see that they have both learned a valuable lesson of acceptance and having courage in the face of fear. They confess their feelings for each other and kiss, hopeful for their future together.

BRAINSTORM PROMPTS FOR THE HAPPY-FOR-NOW:

- What conflicts still need to be resolved for the characters to be happy for now?
- How do the characters' decisions throughout the story lead them to the happy-for-now ending?
- How can you create a sense of optimism and hopefulness in the ending without resolving all the conflicts in the story?
- Are there any loose ends or unresolved conflicts that can be left open for a potential sequel or to let the reader speculate about what might happen next?

- Will the happy-for-now ending be believable and realistic, given the characters and the world of the story?

10. THE TRIUMPH

End on a high note! The triumph doesn't have to be reserved for sports stories or courtroom dramas. Although most commonly found in these genres, the triumphant ending can be used in any story where the protagonist is persevering in the fight for something they believe in with their whole heart. The story ends on a triumphant note, with the protagonist having won the battle, conquered the opposition, or overcome the challenges they faced throughout the story.

STORY CASE STUDY: *AMAZING GRACE*, A 2006 FILM BY MICHAEL APTED

A great example of the triumph ending can be found in the film *Amazing Grace*, which tells the story of William Wilberforce, a British politician who campaigned tirelessly for the abolition of the slave trade. Throughout the film, we see the highs and lows of Wilberforce's fight in parliament. But at the film's climax, Wilberforce's efforts are finally successful when the British parliament votes in favor of the abolition of the slave trade. The closing scene is triumphant and powerful, as Wilberforce, who has been struggling for years to make this happen, is overcome with emotion when he finally sees his dream become a reality.

BRAINSTORM PROMPTS FOR THE TRIUMPH:

- What is the goal that the protagonist has been fighting for?
- What are the obstacles or challenges that the protagonist has struggled to overcome in order to achieve their goal?
- How can you make their victory feel earned and not too easy or convenient?
- What impact does the victory have on the protagonist and other characters?
- How does the victorious ending reinforce the story's themes or messages?
- What is the final image or the final feeling you want to leave with the reader?

Bottom line: **Make your ending matter.**

Part 3

BRINGING YOUR STORY TO LIFE

"Words—so innocent and powerless as they are, as standing in a dictionary, how potent for good and evil they become in the hands of one who knows how to combine them!"

—Nathaniel Hawthorne

Chapter 21

CRAFTING A CHAPTER-BY-CHAPTER OUTLINE

Are you ready to expand your notes on story structure by transforming it into a chapter-by-chapter outline? The outlining method we'll explore in this chapter will help you enhance your story's framework while still allowing for creative flexibility. You'll learn how to create well-rounded chapters designed to hook the readers' attention, draw them in, and keep them engaged. We'll also delve into the brain science behind impactful chapter breaks and examine how to leverage this psychological tool to captivate your readers and keep them turning pages late into the night.

The Psychology of Powerful Chapter Breaks

What if there was a psychological tool we could use at the beginning and end of every chapter of our books to literally addict readers to the story? Believe it or not, there is a scientific explanation for what makes a book addictive. We're going to explore that science right now, and by the end of this chapter, you'll have a clear understanding of what makes readers want to keep flipping pages and how to leverage this tool in your own writing.

The Zeigarnik Effect

In the 1920s, Russian psychologist Bluma Zeigarnik uncovered something intriguing about the human attention span. She observed that waiters in restaurants seemed to remember orders they had not yet fulfilled more clearly than those they had completed. Once the orders were finished, the waiters' memories of them seemed to fade—even if they took both orders at roughly the same time.

This phenomenon is called the Zeigarnik Effect. It suggests that when a task is left incomplete, it creates a kind of mental tension or cognitive dissonance that keeps the task active in our minds. This tension drives us to seek resolution, which helps us remember the task until we can complete it. Once the task is finished, the tension is relieved, and the memory of the task tends to fade because the brain no longer needs that information.

So, how does this apply to writing? We can leverage the Zeigarnik Effect to create binge-worthy chapter breaks by using what I like to call the *open loop method.*

The Open Loop Method

Ending each chapter with an open loop essentially poses a question—sparking curiosity in your reader's brain. This open loop promises that, in the next chapter, the loop will be closed. The reader will receive an answer to their question and be rewarded for their curiosity.

So how do we open a new loop in the reader's mind? First, we ask a question or present a new problem, knowing that the solution won't unfold quite how the character thinks it will. As your reader predicts what might happen next, their curiosity is stimulated. Next comes the reward, but in between that curiosity and reward, we insert a chapter break. See what we just did there? By inserting a chapter break between the curiosity and the reward, we create mental tension that the reader must resolve—an itch in their brain that they *need* to scratch.

When you study your favorite, most engaging books, you'll notice this pattern:

Open Loop → Chapter Break → Closed Loop → More Conflict → Open Loop → Chapter Break → Repeat

We want to leverage these patterns of curiosity and reward because they hook readers into your story. Brain studies have revealed that addiction stems from curiosity. The desire to find answers activates the pleasure-and-reward center in your brain, creating a similar effect to using an addictive drug. It releases the neurotransmitter dopamine and tells you that you're really enjoying this experience. You get that same feeling when you watch an exciting, binge-worthy TV series, and your brain begs you for just one more episode! The same holds true for books. Instead of clicking to the next episode, you keep reading chapter after chapter until a book is finished, driven by a series of open loops that demand closure.

The Trap of Fake Tension

Before we explore the open loop method in action, it's crucial to mention that you should avoid using fake tension to create cliffhangers at the end of your chapters. Fake tension occurs when you set up a situation that seems threatening, dangerous, or potentially life-or-death, leaving your characters hanging at the end of the chapter. You're basically tricking your reader into turning the page to see what happens next. However, once they turn that page and read on, they quickly realize that there are no real consequences.

Here's a quick example: Your characters are driving in a car, about to crash in an accident. The chapter might end with the line "The car careens toward the edge of the cliff!" Then, after a chapter break, the following chapter begins like this: "We swerve off the road, and everything is okay."

If you use fake tension like this, making your characters dodge bullets left and right, you will lower the stakes for the entire story and lose readers' trust. Because they are emotionally invested in these characters, they don't just want a cliffhanger for the sake of tension and excitement. They want every open loop to present a *real* problem or question that has an impact on the story going forward.

So make your tension real, especially if you're going to incorporate a life-or-death situation later in your story. Using fake tension has a similar effect to the boy who cried wolf. If we become *too* familiar with seeing characters in peril, we start assuming there will never be any consequences for their actions. This kills any sense of suspense or excitement for the reader.

How Long Should a Chapter Be?

Should it be 5,000 words? 2,000 words? 400 words? How many pages should a chapter have? Should it contain multiple scenes or just one single scene? It depends on the story you're writing and your writing style, but I will say this about chapter length: Based on my reading preferences and conversations with readers, shorter chapters encourage us to read longer. It might sound contradictory, but once again, this is how the human brain is hardwired.

When you can quickly read a short chapter, and you see that there's another short chapter right after it, your brain thinks, *I've just made a lot of progress!* because you've read a whole chapter. Next comes the thought: *This next chapter is super short, so it's not like I'm making a huge commitment to read it.*

You've probably experienced this internal dialogue many times while reading a good book or watching TV. It's similar to the five-more-minutes effect. When you want to start the next episode of that highly addictive TV drama instead of going to bed, like you know you should, you tell yourself, "I'll only watch another five minutes." It's easy to say yes to short-term commitments. However, if your reader sees that the next chapter is twenty-five pages long, they might set the book aside for now and pick it back up later. Ideally, you don't want your reader to put your book down. Ever. You want them to keep reading and reading and reading until it's two o'clock in the morning and they have no idea where the time has gone. How did that happen? Through the brain's autopilot system of perceived progress and minimal commitment.

I frequently write short chapters in my novels, using the open loop method to push my reader through the revolving door of curiosity, reward, curiosity, reward, curiosity, reward. Here's what this technique looks like in action.

STRATEGIES IN ACTION: THE OPEN LOOP METHOD

Let's analyze the first four chapters of *The Otherworld* through the lens of the Zeigarnik Effect. We'll look at the opening hook, main conflict, and unresolved questions each chapter ends with.

Chapter 1: Orca's Point of View (3,641 words)

Hook: Orca eagerly wakes up on the morning of her eighteenth birthday, filled with excitement, as she is finally old enough to visit the mainland.

Main Conflict: Orca's father dashes her hopes when he tells her that he has to go to the mainland for a meeting with the Coast Guard and that she won't be going with him. Orca is deeply disappointed. We see how desperately she longs for the Otherworld and how lonely her life is. Later that day, as Orca strolls along the beach, she stumbles upon a mysterious backpack that has washed ashore. Curiosity piqued, she opens it and discovers a ringing cell phone that she can't answer in time.

Open Loop: Realizing that this backpack has come from the Otherworld, Orca decides to keep it a secret from her father. But who does this mysterious backpack belong to? And who was trying to call on the phone?

Chapter 2: Jack's Point of View (4,077 words)

Hook: When we first meet Jack, he's grappling with grief and inner turmoil, torn apart by the thought of losing his brother, Adam.

Main Conflict: Jack's parents receive heart-wrenching news from the Coast Guard that they are about to end the rescue search for Adam. Jack's frustration flares up as he accuses his parents of giving up. Taking matters into his own hands, he boldly sets out on a rescue mission, flying over the straits despite the threatening weather, determined to find his brother—but his search is fruitless. Later that day, Jack's mother gently encourages him to let Adam go, but Jack isn't ready to listen. He reaches an emotional tipping point, where he finally loses control and breaks down crying.

Open Loop: Orca calls Jack on Adam's phone, reigniting a spark of hope in Jack. Is his brother alive, after all?

Chapter 3: Orca's Point of View (2,115 words)

Hook: Thrilled by the idea of hiding treasures from the Otherworld, Orca decides to keep her discovery a secret from her father.

Main Conflict: Orca figures out how to call Jack and learns that he is the younger brother of a pilot who recently crashed his plane near her island—the pilot to whom this backpack belongs. Frantic with worry and urgency, Jack pleads with Orca to help search for his missing brother.

Open Loop: Sufficiently pushed outside her comfort zone yet excited by the prospect of a new adventure, Orca eagerly agrees to assist Jack in his search. But how will she keep it a secret from her overprotective father?

Chapter 4: Jack's Point of View (1,411 words)

Hook: At first, Jack can hardly believe that Orca is real. But as she opens up about herself, Jack is truly fascinated by her unique way of life and how different it is from the modern culture he knows.

Main Conflict: Since the Coast Guard and his parents have given up, Orca becomes Jack's only hope during this dark time. Her unwavering optimism and determination spark a flicker of optimism in Jack that his brother might still be alive. Together, they devise a secret plan to keep in touch while Orca searches the island for any sign of Adam—before her father returns from his trip to the mainland.

Open Loop: With her father away for a few days, Orca is determined to spend this time exploring the island in hopes of finding Adam. Will she succeed in her search, or is it too late?

And that wraps up the first four chapters of *The Otherworld*. As you can see, the lengths of the chapters vary significantly, but word count is less important than making your reader empathize with the character's deepest conflicts. You might even discover new ways to refine the pacing as you go through the revision and editing process. In my first draft of *The Otherworld*, I took six chapters to cover all the scenes I just summarized. During the revision process, I trimmed that down to just four chapters by merging and cutting scenes. My goal was to conclude with the most tantalizing open loop to ignite my readers' curiosity and make them hungry for more. I wanted to make it so that there was no good place to put the book down.

Now it's your turn. Flip to page 30 of your companion workbook to outline the first few chapters of your story using the open loop method.

If you're a minimal outliner, this might be all the guidance you need to confidently start crafting juicy, unputdownable chapters for your story. However, if you need a bit more direction in planning each scene, let's move on to the next chapter to explore my tried-and-true Scene Card Template and how to use it to ensure that every scene in your story matters.

KEY TAKEAWAYS

- Use the Zeigarnik Effect to open loops of curiosity in your reader's mind, promising to provide the answer (close the loop) in the next chapter. This taps into the brain's natural psychological drive to seek closure and resolution for an incomplete task.
- Don't be afraid to make your chapters shorter and more frequent. A chapter can consist of a single scene or a fragment of a scene. Shorter chapters typically help you move through a book more quickly due to the combination of perceived progress and minimal commitment.
- Avoid using fake tension to create cliffhangers—not only does this reduce the overall stakes of your story (characters dodging bullets left and right), but your readers may lose trust in your ability to commit to conflict.
- Study your favorite unputdownable books and decipher the pattern of closed loop, conflict, and open loop to better understand what this looks like in different stories. Make it so there's no good place to stop.

Chapter 22

SCENE CARDS

What if you could follow a guide to help you write stronger, more engaging scenes that draw your reader into the story, keep them asking questions, and make them desperate to know what happens next?

Good news: There *is* a guide for this, and I'm sharing it in this chapter. The scene card is designed to help you pinpoint the focus of each scene in your story, ensuring each one matters to your narrative—and, consequently, to your reader. Spoiler alert: It just might transform your writing life.

What Is a Scene?

Is it just another word for chapter? What if you're not writing a book with chapters? Does a scene need to occur in just one location? In just one brief window of time? Can you make cuts or shift to another character's perspective within the scene?

These are all questions I've been asked about writing scenes, as the word *scene* is quite subjective. So let's redefine it, shall we? Instead of thinking of this card as a guide for writing a scene set in one location, I'd like you to view it as a guide for crafting a *sequence*.

As award-winning director Ron Howard highlights in his online

MasterClass, "Good stories work in sequences. And when you have the overarching narrative question, the characters in conflict, but the sequences have their own beginning, middle, and end that are satisfying . . . it really pulls you along. And suddenly you can't wait for the next chapter."[10]

When Howard mentioned "chapter," he was referring to an eight- to ten-page segment of a screenplay. However, it could also be an actual chapter in a novel, an episode of a web comic, or a musical number in the Broadway musical you're writing. Regardless of the type of story you're crafting, imagine it being divided into a bunch of eight- to ten-minute sequences.

The sequence might be one scene. One location, one topic, one conversation, one short window of time. Or it might involve a few scenes. It might switch the point of view. It might be a montage showing the passage of time. In other words, no two sequences are created equal. But every good sequence has the same structure.

Beginning, middle, end.
Setup, conflict, resolution.

Does this sound familiar to you? That's right—it's the backbone of the three-act story structure! Every sequence in your story has an arc that takes us on a small journey and leaves us somewhere new.

We could call it:

Setup → Conflict → Resolution

But really, it's more like:

Setup → Tension → Conflict Crossroads → Decision → Outcome

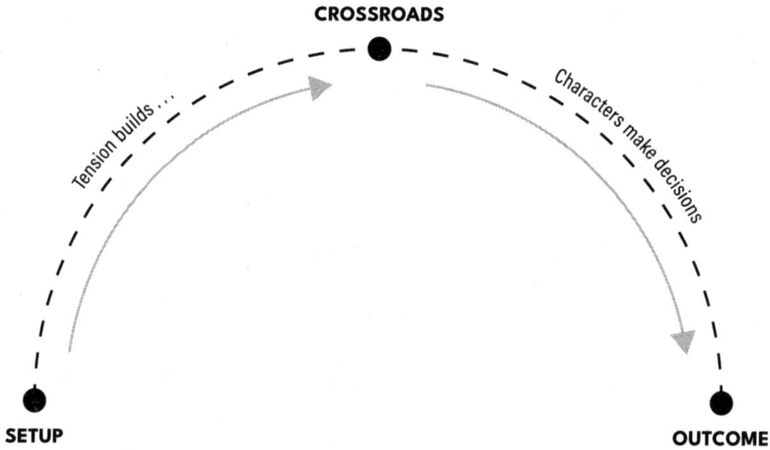

Let's examine each beat of this arc, starting with the **Setup**. This is where your characters begin the scene, filled with internal conflict and likely confronting some external conflict as well. Regardless of what's happening, tension should build, drawing us closer to the main conflict of the scene, which is unveiled at the midpoint or **Crossroads** moment. This represents a pivotal moment when the scene could unfold in two different ways, depending on your characters' decisions and how they respond to the external conflict. Their decisions are, of course, influenced by their own internal conflict—their desires, fears, and false beliefs. How they respond ultimately leads to the **Outcome**.

Obviously, we don't want to resolve *everything* in the outcome. Instead, we want to raise the stakes. We want our audience to ask more questions, and we want every chapter to end in an open loop that makes the reader want to keep reading. You don't need cliffhanger endings for every chapter as long as the reader is always asking new questions and something is always *changing*. It doesn't matter what's happening. What's important is that we, the readers, understand *why it matters*.

The Scene Card Template

CHAPTER/SCENE #
POV CHARACTER:
GOAL OF SCENE:

SETUP
What are the characters dealing with, both internally and externally, when the scene begins?

CROSSROADS
The crux of the scene is revealed . . . the scene could go two ways from here. Characters make decisions based on their internal conflict.

OUTCOME
Where does this leave the characters? What has changed?

THE NEW QUESTION:

At the top of the scene card, we will fill out some basic information for the scene: the chapter number, the POV character, and a one-line description of the scene's goal. Following that, we have our three beats: setup, crossroads, and outcome. After that, we are left with the new question.

If we were to get super analytical, we could argue that every scene in your story asks a question and the following scenes provide answers. You never want the readers to have all the answers . . . not until the story is over. This means you have to keep your readers asking questions.

Remember how essential it is to keep our readers curious? That's what we're leveraging here—the curiosity factor. We love watching people make impossible choices! We love seeing characters we care about struggle with pain versus pain. To make every scene or sequence in your story satisfying, you need to show the readers why what's happening matters to the characters and how it impacts the story moving forward.

This scene card will help you tremendously in giving every chapter of your story a sense of momentum and meaning.

The Scene Card in Action

Let's examine this scene card in action by revisiting *The Otherworld.* Here's a good example of how I would use this scene card to outline a chapter in my book:

CHAPTER #2

POV CHARACTER: Jack Stevenson

GOAL OF SCENE: Jack discovers that the Coast Guard has ceased the search, flies out to look for Adam, and ultimately reaches an emotional breaking point.

SETUP: The chapter opens with Jack waking up from a nightmare about finding his brother dead in the wreckage of his plane. Over coffee, he speaks with his parents, who are both grieving Adam's loss. They've just received word that the Coast Guard is giving up the search, believing Adam's chances of survival are zero. Jack is not ready to accept the grim possibility of his brother's death.

CROSSROADS: Jack reaches a crossroads moment: He can either accept Adam's loss and grieve with his parents or continue to hold out hope that Adam is alive and actively participate in the search. Fueled by furious desperation, Jack storms out of the house and drives to the port, determined to look for Adam himself. He pilots a seaplane in dangerously overcast weather, having a flashback to when Adam taught him how to fly solo. His search proves futile and risky.

OUTCOME: Jack stays out for the rest of the afternoon, unable to confront the crushing weight of his parents' grief at home. When he finally returns in the evening, he talks to his mother, who urges him to let go of Adam and accept the truth so that he can help her bear it. But Jack is still not ready to accept it, at war with himself over his mounting grief and rage, feeling like it should have been him, not Adam, who went down. Jack storms out of the house again, reaching an emotional tipping point as he breaks down in tears. Then, in his darkest moment of despair, his cell phone rings. It's Adam.

THE NEW QUESTION: When Jack answers the call, he's greeted by the unfamiliar voice of a girl. Who is she? What is she doing with Adam's phone?

There you have it! A solid, detailed outline for chapter 2 using this scene card template. As you can see, the flow of this outline encompasses more than just a single scene. We transition between multiple locations and times of day, yet the entire sequence is contained within a single chapter and has a distinct *beginning, middle,* and *end.*

Take this scene card template and start breaking your outline into smaller sequences, identifying the natural flow of setup, crossroads, and outcome until you've defined the lines of each scene. This is my favorite way to determine where a chapter should begin and end to prevent readers from closing the book. We want them hooked and curious enough to keep reading! We achieve this by making something change with every chapter and leaving our readers with a new question at the end.

Now it's your turn. Flip to page 31 of your workbook for the Scene Card Template. Start by filling out the template for the opening scene or sequence of your story.

Chapter 23

HOW TO CRAFT POWERFUL SUBPLOTS

Now that you've finished crafting a compelling plot for your protagonist, you may be wondering: *What about my side characters? Should they go on a journey, too, or simply stand by and watch the protagonist from the sidelines?*

While we briefly developed side characters earlier in part 1, we haven't fully explored what it means to take those side characters on a journey of their own through a subplot.

What Is a Subplot?

A subplot is, essentially, a secondary story that receives less screen time (or story time) and less emphasis than the main plot. At their best, subplots should enhance the dominant theme and conflict of the story, without distracting from the main character.

Behind every good subplot is a side character who matters to the protagonist. If you want the reader to care about this side character, they must first understand why the *protagonist* cares about them.

If executed properly, subplots can add new layers of conflict, meaning, and depth for the reader to engage with. However, if not well executed, subplots can slow down your story's pacing and cause your readers' attention to deviate away from the protagonist's story.

In this chapter, we will explore the key ingredients to making your subplots every bit as engaging as the main plot, without letting them take over your whole story.

THE INTERSECTION OF THE MAIN PLOT AND A SUBPLOT

Remember how, in part 1, we developed our side characters using the CRAI method (Character, Role, Agenda, Impact)? As we meet your side characters and understand their connection to the protagonist, we see how their agendas and actions impact the protagonist's life. This interaction of conflict is where your subplot progresses, because it's in these moments that the main plot and the subplot intersect.

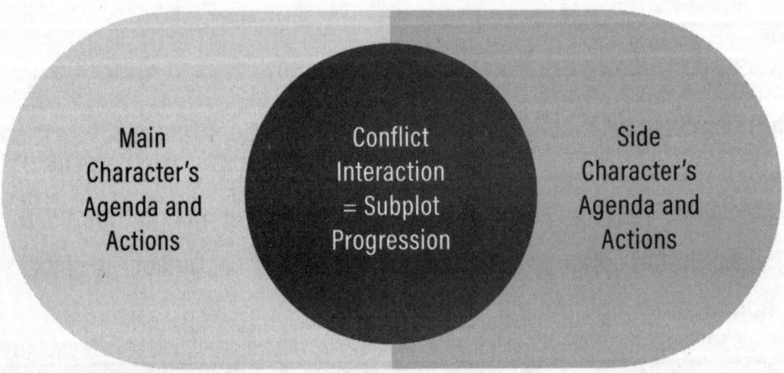

As you can see from this figure, there is an overlap between the main character's agenda and actions and the side character's agenda and actions. Like your protagonist, the side characters consistently make fear-based choices in pursuit of their goals. Remember, they are the heroes of their own stories.

How to Organize Your Subplots

If you feel like your subplots are a jumble of disorganized ideas, you're not alone. Many writers start out with a tangled knot of side characters who all bring different conflicts and personalities to the story. So, what is the best way to organize your subplots? How do you integrate all your subplots with the main plot in a way that feels seamless and natural?

It's important to remember that while all plotlines run parallel to each other, that doesn't mean they receive the same amount of attention. The main plot is the protagonist's journey, so when the main character encounters the side characters, we also encounter their subplots.

Here's another way to look at it:

Main Plotline vs. Sub-Plotlines

Because the main plot is the main character's journey, you can think of it like a line, encountering the sub-plotlines occasionally:

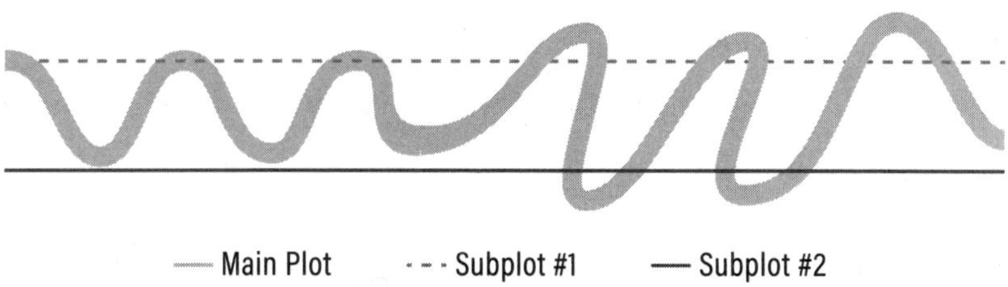

Since the main plot revolves around the main character's journey, you can envision it as a line that occasionally intersects with sub-plotlines. As illustrated in the figure above, the main plot will receive significantly more screen time than the subplots. However, there's no need to pause the protagonist's story to progress with the subplots. Instead, look for opportunities to move the subplot forward without slowing down the main plot.

I like to outline my subplots alongside my main plot so that I know exactly where I'm making room for them. I usually start with a bullet-point outline of my most important plot points for the protagonist's journey, and then I can look for places where the subplots can intersect.

Remember how, in part 1, we used Jane Bennet as an example of a well-written side character? Well, this time, let's pretend we are Jane Austen outlining *Pride and Prejudice,* starting with a bullet-point outline of the most important plot points in the story, while preparing to make room for Jane's subplot.

Bullet-point outline *without* subplots:

- Netherfield Park is let at last! Mrs. Bennet wants to marry off one of her daughters to the Young Man of Large Fortune next door.
- Elizabeth, our protagonist, is too headstrong and independent to contemplate marrying anyone for money and security alone.
- Elizabeth and her family meet Mr. Bingley, who is nice enough . . . but his friend Mr. Darcy is a total jerk to Elizabeth (inciting incident).
- Somehow, Elizabeth has to spend more time with Darcy, and they clash a lot.
- Darcy is a pompous jerk, and Lizzy dislikes him more and more.
- Elizabeth meets the charming Mr. Wickham, whose life was apparently ruined by Darcy back in the day.
- Bingley hosts a ball (for Jane, basically), and Lizzy and Darcy argue over Wickham.

This rough outline looks pretty good so far . . . but how do we make room for Jane's subplot? Let's go back to that CRAI description we wrote for Jane's character.

> Jane Bennet is Elizabeth's closest sister and confidante, on a quest to make a good match and find true love. Her biggest flaw is that she "never thinks ill of anyone." When she falls in love with the wealthy and charming Mr. Bingley, their relationship raises red flags for Bingley's friend Mr. Darcy, who separates the couple. It's not until Darcy mends the rift between Jane and Bingley that he can prove he has transformed his character, which helps Jane achieve her

goal and grow as she learns some people cannot be trusted. Ultimately, she forgives Bingley for his mistake, and they both live happily ever after.

Now, with that character journey in mind, let's see how we can incorporate Jane's subplot without slowing down Elizabeth's side of the story.

Bullet-point outline *with* Jane's subplot:

- Netherfield Park is let at last! Mrs. Bennet wants to marry off one of her daughters to the Young Man of Large Fortune next door.
- Elizabeth, our protagonist, is too headstrong and independent to contemplate marrying anyone for money and security alone.
- **But Jane and Mr. Bingley hit it off as soon as they meet.**
- Bingley's friend Mr. Darcy is a total jerk to Elizabeth (inciting incident).
- **Jane is invited to dine at Netherfield . . . the Bennets hear wedding bells!**
- **At Netherfield, Jane catches a cold and needs to stay for a few days.** That's when Elizabeth goes to visit, spends more time with Darcy, and they clash a lot.
- **Romantic development between Jane and Bingley on the side.**
- Elizabeth meets the charming Mr. Wickham and hears his tragic backstory.
- Bingley hosts a ball (for Jane, basically), and Lizzy and Darcy argue over Wickham.
- At the ball, both Elizabeth and Jane are embarrassed by their family's lack of propriety, **which is the last straw that makes Darcy advise Bingley to dump Jane ASAP.**

This is what I do when outlining a subplot: I start by creating a bullet-point list of the most important plot points for my protagonist. Then, I take the main plot points of my subplot and identify natural places to incorporate the side character's plot. Even better if you can find moments where both plots progress simultaneously.

Do You Need to Advance Your Subplots in Every Chapter or Scene?

No. Sometimes, you only need to touch on the subplot by adding a brief mention or a status update. You rarely need an entire scene dedicated to advancing a single subplot; you just need to give the reader a peek at it from time to time.

Many stories accomplish this well. Next time you read a book or watch a movie, notice how the writer progressed the subplots. How did they unfold? What kept you engaged? Did the writer ever pause the protagonist's story to move a subplot forward, or did both plots progress naturally in tandem?

Every Subplot Has a Beginning, a Middle, and an End

When you view your subplot as its own story arc (or side character's journey), you gain a clearer understanding of the big picture. Since you're not visiting your subplots as frequently as the main plot, they may have a smaller arc compared to the protagonist's journey. Readers won't witness every plot point of the side character's journey—and that's fine, because the focus is on the main character, not the side character.

Understanding the scope of your subplot will help you tremendously with pacing. When you know the beginning, middle, and end, you'll see how to pace the subplot throughout the grand scheme of the story.

What About Writing a Large Cast of Characters?

If you have no single character who acts as the main protagonist of the story, here are some tips to help you make your subplots feel equally important. It takes a lot of skill to write a large cast of characters and make the audience care about everyone's story—but don't let that intimidate you. The most important thing to focus on is creating a *central conflict* that brings all the characters together.

ASK YOURSELF:

- What do all these characters have in common with each other?
- What is the central conflict they are all affected by/engaging with?
- Why do they matter to each other?

The central conflict provides us with an anchor point, rather than relying on a single character as our reference. This central conflict connects every character to the same meaningful point in our minds—it makes them all significant to one another and significant to the reader.

Let's study a few of my favorite large-cast stories and decipher how the writers made us care about all the characters, even without a single protagonist around whom the conflict revolves.

STORY CASE STUDIES: LARGE CAST OF CHARACTERS

- ***Downton Abbey* (TV series, 2010-2015)**
  The series begins with a pivotal crisis—the heir to Downton Abbey perishes on the *Titanic*, catapulting everything into chaos. Lady Mary, the Earl of Grantham's eldest daughter and the intended bride of the deceased heir, grapples with an uncertain future devoid of inheritance. Next in line for the inheritance is Matthew Crawley, an upper-middle-class lawyer who is distantly related and lives outside the realm of aristocracy. He is

viewed as an outsider by Mary and her family. This central inheritance conflict leads to many other disputes, drawing every character into the story. The entire cast operates within Downton Abbey, the Crawley family's residence. Whether we are following the aloof and conniving Lady Mary upstairs or sharing in the domestic dramas unfolding in the servants' quarters downstairs, writer Julian Fellowes masterfully weaves all these characters' stories together in a way that keeps you on the edge of your seat, wondering what's going to happen next.

- ***War and Peace* by Leo Tolstoy**
  This timeless classic unfolds across Imperial Russia, where we follow a sprawling cast of characters—including the introspective Pierre, the earnest Prince Andrei, and the warmhearted Natasha—as their personal lives intersect with the sweeping upheaval of the Napoleonic Wars. As these characters fall in love, chase ambition, suffer loss, and question the meaning of their own existence, the war itself acts as a constant anchor point, drawing their paths together and shaping their individual transformations. Each character carries a deeply human, self-contained emotional arc, yet none of their stories are isolated; every triumph and tragedy is somehow connected to the war. This central conflict ties them together and pulls them apart, creating inescapable tension that reaches into every character's life, no matter how large or small their role.

But don't just take my word for it! As I always say, delve into your favorite stories and subplots to discover what resonates with you and keeps you reading (or watching) past your bedtime. You can use my Story Study Guide templates to analyze your favorite (or least favorite) stories to learn from them and enhance your writing skills.

Now, it's your turn. Turn to pages 32–38 of your companion workbook for the Story Study Guides.

KEY TAKEAWAYS

- Outline your subplots by first identifying the main plot points of your protagonist's journey, then looking for logical places to insert a plot progression for the side character.
- Don't be afraid to let these plotlines intersect from time to time. Remember, we don't necessarily need to leave the protagonist to get an update on the subplot.
- When writing a large cast, ensure you provide your reader with an anchor point, which is a central conflict around which all the characters revolve. Although each character has a unique narrative, you must identify the element that unites them and makes them significant to each other and to the reader.

Chapter 24

SHOW, DON'T TELL

If you've spent any time in the writing world, you're probably familiar with this advice: Show, don't tell. But what does that actually look like on the page? Here's a quick example of telling versus showing.

Telling: She was tired.
Showing: She yawned, her eyelids heavy.

The difference is clear: The first flatly states what a character is feeling. The second shows the character in action and gives descriptive detail. Most of the time, showing is more effective than telling. It pulls readers into the scene and allows them to interpret what's happening. However, when it comes to the unseen things, like false beliefs and internal conflicts, showing rather than telling is easier said than done.

How much of your character's internal conflict should you reveal? Are they supposed to know their false belief or keep it hidden? Do they understand what they want? Are they aware of what they fear? How can we convey all of this to the reader without making them feel like they're simply reading a character profile?

I get questions about this all the time from writers, and I feel their pain because this is *not* easy. You might have done all the groundwork to craft a deeply flawed and conflicted protagonist, but if you don't know how to illustrate those conflicts on the page, your character may still come off seeming one-dimensional.

Here are some really simple techniques that will instantly improve your writing, highlight your characters' innermost conflicts, and make your story unputdownable.

THE GOLDEN RULE OF SHOW, DON'T TELL

Revealing your characters' internal conflict using the show, don't tell rule can be challenging. We know that every compelling character grapples with these things:

- A desire
- A fear
- A false belief

Characters, however, aren't always aware of what they're grappling with. Yes, they are generally aware of their desires. They may have some inkling of their fears (though expressing them can be difficult). But they often remain blissfully unaware of their false belief and their deepest flaws. If they possessed total self-awareness, they would have no transformative journey to make, and there would be no story.

Every one of us has a false belief (or two or three), but most of us have no idea what it is. In fact, we often see our greatest weakness as our greatest strength. We constantly reframe our faults as virtues to stay in the comfort zone of our established personality. For example, a tough and defensive character could be proud of being able to take care of themselves. They are oblivious to their inability to trust or be vulnerable with others, which shuts them off from forging deep relationships.

This is why internal conflict can feel forced or cheesy if a character appears overly aware of their own flaws. If they start to sound like their own therapist, objectively analyzing aspects of themselves that psychologically trip them up, chances are you're revealing too much of their internal conflict.

Let's say you've crafted a deeply flawed and conflicted character named Pam. She wants to be a great writer, but she fears rejection and criticism, so she's never put her work out there. She believes she needs to be perfect and above criticism. This false belief is rooted in her past. She grew up with very strict parents who rewarded her for perfect behavior and punished her if she fell short.

That's a great start. But how do we *show* Pam's internal conflict without making her come right out and say to herself, "I want to be a great writer, but I'm afraid of being criticized. I want to be perfect, but I worry that I never will be because my parents always made me feel like I fell short"?

Let's be honest—no one in real life has objective, unbiased insight into their own flaws like this. That's why it's essential to ask yourself, *How much does my protagonist truly understand their internal struggles?*

Be careful about how you disclose this conflict to your readers. You want to reveal just enough to allow them to understand what the character is struggling with . . . yet, at the same time, you don't want to lay it all out so clearly that there's no mystery, no intrigue, and no motivation for your readers to burn the midnight oil turning pages.

Pam the Writer (Telling)

I'm sitting at my desk, ready to hit Send on a query letter to the agent of my dreams. I'm so nervous that if I make a mistake, it will make me look like an amateur, which is exactly what I am.

I want so much to be a bestselling author, but I'm just so afraid of being criticized and rejected. I know criticism and rejection come with the territory of being a published author, but it's different for me. I had to grow up with parents who constantly pushed me to do better and never allowed a mistake. They only ever rewarded me with love when I made them proud and did something they approved of. And if I failed at something, they made me feel like I fell short.

I can't help but feel like my best will never be good enough, and my dreams will never come true.

This is way too on the nose! You could write out this kind of emotional processing in your character profile or story outline, but it should never appear so transparently within the context of the narrative itself. Why? Because while Pam is rife with internal conflict, she is not an omniscient observer of that internal conflict. She's stuck in her own limited perspective, meaning that her false beliefs define her worldview, even if she can't express why.

What if we take this same character, with the same internal conflict in the same situation (sending a query letter to her dream agent), and make the internal conflict more subtle and nuanced but still present?

Pam the Writer (Showing)

You never have a second chance to make a good first impression.

That's a motto my mother instilled in me at a young age. And it's Mom's voice I hear now, whispering those words in the back of my mind as I proofread my query letter for possibly the hundredth time.

Mom's rule rings especially true when it comes to introducing yourself to a high-demand professional like Sandy Griswold. She's represented some of my favorite authors and landed publishing deals that sent books soaring to the top of *The New York Times* bestseller list.

Is it possible she'll be interested in my novel, too? It's a long shot, especially for a debut author with no accolades, awards, or credits to my name. But with flawless grammar and attention to detail, I may just have a slim chance of impressing the agent of my dreams.

My heart thunders in my chest as I hover my cursor over the Send button. *Here goes nothing.*

Much better! We *see* Pam's anxiety and hear her perfectionistic inner critic hovering at the back of her thoughts. All the same inner conflict is there, but we readers are solving the mystery ourselves and actively engaging with the story instead of being told what to think.

Balancing this can seem daunting, but don't worry—you have what it takes to pull it off. The key is to fully immerse yourself in your character's perspective and allow them to naturally uncover and confront their internal battles as they move through life. Allow them to struggle, pursue their desires, grapple with their fears, and evolve as a result of their journey.

THE POWER OF DIALOGUE

Dialogue can be a powerful tool for showcasing your character's beliefs, inner conflict, and deeper fears. But be careful when revealing this conflict in dialogue! A common mistake many writers make is letting their characters be too objective about their flaws and inner wounded child, which can sound stilted and cheesy if it's too on the nose.

Bottom line: If you can't imagine someone you know in real life saying this, don't make your character say it.

A Bad Example of Revealing Conflict in Dialogue

"Why are you so nervous about querying agents?" my best friend, Fiona, asks me the following afternoon as we sip cappuccinos in our favorite café.

"I don't know," I say with a sigh. "I just feel like I can protect myself emotionally if I never let anyone read my writing. If I never open myself up to rejection or criticism, then I'll never be disappointed or feel like I'm not good enough to be a published author. My parents always wanted me to go to an Ivy League school, and I don't want to disappoint them." I give a sad laugh, shaking my head. "See? That just goes to show how much my parents have psychologically abused me into feeling like I'm not good enough."

"Yeah," Fiona says. "Why should you care about disappointing them? They've never been on your side about your writing."

"You're right. They just want me to fulfill their ambition of having a Harvard graduate for a daughter."

Remember what we discussed earlier: We don't want our characters sounding like their own therapist. But that's exactly what Pam is doing in this scene! She's pinpointing her fatal flaw, objectively observing her faults, and spelling out her parents' psychological abuse as if she is detached from the situation. This comes across sounding strange and stilted, even when packaged in dialogue, because people typically don't talk about themselves like this.

Even saying "my best friend, Fiona," is telling because we are delivering information to the reader that normally wouldn't cross Pam's mind at this moment. When interacting with our best friend, we don't think to ourselves, *This is my best friend.* However, we might find a way for Fiona to naturally reveal that she's known Pam for a long time.

A Good Example of Revealing Conflict in Dialogue

"What's wrong?" Fiona asks, frowning over the rim of her cappuccino. "And don't say, 'Nothing's wrong,' because I've known you since first grade, and I can tell when you're hiding behind a brave face."

I sigh, dropping my face into my hands. "I don't know. Maybe I shouldn't have sent those query letters. I feel so . . . exposed letting someone see my ideas for the first time. What if all I get are rejections in reply? What if my book isn't good enough to publish?"

"Oh, stop with your worst-case scenario planning. What if they love it? What if you become the next J. K. Rowling, and I get to make a fortune from selling your autograph on eBay?"

I'm too sick with anxiety to laugh at her joke. "Maybe Mom is right. Maybe this whole publishing thing is a waste of time, and I should just focus on writing my college application essay. Not some silly rom-com nobody is going to want to read."

"Hey, I like that silly rom-com of yours," Fiona reassures me. "And if you're really that worried about making your mom happy, tell her she can brag about you to her fancy friends when you become a bestselling romance author."

Much better! We've revealed Pam's anxiety and Fiona's heartfelt and upbeat encouragement, all without *telling,* and instead, allowing the reader to *interpret.*

We're going to take a closer look at writing dialogue in a future chapter, but for now, here are some tips for writing dialogue that clearly reveals internal conflict.

DOS AND DON'TS OF REVEALING CONFLICT IN DIALOGUE

Do	Don't
✓ Do let your characters express their fears and beliefs naturally when prompted.	✗ Don't let your characters objectively observe their struggles from an omniscient perspective, like their own therapist.
✓ Do let side characters point out flaws and weaknesses that the POV character can't see themselves.	✗ Don't use side characters to parrot or reaffirm what the POV character has already explained.
✓ Do trust your reader to interpret the subtext of conversations and draw their own conclusions.	✗ Don't editorialize through dialogue and make your characters say exactly what they're feeling.

STRATEGIES IN ACTION: SHOWING VS. TELLING

Let's explore an example of showing versus telling internal conflict in *The Otherworld.* We'll look at two versions to identify the issues and learn how to elevate our writing to the next level. One passage *shows* my protagonist's internal conflict, while the other demonstrates how that same excerpt might read if I had simply *told* the internal conflict. This is from the prologue, where I introduce Orca's internal conflict.

If I were to come right out and *tell you* Orca's internal conflict and fatal flaw, it might look like this:

> *I've never been to the Otherworld, but I long to go with Papa and see what it's like. I've spent my whole life on this island, and I feel like I'm missing out on many things, but mostly relationships and connections—people. However, I'm afraid Papa will never let me go because he thinks I'm not strong enough for the Otherworld. He's always telling me that I'm too delicate and sweet and fragile to handle the harsh realities of the mainland. Really, I think he's just afraid of losing me like he lost Mama.*

This feels like an outline. Literally, just change the pronouns to the third person, and this is how I write an outline. I need to explain to myself what's happening with this character, but the character isn't fully aware of what's going on inside them. If you come right out and explain it to the reader, it comes off as editorializing: dry and flat. You're not allowing the reader to interact with and interpret the story—you're just telling them what to think.

So now, let's look at an actual excerpt from the book, which does a better job of *showing* Orca's conflict through action and dialogue.

> *At times, I have glimpsed lights from the Otherworld, too. Little pinpricks of light, as if some stars had fallen out of the night sky and landed in the water—twinkling for a moment on the horizon before the waves swallowed them up.*
>
> What is it like out there? Will I ever know?
>
> *When Papa spoke of the thunderstorm people in the Otherworld, he emphasized how much we don't belong there. How much I don't belong there.*
>
> *"You're a very special, kind soul, Orca," he'd say, looking deep into my eyes from across the dinner table. "People aren't kind in the Otherworld."*
>
> *"None of them?"*
>
> *"Not many of them," Papa said. "You're like . . . a delicate and unique branch of coral. You belong far away from the violent crashes of the waves on the rocks. You see, corals can't survive in the tide. That's why they flourish in a reef, on the ocean floor. Out of harm's way."*

I understood what he was saying: I wasn't strong enough for the Otherworld. According to Papa, it would smash me and destroy me.

Year after year, I helped Papa keep the light. Occasionally, boats and planes would cross paths with us, always miles out of reach—traveling in too many directions to determine where they came from or where they were going. I amused myself by making up stories about the people in those planes and boats. Where they might be traveling to, and what kinds of lives they led.

Although this excerpt is longer, it does a much better job of allowing you to observe and interpret Orca's feelings instead of being *told* what she feels.

We witness the false-belief reinforcement through the dialogue with her father. We can interpret their conversation and observe how protective he is. We can see Orca's conclusion and false belief taking root. Then, through her actions, we see her curiosity and longing for the Otherworld—watching the lights from the mainland at night, observing the boats and planes, making up stories about people she'll never meet. We *see* how lonely and left out she feels, without needing to be told point-blank that she feels lonely and left out.

Remember, the power of a great story lies in its ability to make us engage with it, not tell us what to think. So, whenever you doubt whether you're showing or telling in your writing, ask yourself this simple question: *Am I explaining, or am I allowing the reader to interpret?*

That's the difference between showing and telling. This forces your prose to improve because instead of writing nebulous, abstract thoughts in the narrative, you're forced to include more action. You're forced to make something happen that the reader can interpret, whether it's an action the character takes or an emotion they struggle with.

When is it okay to tell instead of show? When your character expresses *their* opinion about something, or lets their current mood and beliefs influence their perspectives. This differs from telling in that the character is the one editorializing, not the author. In this case, you're not actually telling so much as writing in deep point of view.

What Is Deep Point of View?
Deep point of view appears when the story is filtered through the narrator's perspective and senses. Writers leverage deep point of view to make the reader feel like they are in the skin of the character, experiencing all the same thoughts, feelings, and physical sensations. This helps us connect with the point-of-view character and empathize with them on a deep level.

For example, in that excerpt from *The Otherworld,* we get a glimpse of deep point of view when Orca thinks: "I understood what he was saying: I wasn't strong enough for the Otherworld." This isn't actually true—it's just how *she* perceives the situation based on her own false beliefs. In this instance, we are telling instead of showing, but the idea being conveyed is not the author's opinion, but the protagonist's.

This rule—show, don't tell—is just one of the building blocks in the foundation of good writing. If you've made it this far, you're serious about taking your writing to the next level and making your style shine. In the upcoming chapters, we'll delve deeper into the most vital elements of well-written prose so you can concentrate on what truly matters and avoid the analysis paralysis that comes from trying to get everything right. This isn't about achieving perfection—it's about discovering your unique voice and making your writing the best it can be.

KEY TAKEAWAYS

- Telling explains what we're observing, while showing lets us interpret what we see and connect with the story emotionally. Don't dictate our thoughts on something; show us how the point-of-view character perceives it and how they feel about it.
- How much does your protagonist truly comprehend their internal struggles? Be careful about how you reveal this conflict to your readers.

You want to show just enough to allow them to understand what the character is wrestling with, but you don't want to make it so obvious that there's no mystery or intrigue left.

- When in doubt, ask yourself: Am I *explaining*, or am I allowing the reader to interpret? This is the difference between showing and telling. Instead of relying on exposition, you're forced to make something happen that the reader can interpret, whether through an action the character takes or an emotion they struggle with.
- When is it okay to tell instead of show? When your character is expressing their opinion about something, or allowing their current mood and beliefs to color their perspective. Rather than editorializing as the author, you're letting the POV character take the reins and show us how they think and feel about things.

Chapter 25

MASTERING THE ART OF DIALOGUE

Are you struggling to make your dialogue realistic and emotionally expressive? Do you find your characters saying exactly what they're feeling, which results in flat, dry, and predictable dialogue? Or do you feel like all your characters sound the same, lacking distinct voices and personalities?

Dialogue is one of those things that, if executed poorly, can pull the reader out of the story. The last thing you want your reader thinking is, *Who talks like this? These characters don't sound like real people . . .*

In this chapter, I will share the seven keys to writing dynamite dialogue—techniques that are guaranteed to transform dull dialogue into a riveting, unputdownable page-turner.

KEY #1: WEAVE YOUR CHARACTERS' MOTIVES AND FEARS INTO THEIR DIALOGUE

Every person filters their thoughts and words through the lens of personal beliefs. Because of this, we don't objectively observe events as they are; instead, we interpret events and others' decisions, formulate opinions, and then we decide which opinions to share based on what we hope to achieve by expressing those opinions.

You might have some juicy, well-developed internal conflict for your characters, but it will fall flat if a character tells us, instead of showing us, what those conflicts and false beliefs are. As we just explored in the previous chapter, having a character come right out and explicitly state their internal struggles can instantly make dialogue feel unrealistic and emotionless. I like to call this *conflict dumping.*

Conflict Dumping vs. Subtext

Subtext is the golden rule of dialogue. It's what makes it feel subtle, realistic, and mind-blowingly good. Subtext, in essence, is the hidden meaning behind what we say. It's the unspoken truth we find when we read between the lines. It's the emotion or intention your character is *not* directly expressing.

Imagine you stumble into your house after midnight, only to be greeted by your partner, who gives you a meaningful look and says, "You're home late." They are stating a simple fact, but there's subtext behind those words. Perhaps they're concerned and really saying, "I was worried about you." Maybe they're jealous and really saying, "Who were you with?" Or perhaps they're disappointed and really saying, "How could you do this to me again?" That's subtext.

However, mastering subtext can be tricky because, as writers, we can see through the masks our characters hide behind. *We* know what the characters are secretly struggling with, but that doesn't mean they should *reveal* that struggle.

Let me show you what this looks like in action. For example, imagine you have two characters—Violet and Kent. They are both students at the same school, and in this scene, Violet confronts Kent about cheating on a test, while he refuses to admit it.

Violet: "I think you cheated on that test, Kent. Your grades have been terrible lately, and now you have a perfect score."

Kent: "How dare you say that! I didn't cheat."

Violet: "Then why are you acting so strange? I have proof you cheated. I found the paper in your backpack."

Kent: "Okay, fine, you're right. I cheated."

Violet: "Why?"

Kent: "Because my father expects me to succeed academically, and I didn't want to disappoint him again. I'm tired of always being the family disappointment. I think that's why I felt the need to cheat—so I can measure up to my father's image of success and feel worthy of his love."

This sounds cringeworthy because it's not how people talk. Is there internal conflict? Yes. But it's all too obvious and on the surface, and Kent is objectively observing his own internal conflict in a way that doesn't feel human. I don't know about you, but I've never met someone who can verbalize their deepest internal conflicts or childhood traumas as if they're reading a Wikipedia page about their life. So if your character starts to sound like their own therapist—identifying the root cause of their beliefs and discussing those issues in casual conversation—it's a clear sign that you need to rewrite your dialogue.

When you're about to write a line of dialogue that conveys your character's emotions, ask yourself, *How can I express what they're feeling without them stating it directly?*

Consider your character's personality and their emotional responses to what's being said. Are they the type to withdraw from conflict and become uncommunicative? Or are they prone to angry outbursts when they feel attacked? Perhaps they even laugh and charm their way out of uncomfortable conversations. Your character's unique coping mechanisms will depend on the nature of the dialogue. However, these three pillars—a character's personality, beliefs, and the ultimate goal of the scene—provide a strong foundation to start from.

Revealing Conflict Through Subtext

Let's return to our dialogue between Violet and Kent and see if we can enhance it. I suspect Kent is a deeply insecure kid, so he tends to hide behind his charm when necessary. However, when he feels threatened, he becomes defensive.

Perhaps he's an Enneagram 3. This insight could help me uncover the root of his false belief—that he must perform well academically to feel like a worthy son.

Violet: "Did you cheat on that test, Kent?"

Kent: [with a forced laugh] "What? Are you kidding me? Why would I need to cheat?"

Violet: "I don't know, because your grades have been, well . . ." [haltingly] "kind of terrible lately . . . and you heard what Mr. Lang said—nobody has ever gotten a perfect score on that test."

Kent: [flashes her a convincing smile] "Well, I guess there's a first time for everything."

Violet: [steps closer, lowering her voice so nobody else hears] "Kent, I found the paper in your backpack."

Kent: [surprised and a little defensive] "What were you doing snooping through my backpack?"

Violet: "I needed an eraser. I wasn't snooping."

[Kent turns away, a muscle ticking in his jaw. He's been caught, and he knows there's no getting out of it.]

Violet: "I'm not going to tell your dad, if that's what you're afraid of."

Kent: [defensively] "I'm not afraid of him. I'm sick of him. I'm sick of watching him congratulate my brothers on everything they do, telling them how proud he is of them, and meanwhile, I just . . ." [he shakes his head, frustrated and ashamed of himself]. "You don't know what it's like, Violet. So just keep your nose out of it. Okay?"

As you can see, the emotional tone in this version of the scene is quite different. It feels more natural for Kent to first deny the accusation, then become defensive, and finally reveal a glimpse of his internal conflict without directly stating his fears and false belief. It becomes clear that he doesn't feel he measures up and believes his father isn't proud of him, which drives his need to cheat. It's what

Kent *doesn't* say—the subtext—that makes us realize something is happening beneath the surface.

KEY #2: KEEP YOUR CHARACTER'S VOICE CONSISTENT IN DIALOGUE

Most people don't speak with perfect grammar. Our vocabularies vary based on our culture, environment, social circles, and other influences. Which means, when crafting your characters' unique voices, you need to take these external influences into account to prevent your characters from sounding identical. A fifty-year-old English professor will speak and think differently from a high school student. If all your characters sound the same—or sound like *you*—they won't feel like real people.

So ask yourself, *What makes one character distinct from every other character in the story? How old are they? How has the community in which they were raised influenced their speech, thoughts, and perceptions of the world around them?* Even if these differences are subtle, make sure you're revealing them to us through the dialogue. Every character should have their own perspective on life and a distinctive voice that reflects their beliefs and personality.

Character Voice Cheat Sheets

One of my secret hacks for maintaining a character's unique voice consistently throughout a story is developing a cheat sheet with clear parameters as to how a particular character speaks and thinks based on their personality, beliefs, and backstory. Here are a few ingredients that might factor into a character's voice:

- How old they are
- Where they grew up
- Who they've spent time with
- What they do for a living
- Personality type

- Sense of humor
- How they see the world
- Hobbies and interests

Once you have completed your character voice cheat sheets, compare them to identify areas where you can further define the characters' voices and ensure they feel distinct from one another.

Kent:

- Age: 16
- Charming and smooth
- Straight shooter
- Defensive when threatened
- Dry humor
- Sees life in terms of success and failure

Violet:

- Age: 16
- Sweet and somewhat shy
- Brutally honest when she wants to be
- Afraid of causing conflict
- Loyal friend
- Assumes the best in people

KEY #3: STRIP DOWN WORDY DIALOGUE TAGS AND DESCRIPTIONS

A few chapters from now, we will explore my golden rule of pacing: You see everything happening at the pace at which you read. When you show your reader two characters having a dialogue, you want the reader to visualize it as if they are watching a movie scene. If you slow down the pacing with long descriptions and wordy dialogue tags, you start to lose the momentum of the scene.

Dialogue tags (such as "she said" or "he shouted") are necessary to show us what character is talking, but too many dialogue tags can distract from what's being said. The last thing you want is to make your reader skim over the "unimportant" details to get to the good stuff. In other words, keep the dialogue rolling so it doesn't lose momentum.

Here's an example of what I mean. Let's take our scene with Violet and Kent and add some dialogue tags—far too many of them.

Violet narrowed her eyes, regarding Kent with suspicion for a long moment. "Did you cheat on that test, Kent?"

He responded with a laugh that sounded somewhat forced. "What? Are you kidding me? Why would I need to cheat?"

Violet didn't know how to begin. How to say it in a way that wouldn't hurt his feelings or make him defensive. "I don't know, because your grades have been, well . . ." She trailed off, her voice halting and quiet. She didn't want to have this conversation, but there was no avoiding it now. "Your grades have been kind of *terrible* lately . . . and you heard what Mr. Lang said—nobody has ever gotten a perfect score on that test."

Kent flashed her one of his classic, unruffled smiles. The smile he gave everyone, with a side of flattery and easy charm. "Well, I guess there's a first time for everything."

Violet stepped closer, lowering her voice to a hushed murmur so nobody else could hear. "Kent, I found the paper in your backpack."

Kent turned to face her, a spark of defensiveness flickering in his eyes. The look was equal parts surprise and guilt. "What were you doing snooping through my backpack?" he growled, every muscle in his body wound tight.

"I needed an eraser," Violet explained, nervously picking at her fingernail. "I wasn't *snooping*."

Kent turned away, a muscle ticking in his jaw. But Violet wouldn't back down from this conversation, and she made that clear by the way she stood her ground, waiting for an explanation. When a long silence passed between them, and it became obvious that Kent wasn't going to explain, Violet spoke again.

"I'm not going to tell your dad," she said gently, "if that's what you're afraid of."

"I'm not afraid of him," Kent fired back, his voice hardening. "I'm *sick* of him. I'm sick of watching him congratulate my brothers on everything they do, telling them how proud he is of them, and meanwhile, I just . . ." He shook his head, and Violet could see an unmistakable glint of frustration and remorse in his eyes. "You don't know what it's like, Violet. So just keep your nose out of it. Okay?"

Talk about slowing down the dialogue! If that were a scene in a book I was reading, you can bet I would skip almost every single dialogue tag and description to get to the important parts.

But, Abbie! What about all the nuances of emotion? All the body language? All the visual descriptions and emotional undertones?

We can still have all those elements without burdening the reader with so much input. We can show the emotion of the scene without telling them every single time someone bats an eyelash or picks at their fingernail. When you over-describe little actions like this, your reader begins to feel as if they are watching a movie in slow motion—zooming in on minor, unimportant details that distract from the heart of the scene.

Let's strip this scene down to the most impactful dialogue tags and descriptions to see how it works.

Violet narrowed her eyes. "Did you cheat on that test, Kent?"

His laugh came out sounding forced. "What? Are you kidding me? Why would I need to cheat?"

"I don't know, because your grades have been, well . . . kind of *terrible* lately . . . and you heard what Mr. Lang said—nobody has ever gotten a perfect score on that test."

Unruffled, Kent flashed her a smile. "Well, I guess there's a first time for everything."

"Kent." Violet stepped closer, lowering her voice so nobody else could hear. "I found the paper in your backpack."

He whirled to face her. "What were you doing snooping through my backpack?"

"I needed an eraser. I wasn't *snooping*."

Kent turned away, a muscle ticking in his jaw. Violet stood her ground, making it clear she wasn't going to leave without an explanation.

"I'm not going to tell your dad," she said gently, "if that's what you're afraid of."

"I'm not afraid of him," Kent fired back. "I'm *sick* of him. I'm sick of watching him congratulate my brothers on everything they do, telling them how proud he is of them, and meanwhile, I just . . ." He shook his head, frustration and regret clashing in his eyes. "You don't know what it's like, Violet. So just keep your nose out of it. Okay?"

Ah, much better! See how, even though this excerpt is shorter, it more effectively conveys the characters' feelings? That's because you don't need an avalanche of descriptions to convey subtle emotional cues and reveal what the characters are feeling.

I encourage you to experiment with dialogue in your own writing. See if you can take a lengthy dialogue tag and condense it to be just as impactful but twice as quick to read. In some cases, a description can be removed entirely without altering the tone or confusing the reader. Other times, you might want to slow down a moment in a conversation to highlight nonverbal communication (such as the POV character experiencing a realization about the true nature of something). But be careful not to pause for too long, or the momentum of the scene will be lost.

KEY #4: MAKE ALL YOUR DIALOGUE SOUND NATURAL AND REALISTIC

When writing dialogue, it's crucial to ensure that every line sounds authentic and true to your characters. One effective way to test this is by acting out your dialogue as if you were in a movie. This simple exercise can give you a better sense of how your characters would speak and the emotions their words would convey. If something doesn't roll off your tongue naturally, rewrite it until it does. Remember, if you can't deliver a line convincingly out loud, your readers won't be able to hear it in their minds, either. Acting out dialogue can help you create more realistic and compelling conversations between your characters . . . even if your neighbors think you're losing your mind. (It's worth it!)

When in Doubt, Trust Yourself

If you're struggling with a specific line of dialogue, try to put yourself in your character's shoes and ask yourself, *What would I say in this scenario?* Not all characters will share your personality or beliefs, but when it comes to emotional reactions, the best approach is usually to do what feels natural and believable—something you can imagine yourself doing or saying in a similar situation.

You can also seek feedback from trusted friends and critique partners on whether your dialogue feels natural or forced. Sometimes an external perspective is all it takes to identify what isn't working so you can fix it.

KEY #5: WRITE YOUR DIALOGUE LIKE A SCREENPLAY

One thing that has helped me strengthen my dialogue is writing in screenplay format when developing conversations between my characters (as we saw in the first example scene with Violet and Kent). Later, I embellish the scene with dialogue tags and descriptions, but during the outlining stage, it can be tremendously helpful to ignore those details altogether and just focus on what matters to the conversation. This keeps the dialogue on topic and meaningful. And you may be surprised by just how little description is needed to paint a colorful image for the reader.

When I write dialogue out of the context of the whole scene, I can focus entirely on the conversation and emotional tone. So, try writing the important parts now and add details of the setting, character actions, and body language later.

KEY #6: EFFORTLESSLY STEP INTO YOUR CHARACTER'S VOICE

How can you do this? Start by listening to people who sound like your character (similar personality, attitude, and internal conflict). Yes, *listen.* The goal here is not to steal someone's voice (fictional or real) but rather to get their attitude and personality stuck in your head like a catchy tune.

For me, reading doesn't achieve this effect as well as listening, which is why I enjoy watching and listening to a character (or a real person) who exudes the same energy as the character whose dialogue I'm trying to write. If I ever struggle to connect with that particular character's voice, it's remarkable how helpful a little time spent listening to a similar voice can be. After conditioning my brain with this person's voice, speaking style, attitude, and personality, I feel as though their vibe has rubbed off on me, allowing me to shift gears effortlessly.

How Would ________ Say This?

As I mentioned earlier, the aim of this exercise is not to appropriate any actual words or distinct quirks from real people or another writer's original characters. Instead, the goal is to internalize a particular energy and attitude, so when you sit down to write, you can already hear your character's voice in your mind.

Find a character or person (on YouTube, or perhaps someone you know in real life) and spend some time listening to the way they talk. Then, when you return to writing dialogue, ask yourself, *How would [my inspiration character] say this?*

This trick is especially helpful when you write dialogue for characters who are not like you. Don't sweat it; just enjoy the process. Experiment, play, and have fun with it.

KEY #7: PRACTICE MAKES PERFECT

Practicing a lot is the best way to improve your dialogue. Sometimes it may feel slow and tedious, but trust me—it's worth it. Each time you sit down to write dialogue, you become better at it. You can also enhance your skills by watching a film or reading a book and then critiquing the dialogue. Analyze both your favorite and least favorite scenes. What is it about bad dialogue that makes you cringe? What is it about good dialogue that makes you quote it, even years later? Watch and read with an observant eye, and turn every moment into a learning opportunity.

ASK YOURSELF:

- What makes this piece of dialogue riveting or dull?
- How would I change it to make it sound more believable?
- Would I make the characters say more or less? Why?
- Would I have the characters say anything in a different tone? What impact would that have on the scene?
- Would I delete or add dialogue tags or description to change the pacing of the scene?

KEY TAKEAWAYS

- Subtext is the magic ingredient of mind-blowing dialogue. When you take the time to *show* your characters' motives and fears (instead of telling), you make your reader emotionally invested in every conversation. It's not about what is said—it's about what is left *unsaid*.

- Use character voice cheat sheets to keep your characters' voices consistent and unique. Compare cheat sheets to see how you can make them different.
- Quicken the pacing of slow scenes by stripping down wordy dialogue tags and keeping the momentum of the conversation rolling. Remember: You see everything happen at the pace at which you read. So, do your dialogue tags hit pause on the movie in your reader's mind? Or do they keep up with the pace of the scene?
- Try writing your dialogue out of context in screenplay format. Let the ideas and emotions flow freely with very little description; then, add tags later.
- Step into your character's voice with ease by listening to other characters/people who have a similar attitude/personality and letting that energy rub off on you.

THE DOS AND DON'TS OF DIALOGUE

✗ Don't make characters say exactly what they're feeling all the time.
✓ Do use subtext to suggest the characters' emotions and beliefs through their dialogue.
✗ Don't make all your characters sound the same.
✓ Do give your characters distinct voices and different perspectives.

BRAINSTORM PROMPTS:

For writing subtext:

- What is my character's desire going into this scene? What are they hoping to achieve by participating in the conversation?
- What fears and insecurities are they struggling with? Where do they *not* want this conversation to go?

- How does their personality dictate their emotional responses to what is being said? (For example, do they shy away from conflict or get aggressive?)

For improving dialogue tags and pacing:

- What happens if I delete this dialogue tag? Does it change the emotional tone of the scene? Will it confuse the reader?
- How do my character's behavior and body language express their feelings? Do I need to add a description to show this, or will the dialogue suffice?
- Can I swap adverbs for a stronger verb? (For example, "she said softly" → "she whispered")
- Can I delete any weak filler words, such as somewhat, slightly, etc.?

Chapter 26

WRITING POWERFUL FLASHBACKS

Flashbacks are among the most challenging elements of storytelling. While they allow you to shed light on a character's backstory, it can be a headache to weave flashbacks seamlessly into a narrative. What if the flashback distracts from the main plot? What if it confuses the reader? What if it makes the reader put the book down and lose interest? You might think you're safer just avoiding flashbacks altogether. But don't let this challenge intimidate you! While flashbacks can be tricky to master, they greatly enhance the emotional depth of a character's journey and make the reader more invested in the story.

In this chapter, we will break down flashbacks step by step, uncovering the most common pitfalls and how to avoid them. We'll explore the essential types of flashbacks—parallel, bite-sized, dual timeline, and mysterious narrator—and examine how to use each one effectively to strengthen your story. We will also delve into the curiosity-to-reward ratio, a powerful technique for keeping readers hooked as they uncover the character's past. With clear dos and don'ts, along with side-by-side examples to illustrate each method in action, we will discover how to craft flashbacks that are captivating, meaningful, and fully integrated into the heart of the story.

THE THREE KEYS TO POWERFUL FLASHBACKS

1. **Clear trigger.** It's essential to have a clear trigger that brings us into the flashback. The reader must understand why they are experiencing this flashback at this particular moment. It needs to make sense to their brain right now, even if they won't see the deeper significance until later on in the story.
2. **Direct impact.** When we emerge from the flashback, does it directly influence our perception of the present story? The power of a flashback lies in its effect on the current narrative. It's not significant just because it impacted your character *once*; it's significant because it's still impacting your character to this day.
3. **Rewards for curiosity.** If you never reward your reader with answers to their questions until the big reveal at the end, they might not make it to the end. Flashbacks are a great way to sprinkle in pieces of the puzzle, and as we fit them together, we begin to see the fuller picture.

THE DOS AND DON'TS OF WRITING FLASHBACKS

Don't Go into a Flashback Without a Clear Trigger

A flashback means hitting pause on the current story to explore the past, highlighting something that will be significant to us. The subconscious mind continually seeks meaning and relevance in what we observe. So, if your reader cannot immediately understand *why* they're entering this flashback at this particular moment, they may feel disoriented.

I see many writers making this mistake. They're like, "Oh, don't worry, it will all make sense later." No, no, no. It has to make sense now. It can take on deeper meaning and greater significance later, but my brain needs to understand why we've paused the current story to flashback to something in the past. I need to see the relevance, even if I don't fully grasp the grander impact until later.

Don't Give the Reader a Flashback That Has No Impact on the Present Story

You know what's even worse than entering a flashback with no clear trigger or reason for its existence? Coming out of a flashback and having no clue why *any* of that mattered! We're left reeling and disoriented, like waking up from a crazy dream, thinking, *What was that all about?*

As I mentioned earlier, relevance is crucial so we can keep the dopamine firing in your reader's brain. We must continuously trigger the curiosity-reward system by providing your reader with answers to the questions they are silently asking.

Maybe those questions are:

- What happened in the past to make this character believe [their lie]?
- What tragedies or struggles have they faced to make them so [defensive, angry, jealous, bitter, etc.]?
- What secrets from their past are they keeping hidden?

Don't Use a Flashback to Info-Dump Your World Building

If you're going into a flashback to tell us, "Long ago in this world, one group of people fought against another group of people, and this magic did one thing while that magic did another, and this government was established, and this army battled that army—"

Nobody cares! If this information doesn't directly affect your protagonist in this moment in the story, we won't understand why it matters. The protagonist is the character we care about, and we measure the importance of everything by how significant it is to them. That's why I always encourage writers to use exposition through action—as in, the world is explained and introduced to us as the protagonist moves through and interacts with it. What matters to them right now is the *only* thing that matters to us. So please, save your world building for the present moment, and avoid lengthy monologues about the history of the fictional world.

As we delve deeper into the story, the protagonist may truly need to uncover more about the history of their world—but let us see this through *their* eyes. That way, we are immersed in their perspective and make discoveries alongside them, rather than being inundated with information that we'll simply skim and forget.

Don't Use a Flashback to Answer Questions We Haven't Asked

Answering questions before your reader asks them is a guaranteed way to kill suspense and lose your reader's interest. You want your reader to feel curious—you want them engaged with the story, asking questions and eagerly anticipating the resolution of the plot's mysteries by piecing together the puzzle.

This is not to say you shouldn't start with a backstory to reveal where your characters' internal conflict originated. As you've probably gathered, I'm an advocate for opening your story with a flashback that shows something about the protagonists' past and how it has shaped them into who they are today, along with the conflicts they struggle with.

If you're having difficulty finding the balance here, my rule is this: Provide enough detail to make me *care* about the characters, but leave out enough to keep me *curious* about them.

Do Give Every Flashback a Clear Trigger

As I mentioned at the beginning, our brains seek relevance. Why does this matter? Why am I being shown this right now? The trigger doesn't have to be something hugely significant—it could be a minor event that causes your POV character to recall a meaningful moment from their past.

Sometimes I write all my characters' backstories in advance and keep them in a separate document. Then, I look through my book for existing natural triggers that could seamlessly lead into flashbacks. I break up the backstory into bite-sized pieces so that it fits effortlessly into the rest of the narrative—without slowing down the present story.

Do Make Every Flashback Change the Way We See the Story Going Forward

When we step out of a flashback, we should find ourselves viewing the characters and the present story in a different light, even if it's just a slight shift.

What makes a flashback powerful is the impact it has on the present story. It's not important because it happened once; it's important because it's *happening still*—the effects of this moment in your character's past are like ripples on a lake, continuing to make waves.

When you come out of a flashback, ask yourself: Does this alter how my reader perceives the protagonist? Does it clarify something we've been wondering about? Does it reveal the origins of the character's current internal conflicts?

Do Use Flashbacks to Answer Questions and Reward Our Curiosity

Throughout my years of studying stories, I've discovered a magic ratio for answering readers' questions. This is especially true in stories with mystery elements or an unreliable protagonist whose motives aren't entirely clear. I call this the curiosity-reward ratio, and I've found the magic numbers to be 2:1. This means for every two questions we have, we receive one answer. This keeps the reader's mind engaged with curiosity, but continually rewards them piece by piece with answers—setting off dopamine in their brain and making them want to keep reading.

PARALLEL FLASHBACKS

Let's begin by exploring my favorite style of flashbacks: the parallel effect. This artistic and engaging technique uses present conflicts and triggers to bring past memories to the surface. With parallel flashbacks, you can contrast the past with the present to illustrate how time has changed things for the characters. It's also an excellent way to weave natural triggers into your story, making the flashback feel more relevant.

A few ways to use parallels as triggers:

- Photographs
- Mementos/souvenirs
- Word-of-mouth stories
- Events that happened before in a different context

- Phobias/fears
- PTSD triggers
- Phrases or jokes that someone used to say
- Habits or quirks of a character from the past

STORY CASE STUDY: *THE OTHERWORLD*

In my novel *The Otherworld*, I used parallel flashbacks to reflect the past and present in several scenes. I'm going to share one of those scenes with you now as a case study of a way to play with this effect and help your reader visualize your book like a movie, cut and edited exactly as you see it in your mind.

In the following scene, Jack Stevenson grapples with the grim possibility that his brother, Adam, may have died in a plane crash. Adam is still missing, and Jack is preparing to fly out to search for him. Meanwhile, he reflects on his first solo flight when Adam was his flight instructor.

> The dock bobs up and down as I walk out to Adam's other plane—the one he uses for passenger flights. I stop at the end of the dock and gaze out over the water. Endless gray waves roll into the fog.
>
> I wish I could believe the sun is burning it off, but there's no way to know for sure. If I take off, pushing the weather, and the cloud base drops any lower . . .
>
> I don't care. I'm going up.
>
> I need to.
>
> Before I can change my mind, I start untying the Beaver from the dock, my hands slick with cold sweat.
>
> *I pulled open the door, sliding in first so Adam could sit beside me. But he hesitated. While I slid the key into the ignition, he just clung to the ladder, watching me with a knowing grin on his face. Standing there in that bomber jacket, he looked like a fighter pilot from World War II.*
>
> *"Are you getting in, or what?" I asked.*

Adam lowered his shades and looked at me, his blue eyes lit up with a spark I hadn't seen before. "No . . . You're on your own, Superman."

My heart stopped. "W-what? No, wait—"

"First solo flight," Adam declared.

My stomach somersaulted.

"Now? Today? You didn't tell me—"

Adam laughed. "Of course I didn't. You'd be a nervous wreck."

Too late. My heart was pounding double time. "But I can't," I stammered. "I can't do this, Adam. I need you."

Adam shook his head. "No, you don't," he said. "You got this." And he shut the door.

Slam. I'm alone inside the Beaver. I take a deep breath, sit back, and try to focus my mind.

Ignition switches: on. I listen as the engine rumbles to life. The propeller spins in front of me, slicing the fog. While waiting for the engine to warm up, I go through my checklist. Fuel levels, oil temp, pressure gauges, tank feeds. Everything is good to go.

I glance out the window at the empty dock.

Adam stood outside on the dock, his arms crossed over his chest, still grinning in the sunlight. A six-foot-one mountain. He always called me Superman, but it was a joke. I knew who the real hero was.

"Good luck," he mouthed, and gave me a two-finger salute.

I saluted him back.

My heart races as I buckle up and slide my fingers to the worn grooves of the yoke . . .

When flashing back and forth like this, be mindful of your reader, and don't overwhelm them with too many transitions between the past and the present. Look for the smoothest places to transition by identifying those triggers and ensuring they make sense. Your reader's flow of thought shouldn't be interrupted; it should just keep flowing, like a movie scene playing in their mind.

DUAL TIMELINE FLASHBACKS

Dual timelines can be a great way to juxtapose the past and the present. Unlike other kinds of flashbacks, a dual timeline is almost always linear and is designed to run parallel with your present plot. Remember, the relevancy rule still reigns supreme here! The reader must understand why they are journeying to the past to witness another story timeline. If it's completely disconnected, your reader won't see why it matters—and their attention will be lost.

Building a Relationship Between Two Stories

Crafting a powerful dual timeline story is challenging because you continually hit pause on the present to reveal events from the past. It can be executed effectively, as long as you prioritize relevance and meaning. It's not just about constructing two compelling stories happening at different times; it's about creating a connection between them. It must be clear how these two stories link and why we care just as much about what happened in the past as we do about what's happening in the present. Even here, look for triggers and mirrors to create that clear connection for your reader.

With dual timelines, don't feel like you have to include every single event that occurred in your character's past. Instead, concentrate on the pivotal, character-defining moments—the moments that *matter* the most.

STORY CASE STUDY: *100 DAYS OF SUNLIGHT*

When I wrote my debut novel, *100 Days of Sunlight,* I knew I wanted to include a lot of backstory for my male protagonist, Weston—which meant entire chapters consisting solely of flashbacks from his perspective. I established the first trigger when Weston began to recount to Tessa's grandparents how he became an amputee, which led to the rest of his backstory being revealed in flashbacks throughout the book.

Even though I got the ball rolling in that first chapter, I still looked for moments to trigger the following flashbacks, allowing each one to reflect something occurring with Tessa's story in the present day. For example, when Weston tells Tessa, "There's nothing you can't do," he immediately recalls a moment from his past when he overcame a challenge and embraced this motto.

ASK YOURSELF:

- Is there another story to be told here?
- How have my characters' pasts shaped who they are today?
- What are some things they wish they could go back and change about the past (regrets, failures, etc.)?
- How do they see the events of the past differently, in retrospect?
- Is there any advice they wish they could give to their younger self?

BITE-SIZED FLASHBACKS

You might not have the space to include full-length flashbacks in your book, but you still want to offer your readers glimpses of the past. My favorite method for achieving this is through bite-sized flashbacks.

Sometimes, the smallest memories leave the biggest impressions on us. We remember our pasts in bite-sized moments far more often than we sit and contemplate large portions of our lives. That's why quick glimpses into the past can feel more realistic (and more powerful) than pausing to dive into a lengthy portion of the backstory.

There is a time and place for longer flashbacks, especially when delving into the root causes of your character's fears and false beliefs. However, you can incorporate smaller flashbacks more frequently without distracting from the present story or slowing down the pacing.

STORY CASE STUDY: *THE OTHERWORLD*

Let me share a few more excerpts from *The Otherworld* to illustrate what this looks like in action:

Excerpt from chapter 1, Orca's POV:

My gaze drifts down to the cracks in the old kitchen table. I know every line and scratch, exactly how it got there. This one from the bread knife I dropped a few weeks ago. This one from the year I learned to write the alphabet and accidentally scrawled past the edge of the page. This one from Lucius's claws, attempting to steal a cooling pie before I wrestled him to the floor.

Eighteen years I have sat at this kitchen table and looked across at Papa's sweet, familiar face.

Six thousand, five hundred and seventy days.

Perhaps I was foolish to hope, to wait, to expect that one of those days would be the day. The day Papa told me I was old enough, strong enough, wise enough to go to the Otherworld with him.

Excerpt from chapter 2, Jack's POV:

Choking on air, I race across the driveway and duck into the shadow of our woods. Sappy wet pine branches slap my legs, my face. I don't know where I'm going, but I know I can't stay in the house for one more minute with Mom's grief hanging in the air.

He's gone.

My hands shake uncontrollably. I squeeze them into fists. Out of breath, I stop behind the barn—where I first caught him kissing a girl, where he first caught me smoking cigarettes. There's no place I can go to get away from his memory.

He's gone.

Excerpt from chapter 52, Adam's POV:

I inform Mom that I'll be sleeping at my hangar until Jack cools off. She tries to talk me out of it, but I know it's for the best.

I miss the times when our fights were stupid and small. When Jack was little and would forgive me in a heartbeat. Like that time when I was fifteen, and he caught me kissing my first girlfriend behind the barn. I was so mad when he stumbled out from his hiding place and started laughing his head off. I yelled at him and called him a snot-nosed brat, which made him run off and lock himself in our room with a "keep out" sign taped to the door. I apologized through the crack and then took him out to the diner and bought him chocolate chip pancakes, and everything was okay again.

But Jack isn't five years old anymore. It will take much more than a simple "Sorry" to make this right.

How to Do This in Your Own Writing

- Find triggers that easily connect the dots to your character's past.
- Connect these flashbacks to a relationship between characters to add emotion to these memories.
- Challenge yourself to illustrate a clear and colorful story in as few words as possible.
- Use these bite-sized flashbacks to emphasize and underscore what matters in the present moment by drawing attention to the common theme or deeper meaning of the memory.
- Don't overwhelm the reader with too many glimpses of the past; only use them when bringing attention to something that matters.

MYSTERY FLASHBACKS

Flashbacks told by a mysterious narrator can create intrigue and suspense, but they may also leave the reader feeling disconnected from the protagonist, making them some of the trickiest flashbacks to write. Let's explore how to navigate this without losing your reader's attention.

A Mysterious Flashback Is a Promise

Remember, curiosity stimulates the pleasure-and-reward center in our brain, making the act of solving mysteries a deeply satisfying experience for the reader. That said, it's essential to recognize that you're making a promise when you pose a question and allow your reader to ponder the clues. You're giving them a shot at finding the answer. Think of your mystery flashbacks as pieces of a grand puzzle. Are there enough clues for them to put together the picture and uncover the greater significance of the puzzle? Is it clear that there is a puzzle to solve, or do these flashbacks seem unrelated? Pique curiosity; don't confuse your reader.

STORY CASE STUDY: *WORLDS BENEATH* BY K. A. EMMONS

In the second book of The Blood Race trilogy, we find our two main characters, Hawk and Icarus, confronting a formidable enemy who has followed them since book 1 (and has been pursuing Hawk from her past). When the book first opens, we don't know that this enemy is still alive and poses a threat to the protagonists, but we read occasional flashbacks from his POV through short, mysterious journal entries. As the dates inch ever closer to the present day, the mystery begins to unfold . . . and the big reveal moment when Hawk discovers the truth is both chilling and unforgettable.

ASK YOURSELF:

- How is this mysterious narrator related to the protagonist's story?
- What clues do I want to give my reader to hint at the connection between this mystery character and the protagonist?
- Can I show the mystery character's goal while keeping their motivations unclear?
- Is there an impending threat to the protagonist? (Add a ticking clock if possible!)

CURIOSITY AND REWARD

If curiosity fires dopamine in your reader's brain, how can we harness this chemical reaction to encourage them to stay up past their bedtime reading? To answer that question, we first need to strike a balance between curiosity and reward.

As I highlighted earlier, the ideal ratio to aim for with curiosity to reward is 2:1—twice as many questions as answers, but those answers continually fire dopamine in the reader's brain. If you don't provide your readers with any answers to their questions, you might lose their attention before they reach the big reveal at the end. Remember, the past is like a puzzle. We find satisfaction in putting the pieces together until we see the full picture.

CASE STUDY: *THE WOMAN IN WHITE* BY WILKIE COLLINS

Wilkie Collins's intricately plotted classic unfolds through witness statements from a diverse array of characters as they unravel a cunning conspiracy against an innocent woman, Laura Fairlie, who has allegedly been murdered by her husband. The first episode of the BBC miniseries begins in the present day, with

Laura's half-sister Marion reflecting on the initial events that started Laura's downward spiral toward her "murder." We, the viewers, have no idea what led to Marion's present desperation, but the questions are gradually answered with each new flashback from a different character's perspective, piecing together the puzzle one fragment at a time. The current mystery holds the promise of an answer. We know that, if we keep watching, we will eventually see the full picture.

KEY TAKEAWAYS

- Flashbacks are a powerful way to deepen your character's conflict and make them care more about the story.
- Whether you're showing us a lot of backstory or just a pinch here and there, the past always gives us deeper insight into what these characters have been through and how their pasts have shaped them into the individuals they are today.
- Remember to always leverage curiosity and give your audience enough to make them relate to the character in the present day before rolling out the flashbacks.
- When in doubt, ask yourself the most important question of writing: *Why does it matter?*

Chapter 27

THE SECRET TO PERFECT PACING

Many writers struggle with pacing—striking a delicate balance between a character's thoughts and feelings and the action that's happening externally. If we focus too much on external events, the reader may feel detached from the character, rather than anchored with them. However, if we spend too much time on the character's inner thoughts, readers might lose track of what's happening *around* them.

In this chapter, we will explore the science of pacing—fast, slow, and montage pacing—essentially, what works and what doesn't, with side-by-side examples.

THERE IS NO ONE-SIZE-FITS-ALL RULE FOR PACING

While it would be great to have a foolproof guideline to follow, pacing changes dramatically from author to author and scene to scene.

The golden rule to remember about pacing is that your reader sees everything happening at the pace they read. This is exciting because it means you can slow down or speed up the film playing in their mind by adjusting how you pace a scene.

It's not that slow pacing is always bad or fast pacing is always good; it all depends on the scene and how quickly or slowly you want your reader to *perceive* the events unfolding. Let's look at a few examples of different pacing styles to compare and contrast what works and what doesn't.

Fast Pacing That Works

I spring into action, lunging at my opponent with a combination. Jab, straight right, uppercut in the ribs.

The finish lands harder than I expected, knocking the air out of his lungs and making him stumble over his feet. He counters, but I swat his punches away like flies—bobbing and weaving around his shots with ease.

Get your anger out now, you jerk.

I duck and move in, slugging a hard right hook into his ribs. He staggers forward, trying to ram his knee into my gut. But I don't give him the chance. I trap his arms and pivot on my feet, throwing him over my shoulder like a rag doll.

He lands on his back with a bone-rattling *thud,* gasping as he stares up at me.

TAKEAWAYS

- Because this is a fight scene, we want the reader to see it unfolding super fast—like a high-adrenaline scene from an action movie.
- We don't spend much time describing each movement or the thought processes the POV character has.
- The action focuses on the movements that affect the POV character, anchoring us in their perspective.

Slow Pacing That Doesn't Work

I spring into action, moving with swift and practiced precision as I cross the length of the fighting ring. My muscles tighten, propelling me forward with the kind of tactical, brutal grace that only comes from months of repetition, of bloodied knuckles and aching joints. My shoes scrape against the canvas with a whisper of friction as I cross the breadth of the fighting ring, each step deliberate, heavy with momentum and intent. I can feel the uneven give of the floor beneath me, the stale, metallic scent of sweat hanging thick in the air, mingling with the sharper sting of adrenaline as it floods my system.

I rely on a solid three-punch combination that I've been practicing on the heavy bags for weeks. Jab, straight right, uppercut to the ribs. Each strike lands with its own unique rhythm, its own voice in a rising chorus of violence—*thud, crack, thump*. There's a flicker of something primal flaring hot in my chest as I see him stagger, retreating with a clumsy shuffle into the opposite corner of the ring like a marionette with one too many strings cut.

Sweat trickles down my face as I catch my breath and prepare to defend his counterattack. All I can hear is the steady, unrelenting beat of my heart hammering in the back of my skull, like a drum leading me deeper into the fight.

TAKEAWAYS

- From the first line, it's a slow and arduous reading experience—like watching a fight scene in slow motion.
- There are too many thoughts and pauses between the actions.
- We become lost in the overload of description, losing sight of what we are observing and feeling detached from the POV character.

When writing a high-stakes fight scene, you want to embrace fast pacing so that your reader experiences the story unfolding like a movie in their minds. However, there is a time and place for slower pacing—specifically, when you're trying to emphasize how slowly time seems to be passing for your characters.

Slow Pacing That Works (Excerpt from *The Otherworld*)

The day passes slowly. Side by side, Lucius and I scout the entire coastline of the island—picking our way through fields of driftwood, climbing up rocky slopes, edging along the tree line to peer down at the tidewater smashing against the shore. My legs grow tired of hiking, and my eyes grow weary of surveying the landscape, but my heart never ceases to anxiously press against my ribs, thudding with equal parts hope and dread.

I still haven't sorted out what I'll do if he's badly injured or unconscious. Or even worse, what if he's dead? I couldn't leave him wherever I found him—but I couldn't drag his body back to the lighthouse, either. How would I manage?

How would I tell Jack?

The lighthouse is coming back into view now—rising from the northern tip of the island to shine courageously across the dark gray sea. The clouds at the horizon have split open to allow the sun her one and only appearance of the day, skipping orange flares across the tops of the waves before the ocean swallows her up.

TAKEAWAYS

- Slow pacing works here, as we are emphasizing how time seems to stretch on forever as Orca fruitlessly searches for Adam.
- We slow down to spend time on Orca's inner turmoil, which plunges us into deep POV.
- The description of the lighthouse at sunset incorporates Orca's unique character voice, keeping us grounded in her perspective.

Sometimes, slow pacing is better than fast pacing because it allows us to linger on the characters' emotions and explore their inner turmoil. If we were to edit this scene and make the pacing faster, it would feel completely different. Below is an experimental rewrite of the same scene from *The Otherworld* with fast pacing instead of slow pacing.

Fast Pacing That Doesn't Work

The day passes slowly. Lucius and I scout the entire coastline of the island—but we don't find anything. I try my best to look for Adam, but my efforts prove fruitless, and eventually, I'm so tired that I can't see straight.

I still haven't sorted out what I'll do if he's badly injured or unconscious. Or even worse, *what if he's dead?* I don't know what I'll do or how I'll tell Jack.

The lighthouse is coming back into view now, shining in the glow of the setting sun. Lucius pants beside me, and I scratch his head as we walk back up to the house.

TAKEAWAYS

- The wording feels cut-and-dried and doesn't reflect Orca's poetic voice at all.
- The quick pacing fails to emphasize how arduous and long the day has been.
- We don't feel the longing, desperation, and disappointment of Orca's fruitless search.

You can use these techniques to leverage your character's feelings and their experience of time passing, depending on what type of scene you're writing. For instance, if your character is caught in the middle of a battle scene, time seems to pass at lightning speed. But if they're stuck enduring an awkward family dinner, time might feel like it drags on forever.

Now, what about montage pacing, where you want to quickly show a series of events or time passing without lingering for too long on each scene? We see this executed in film quite often, when the editor is able to cut between scenes at lightning speed. But how do we pull this off in writing, when we don't have the shortcut of movie scenes to visualize the passage of time?

Imagine you're editing a movie in your reader's mind. Each sentence serves as a fragment of the scene—and you can speed up or slow down this mental film by playing with sentence length. Start by showing the reader quick glimpses of scenes instead of lingering to paint a complete picture. Remember: We see everything happening at the pace at which we read. Sometimes, you only need a few words to create a clear visual. Here's an example of what I mean.

Pacing for a Montage (Excerpt from *100 Days of Sunlight*)

I set my alarm for 6:30 every morning. I had to get used to waking up early, for when I went back to school. Regular school, with Rudy and all my other friends.

Nobody was standing in my way except for me, right?

Right.

Rudy met up with me at the track every afternoon (except for the afternoons I was stuck at the prosthetist's, getting my running blades adjusted for the millionth time). I ran faster every training session. Three minutes per lap became two and a half minutes per lap. We must have looked like quite the pair—one boy sitting on a bench with a serious frown and a stopwatch, one boy without legs running laps in the freezing cold and cheering every time he beat his personal best.

I blasted the heavy bag in my garage every chance I got. One-minute rounds turned into two-minute rounds turned into three-minute rounds. Finally, I was able to beat that thing like it was out to kill me. My knuckles bled and I flurried the bag and Led Zeppelin screamed at me from the radio. I felt like I was dying—but at the same time, I finally felt alive again.

I did one hundred push-ups without stopping.

I broke a new record at the track—a two-minute-and-thirteen-second lap. I woke up at 6:30 every morning, and I never hit the snooze button.

TAKEAWAYS

- If you were editing a montage in a film, you would spend mere seconds on each scene. I did this in prose by flashing through each scene lightning fast, dedicating only one or two lines to a specific scene.

- Rhythm helps with this, such as "one-minute rounds . . . two-minute rounds . . . three-minute rounds"—allowing the reader's mind to interpret this progression as the passage of days or even weeks.

STUDY PACING THAT WORKS

The best way to improve your pacing is to pay attention to what proper pacing looks like. This can be difficult to notice in books because when pacing is truly effective, you should forget that you're even reading. During these moments of deep immersion in the story, pause and ask yourself: *What about this pacing works? What is the balance between emotion and action?*

Annotating books will help you identify the balance between the internal and external worlds, as well as how the author has leveraged reading speed to make you see the scene unfolding at a specific pace.

BRAINSTORM PROMPTS:

- What needs to be accomplished in this scene? Create a brief bullet-point list of action steps for your reference.
- What is the primary source of conflict in the scene? Who is it impacting the most, and why?
- What are your characters' goals? How will they respond to the external conflict based on their goals?
- How quickly or slowly do you want your reader to see the scene unfolding? Your answer will influence how much time you devote to action versus emotion.

Good pacing is just one ingredient to great writing. If you want to improve your prose, find your unique voice, and make your writing the best it can possibly be—you won't want to miss what we're unpacking in the next chapter.

Chapter 28

REFINING YOUR WRITING STYLE

We've already covered many fundamentals of strong writing: showing instead of telling, writing realistic dialogue, incorporating flashbacks, and mastering perfect pacing. Now, let's take it to the next level by refining our prose.

In this chapter, we'll explore:

- the three key ingredients to beautiful prose: rhythm, flavor, and emotion
- crafting immersive descriptions that create an atmosphere (plus describing characters)
- writing in deep point of view and mastering character voice for a more immersive reading experience
- expanding your vocabulary in fun, creative ways that won't feel like work

THE THREE KEY INGREDIENTS TO BEAUTIFUL PROSE

This may seem counterintuitive, but if you want to improve your prose, you shouldn't embark on a mission to *write* beautiful prose. Why? Because, above all, your prose should *mean* something, not just *sound* beautiful.

Think of your prose as a frame that displays the story. Like a picture frame, your writing should enhance the story and draw us in without distracting from it. Some stories feature strong characters and conflicts, but they are conveyed in dry, wooden prose, while others become so overwhelmed by showy, ostentatious prose that it distracts from the story. Needless to say, you want to find a happy medium between these two extremes.

What Makes Prose Beautiful?

That question has stumped writers for generations. Everyone's opinion differs, which means there is no right or wrong way to write prose. What some readers love, others hate, and vice versa. You can't please everyone, so the best course of action is to simply do your best and let your own voice shine in a way that you can be proud of.

That said, there are a few essential ingredients that contribute to beautiful prose.

Key Ingredient #1: Rhythm

Words, whether read or spoken, carry sound. They can have a melodic rhythm, or they can fall flat. For example, let's say I'm writing with short sentences. I like short sentences. Everyone likes short sentences. They're easy to read. But they're hard to listen to. Because everything sounds the same. It becomes predictable. Like a broken record.

The same problem can unfold in a different way when every sentence is so long and difficult to wade through (with no end in sight for the reader's eye) that you literally fatigue their brain as they desperately try to find a rhythm amid this raging sea of words.

Do you see the difference between those two paragraphs?

Here's an example of how I used rhythm when writing *The Otherworld.*

Remembering our argument in the driveway is enough to stoke the fire of jealousy still smoldering inside me, every single paper cut of doubt stinging me all over again.

How she snuck off this morning with him.

How she picked out his favorite music in the store.

How she said, *Adam says he probably did it to protect me. Adam says he'll take me to see my mom if I want to. Adam says, Adam says, Adam says . . .*

I want to stop dancing right now and make her look me in the face and tell me which of us she would choose—him or me. I want to hear her say the words.

I would choose you, Jack.

Only you.

Always you.

Using repeated phrases (like "how she" or "Adam says" in this example) can bring a lyrical flow to your prose that almost makes it feel like a poem—without coming off sounding too ostentatious and flowery.

Try annotating a book that you think has beautiful prose by making notes on how the author uses rhythm in their writing. You can learn a lot about writing with rhythm by simply noticing where your favorite books sound like music in your mind.

Key Ingredient #2: Flavor

Some might argue that having an expansive vocabulary is essential for giving your prose more flavor. However, you don't need to learn a plethora of complex, descriptive words to make your writing flavorful. Often, the most impactful writing relies on simple, everyday words. It's how you arrange them that brings the writing to life so vividly that you can almost taste it.

This isn't just about writing yummy descriptions—it's about infusing your character's unique voice into the narrative and showing us how *they* see the world.

Here's an example of how I used flavor in *The Otherworld* to make my prose more vivid:

> Reaching over the sink, I push open the window and invite the morning breeze inside. Beyond the window, a knoll of soft young grass slopes down to the land's end where massive, craggy rocks meet the sea. My gaze follows a pathway of golden sunlight glittering on the high tide like crushed diamonds. Waves crash, and seagulls cry.
>
> Our world carries on, ever the same.
>
> But today is different.
>
> The aroma of chamomile and lavender fills the kitchen as Papa strains freshly steeped tea into two ceramic mugs for us. A sickle of morning light crests the side of his face, contrasting with the scruffy, salt-and-pepper beard that lines his jaw. Steam curls around his weathered hands as he pours the tea, his gray eyes solemn and thoughtful.

Notice the active verbs I'm using here for inanimate objects. The grass *slopes,* sunlight *glitters,* waves *crash,* and steam *curls* around Papa's hands. It would be easy enough to say, "It's a bright and sunny morning. The sound of waves and seagulls can be heard from outside as Papa makes tea." But that doesn't bring the scene to life in a vivid, flavorful way like active verbs do.

If your writing feels flat or lacks flavor, try replacing some of the adverbs with stronger verbs—even if that means bringing inanimate objects to life with movement, sound, and color.

Key Ingredient #3: Emotion

Strong prose should, above all else, make you feel something by conveying the emotions of the characters in a palpable way. Mastering this skill takes time and practice, so don't become frustrated if you haven't fully grasped it yet.

Sometimes, the pressure to write well can lead to analysis paralysis, leaving you feeling stuck and unable to write anything at all for fear it won't turn out the way you want.

My advice when this happens is to *write ugly.* Write messily, passionately, intensely, with rough strokes. It might seem chaotic right now, but the most important thing is that you make your reader feel something. The best writing is not always the most eloquent—rather, it's the writing that hits your reader like a punch in the heart.

Let's return to *The Otherworld* to look at one of the most emotional scenes in the book.

> When morning comes, I lie staring at the ceiling—haunted by my brave words from the past week. All the times I stubbornly back talked Mom and Dad, insisting that Adam was still alive. Refusing to grieve. Pissing Dad off. Making Mom cry. Holding out that flicker of hope like a burning match in a hurricane, desperately cupping my hands around it, bending my reality around it, losing my mind because of it.
>
> Dad accused me of causing trouble by not accepting that Adam is gone.
>
> But he doesn't understand.
>
> Even if I did what he wanted, "accepting it" wouldn't be a one-time decision.
>
> My brother is dead.
>
> I couldn't accept it once and move on.
>
> I would have to accept it over and over again every morning when I woke up and remembered that he's not here anymore.
>
> Every morning for the rest of my life.

In this scene, I aimed to emphasize how broken and hopeless Jack felt as he confronted the idea of accepting his brother's death. I wasn't trying to make my prose beautiful while writing this scene—just the opposite. I wanted it to be ugly and desperate, capturing the raw emotion Jack experienced at this pivotal moment.

CRAFTING IMMERSIVE DESCRIPTIONS THAT CREATE AN ATMOSPHERE

You're not describing things as they are—you're describing things as your character sees them.

This is the golden rule of any immersive description. It doesn't matter whether you're writing in the first person or third person; you should filter everything the reader sees through the lens of what the POV character perceives—and how they feel about it. Our emotions shape our perceptions, which in turn influence the way we see things. Our perception shapes our reality. (That's a fundamental rule of psychology.)

Instead of asking yourself, *What does this look like?* (when describing something visual), consider asking, *How does my character perceive this based on their beliefs and attitudes?*

Remember: They do not simply observe how things are; they *interpret* how things affect them. They actively participate in the scene—and that's what makes your reader feel like they are an active participant in the scene as well.

Flat Example:

Teresa stood on the walkway, staring up at the creepy old house. It was two stories tall with peeling paint and broken panes in some of the windows. It had a wraparound porch with a weathered swing that creaked as it moved back and forth. The front door had been left open, like the ghosts were expecting her. Storm clouds were darkening the sky, which made the whole place look scarier. Teresa didn't want to go into the house and find out whether it was really haunted, but she didn't have much of a choice.

Stronger Example:

A chill raced down Teresa's spine as she stood on the pathway, staring up at the old Victorian house that loomed before her. Were the rumors true? Was this place really haunted? It certainly looked like a breeding ground for ghosts; a hollow shell of a house sagging with rot and smothered in moss, like an infection that had spread to every shutter and floorboard.

On the wraparound porch, an old swing creaked eerily as it drifted back and forth, like an invisible hand was pushing it. But that wasn't what terrified Teresa the most—it was the front door, which had been left open as if expecting her arrival. All she could see when she looked at it was a hungry, gaping mouth, ready to swallow her.

Stop it, Teresa scolded herself silently. *Ghosts aren't real.*

She ignored the coil of dread tightening in her stomach and took a step toward the old house.

What's the Difference?

One is flat, while the other is more creative and colorful. Why? Because in the second example, we see the house as *Teresa* sees it. Her observations are subjective—the moss is an infection, an invisible hand pushes the swing, and the front door is a hungry mouth ready to swallow her . . . these are all Teresa's *interpretations* of what's happening, not necessarily what is actually happening.

Describing Characters

Some of the most challenging descriptions to write are physical descriptions of other characters. Many writers get carried away with detail, while others don't describe enough detail, leaving us to create our own (often inaccurate) mental images.

Some features to describe:

- Facial features (eyes, lips, nose, etc.)
- Build and height
- Skin tone
- Hair color and texture
- Scars or tattoos
- Makeup
- Clothing
- Voice/accent
- Body language
- Scent

Again, consider the POV character who is doing the describing. What things would they notice? Why? How do their preconceived ideas and opinions affect their perception of this person? For example, I once wrote a story where my POV character was a pickpocket describing a woman he intended to steal from. Instead of focusing on her physical appearance, I put more focus on the jewelry that my POV character was planning to steal from her.

Remember, you don't have to describe everything at once when introducing the new character. You can provide enough detail to create a mental image, then add more details gradually as time goes on. This is one of my favorite methods.

Flat Example:

She had long, curly hair the color of honeysuckle and eyes as blue as a morning sky in late June. Her skin was tan from the sun, and her strawberry-pink lips were always smiling. She had dimples in her cheeks, freckles across her nose, and a peace-sign tattoo on her left ankle from her freshman year in college when she and her friends had all dared each other to get tattoos. She never wore makeup, but she didn't need to—she was a natural beauty. Today she was wearing a Rolling Stones T-shirt and denim shorts, but she still looked glamorous.

Stronger Example:

She was like sunshine in human form: honeysuckle hair, sky-blue eyes, and a laugh like the first day of summer. Effortlessly glamorous, even in a Rolling Stones T-shirt and denim shorts. It was impossible not to notice her dimples because she was always smiling—and that was the most beautiful thing about her. She was genuinely happy in a way that made everyone around her feel like the sun had just come out from behind a cloud.

What's the Difference?

One is like an inventory list of the character's physical features; the other tells us not just how she looks but *who* she is. You don't need to overdo it by describing every detail. Typically, less is more, especially when it comes to metaphors. As we've observed in these examples, metaphors can powerfully paint an image in the reader's mind, but too many can make your writing feel muddy and bogged down. If you keep comparing things to something else, the reader begins to lose sight of what they're actually looking at.

Ultimately, writing stronger prose requires time and lots of practice. When you genuinely enjoy the process of playing with words, your unique voice will begin to shine through on its own. Let go of expectations, take the pressure off, and just have fun with it. With each session, you'll notice your writing improving and growing as you gain more experience.

Don't take yourself too seriously. Remember why you love writing, and do it for the joy of the practice.

MASTERING CHARACTER VOICE FOR AN IMMERSIVE READING EXPERIENCE

Another key element of juicy, colorful descriptions is incorporating your character's voice and personality into the narrative. We think in the style we speak. How do your character's personality and voice influence the way they describe scenes, situations, and other people?

Imagine you're writing from the perspective of a cheeky character who is overly confident and self-centered. Picture him walking into work, knowing his boss is about to promote someone in the office—and he mistakenly thinks he will be the one to receive the promotion.

Flat Example:

Today was going to be a great day—I could feel it. The sun was shining, the birds were singing, and I was walking into the office on my first day as the senior creative director. What could possibly go wrong? *Nothing*, I thought—until my annoying cubicle neighbor Emily walked up with a taunting smile and said, "Good morning, Bryce."

"Good morning," I replied with suspicion. "Why do you look so pleased with yourself?"

"Because I just got the promotion!" she burst out, rubbing it in by sticking her hand out for a shake, as if we'd never met before. "You're speaking to the new creative director."

I stared at her, dumbstruck. I couldn't believe it.

Stronger Example:

Today was going to be a great day—I could feel it. The sun was shining, the birds were singing, and I was striding into the office on my first day as the senior creative director. Okay, maybe I was *strutting* more than *striding*, but who cares? I deserved this promotion.

"Good morning, Bryce." Emily greeted me when I entered the office.

Good old Emily—she may have been the most annoying cubicle neighbor I was ever forced to work with, but I had to hand it to her: The girl had real sportsmanship. Nobody (besides me) had fought as hard for the promotion as she did. But her smile was full of admiration and respect.

Heck, I was almost going to *miss* sitting next to her in that dingy little cubicle.

"It *is* a good morning, isn't it?" I said with a grin, straightening my tie. "Always a good morning when you're the senior creative director in a place like this."

Emily laughed and tossed her silky hair over one shoulder. "I know, right? It's so exciting. I can't wait to get started. I have to admit, I was surprised they didn't choose you for the promotion. But don't worry, I'm sure it's nothing personal. I was just the better person for the job."

The realization hit me like a punch in the stomach. "What?"

What's the Difference?

Not only are we emphasizing character voice and internal dialogue here, but we're also playing with comic timing and the contrast between expectation and reality. Allowing your characters to assume a situation and then surprising them with a different outcome is a fantastic way to maintain your reader's interest. Essentially, you can incorporate plot twists in places even where they don't exist.

Remember the character voice cheat sheets we created in the chapter on writing dialogue? You can refer to those cheat sheets here to refine your character's voice and enhance your writing style with *their* unique personality.

Here are a few final tips for making your character's voice more unique, iconic, and recognizable—so that we don't even need to look at the chapter heading to know whose perspective we're about to read from.

Tips for making your character's voice unique:

- Leverage the character's personality to give them unique quirks that pair well with their attitudes (e.g., optimist versus worst-case-scenario planner).
- If you're uncertain about how they might describe something, ask yourself: How would they *speak* it?
- Incorporate their negative traits into their voice (e.g., a suspicious character who constantly thinks others are up to no good; a selfish character who always blames others; an oblivious character who misses appointments and doesn't know the time).
- Keep some vocabulary specific to one character (i.e., in dialogue and internal thoughts).

FUN AND CREATIVE WAYS TO EXPAND YOUR VOCABULARY

You might think that to expand your vocabulary and begin writing beautiful, colorful, lyrical prose, you need to read Pulitzer Prize–winning novels and adopt the vernacular of an Oxford academic. This is simply not true!

I firmly believe that there is no such thing as a gold standard in writing style. Literature is a form of art—and just as there is no right or wrong way to paint a picture, there is no right or wrong way to style your prose. Every author's voice is unique, and every reader's taste varies. Some may enjoy poetic literary prose, while others might prefer raw, gritty writing that cuts right to the heart. Pay attention to the prose that resonates with *you*, and read more works that inspire you with their style.

Tips for expanding your vocabulary:

- Use a reverse dictionary such as OneLook.com to discover alternatives for frequently used words.
- Imitate the speech of a speaker whose vocabulary and articulation you admire.
- Play word games such as Scrabble, or do crosswords.
- In casual conversation, challenge yourself to find new words to explain familiar concepts.
- Read poetry by multiple authors.
- Watch foreign films with subtitles to expose yourself to new vocabulary and speech patterns.
- Rewrite the lyrics of your favorite song while preserving the same meaning.

When you love writing and enjoy the process of playing with words, expanding your vocabulary and creating an immersive reading experience becomes truly joyful. Always remember that your unique voice should not mimic someone else's, and what matters most is making your reader *feel* something.

KEY TAKEAWAYS

- Rhythm, flavor, and emotion are three key ingredients in crafting beautiful prose. How you arrange these ingredients is up to you as the writer, so allow your creativity to lead the way.
- Don't try to mimic another writer or aspire to the prose of a Pulitzer Prize–winning novelist. Instead, pay attention to the writing styles that resonate with you. Try to incorporate more of these techniques into your own writing.
- When writing a description, frame it through your POV character's opinions and personality. Everyone perceives the world differently, and

while reading a story, we want to experience it through the character's eyes.

- Expand your vocabulary in fun, creative ways that deepen your love for language. If you enjoy reading, that's wonderful! However, if reading isn't your thing, it doesn't mean you can't enhance your writing skills. There are numerous methods to learn new words and writing styles without overwhelming yourself with reading assignments.

BRAINSTORM PROMPTS:

- What is actually happening right now?
- How does my character see what's happening?
- What descriptors, metaphors, and similes would my character use, given the person they are?
- How would it feel to experience this moment if I were this character?

Chapter 29

STAYING MOTIVATED TO WRITE YOUR BOOK

If you're feeling a bit overwhelmed because your book isn't written or finished yet, don't worry! You're not alone. Many writers feel daunted when facing the mountain of the novel-writing process. But remember: You were born to conquer this mountain. Your story is burning in your heart with the fire of a thousand suns, and only you can bring it to life in the uniquely beautiful way it was meant to be told.

So don't retreat from this epic quest—don't shrink back into your comfort zone just because it feels safer there. You know what lies within that comfort zone; it's never going to change. To live your dream as an author, you must climb that mountain.

Perhaps your dream is to publish novels and share your stories with the world. Or you might want to see your screenplays turned into films. Or perhaps you aspire to run your own publishing house. Or maybe you want to craft stories for video games or audio dramas, or you want to pen your memoirs.

No dream is too big. Do you know why? Because *you* created that dream, which means you have already conquered it in your mind. This dream is etched in your heart; this mountain is born from your imagination. And that means you are fully equipped to climb it. You were *born* to climb it.

BECOMING A BULLETPROOF WRITER

Every writer faces it at some point: doubt, discouragement, fear, hesitation, perfectionism, and creative burnout. Sometimes the last thing we want to do is sit down at our desks and write. Why? Because writing is hard! It's a challenge filled with obstacles and conflicts—a lot like your protagonist's journey of change. But just like fictional characters, our goal is to overcome these challenges and obstacles, not allow them to defeat us.

Writers are inherently introspective. We possess supercharged imaginations, which can sometimes backfire. When self-doubt creeps in and makes us question if our books are worth writing, a part of us clings to that fear and uncertainty, causing our creativity to shrink and our motivation to wither.

I don't want to see this happen to you. That's why we're going to identify the top-ten obstacles writers face and how to overcome them. Remember, you are the main character of your own story! Your character arc unfolds through struggle and triumph. So, let's break down the most common ways writers self-sabotage and how to overcome these obstacles.

OBSTACLES THAT KEEP WRITERS FROM STARTING OR FINISHING THEIR BOOKS

01. Perfectionism

The Trap: You think your writing must be flawless on the first attempt. When you write something, you often feel dissatisfied because it doesn't match the quality of the Pulitzer Prize–winning prose you compare it to. You find it hard to make significant progress during a writing session because your perfectionism is keeping you stuck in one place, listening to your inner critic.

How to overcome this: Focus on progress, not perfection. Give yourself permission to write ugly, especially in the first draft. Because, guess what? If you pick up any book in a bookstore, you're not reading that author's first draft. Published books go through multiple rounds of revisions and edits before they ever land on your bookshelf. So take the pressure off to be perfect during the writing stage. First drafts are supposed to be messy. It's through rewriting that brilliance emerges. As I always say: You don't need to be a good writer; you just need to be a good *re*writer. Don't make it perfect. Just make it exist.

02. Imposter Syndrome

The Trap: You believe you're not qualified to write a book because you're not "a real writer." Perhaps you have just recently started writing and don't have as much experience as seasoned authors publishing books. You feel like an imposter because when you imagine your book sitting on the shelf beside titles by your favorite authors, a little voice in the back of your mind whispers, *You don't belong with them. You're not a good enough writer. You'll never be as famous or successful as those authors!* This voice of self-doubt paralyzes you, stifling your creativity and making you feel ill-equipped to share your work with the world.

How to overcome this: Real writers are people who *write.* Your experiences, perspective, and voice are valid and needed. You have something unique to bring to the world that has never been created before. And, guess what? Those successful, famous authors you admire—they all started *exactly* where you are now. They all have bad writing days sometimes. They all make embarrassing typos. They all get one-star reviews from critical readers. They are all human, just like you. Curing imposter syndrome is not about climbing the ladder of success and meeting your idols in the winner's circle—it's about taking your idols *off* those pedestals and seeing them as the ordinary people they are.

03. I'm Too Young/Old

The Trap: You believe your age disqualifies you from writing something meaningful or getting published. Perhaps you're a kid, teenager, or young adult who feels that you need more education and experience before you can be a writer.

Or, maybe you're a senior, reflecting on your life and wishing you had written a book years ago. Whether you think it's too soon or too late to write that story in your heart, both beliefs are dangerous misconceptions that will trip you up and stop you from unlocking your creative potential.

How to overcome this: Creativity doesn't have an expiration date—or a minimum age requirement. Readers crave authentic stories, regardless of the writer's age. Instead of viewing your age as a setback, see it as an advantage! If you're a teen writer, you have a unique perspective that adult writers lack. If you're an older adult, you have invaluable life experience and wisdom that younger writers have yet to acquire. Wherever you are in life, you're in a unique position to offer *your* perspective and ideas to readers who will connect with them.

04. Overwhelm and Decision Fatigue

The Trap: You're getting stuck trying to find the perfect way to outline, draft, or edit, and instead, you end up doing nothing. This is known as analysis paralysis. When you become too caught up in the planning process, you sabotage the writing process. The actual practice of writing always seems just out of reach—after more outlining, more research, more plotting, and more waiting on the muse. This is the equivalent of an Olympic athlete who spends all their time watching others train, buying gear, prepping meals, shopping for workout clothes, and polishing their empty trophy case . . . yet they never actually train in their sport. All those activities support the practice, but without the practice itself, your preparation is futile.

How to overcome this: Choose a method (for outlining, writing, editing, or whatever the case may be), and take that first step. Clarity comes from action. You learn by *doing*! You can never discover what process works best for you if you don't get your hands dirty and start that process. If you've made it to the end of this book, you have every tool you need to start bringing your story to life. There is an untapped creative power within you just waiting to be unleashed! Don't let overanalysis hinder your forward momentum.

05. Fear of Judgment

The Trap: You find yourself worrying about what others (family, friends, readers, reviewers) will think of your story or your writing ability. The thought of having your work out there under scrutiny is literally terrifying. What if your book receives nothing but criticism and bad reviews? Or what if you send your manuscript to literary agents only to face a pile of rejections? Wouldn't it be better to keep your writing under lock and key so nobody can judge you? If these thoughts sound familiar, don't worry—you're not crazy, and you're not alone.

How to overcome this: Do me a favor. Pick one famous book that you've always heard readers praise to the high heavens. The book that seemingly *everyone* loves. Got it? Now, look up that title on Amazon or Goodreads and filter the reviews by one star. Yes, even though many readers love this book, it still garnered a lot of dislike from others. Does that mean the author shouldn't have written or published the book? Absolutely not! The point is: No creative work is exempt from judgment. Arm yourself with this knowledge, and it will give you confidence. Trust that your book will find its readers, and they will *love* it. If some people don't like it, that doesn't mean there's anything wrong with your story. It just wasn't their cup of tea! And that's okay. Remember: You're in good company. Every famous author has endured judgment and criticism. Don't let that fear of judgment stifle your creativity or keep you playing small. You were meant to shine.

06. Comparing Yourself to Other Writers

The Trap: You think your writing isn't good enough because it doesn't sound like someone else's. You read many books by authors you admire and find yourself silently comparing their writing styles to your own—feeling like yours doesn't quite measure up. You know what good writing *should* sound like, so you get increasingly frustrated when you sit down to write, and every page seems to pale in comparison to your favorite books.

How to overcome this: Comparison kills creativity. Your job is not to be them—it's to be you. Embrace your unique style and voice. That's what makes your story different from anything that has been seen before. You might be thinking, "This isn't my style; it's just lackluster writing." And if that's truly the case, then there's only one way to develop your style and improve your writing: time and practice. As I always say: There is no bad writing. Your writing is either great, or it is making you great. Every line you write brings you closer to that place of mastery. And, guess what? It's going to be tedious sometimes! But that's when you know you're getting closer to true mastery. Just like an Olympic athlete must train the same skill or routine over and over again, you need to push through the monotony and keep writing even when it feels like you're getting nowhere. I guarantee you *are* making progress, even when it doesn't feel like it. One day, you'll look back at your writing and see how far you've come—but only if you keep writing.

07. Waiting for Inspiration

The Trap: You believe you can only write when you're "in the mood" or feeling creative. You find yourself waiting for the elusive muse to show up, scrolling Pinterest boards into oblivion, making playlists for your characters, staring out the window, and daydreaming about your story . . . but never actually writing it. The thought of facing that blank page is intimidating enough to make you continually retreat to what's *comfortable*—thinking about your story instead of writing it. You catch yourself saying things like, "I really need to write more," or "This year I'm going to finish drafting my book." But these commitments feel distant and intangible, always pushed off to some future date when you feel like doing it.

How to overcome this: Writing is a practice, not a mood. Show up consistently—even for just fifteen minutes a day—and inspiration will start to show up, too. Train your brain to get used to the habit of sitting down and opening your book project. Maybe on the first day, you won't feel like writing. But I encourage you to try. Don't let the blank page intimidate you. Write something, even if it's just a few lines of dialogue or an outline sketch of what needs to be accomplished in the following scene. Mood boards and playlists are wonderful for getting in the mood to write (these are tools I use all the time!), but you can't let them replace the practice itself. Only *writing* will make you a better writer. So quit waiting for the muse to appear—*become your own muse.*

08. Never Finishing What You Start

The Trap: You get stuck at the beginning of your story or halfway through, losing your motivation. You continuously uproot yourself to start new works in progress, which results in never finishing anything. You just can't summon the inspiration and creative energy needed to endure the marathon of writing a book. Bored and restless with each new story, you jump from one idea to another, hoping to eventually discover "the one"—your magnum opus, the story you will actually finish.

How to overcome this: Finish something, even if it's just a five-page short story. Seeing a project or idea through to completion will give you an incredible sense of accomplishment. Oftentimes, it's not that we lose creative energy for an idea—it's that we lose *confidence* in it. Self-doubt sneaks in, distracting us and making us overly critical of our work. Perhaps the characters, plot, themes, or story world just aren't exciting to you. If that's the case, consider adding something new and unexpected. Can you incorporate a trope you know you love? What if you changed the POV character? What if you blended subgenres to create something truly fresh and unique? Ask yourself, *What would be the most fun, exciting, indulgent thing for me to write?* Adding that layer of enjoyment for yourself as the writer will help you see this project through to the end.

09. Overediting as You Write

The Trap: You constantly backtrack to rewrite and edit the same scene instead of moving forward. Whenever you sit down for a writing session, you struggle to make progress because you pause to tweak every line to perfection. As a result, you leave each session feeling frustrated. While other writers seem to breeze through drafts at lightning speed, you remain stuck on the same chapter you've been working on for a week.

How to overcome this: Separate drafting from editing. Get the story down first—then go back and refine it. Writing a book is a bit like building a house. You can't stage and decorate before the structure and drywall are up! The same goes for your book. Build the foundation first, even if it doesn't look as polished and beautiful as you imagined. The decorating process will occur during revisions and edits. Right now, what matters most is keeping your momentum strong as you write your first draft.

10. Chasing Money, Fame, or Recognition

The Trap: You're writing a book with the primary goal of becoming rich, famous, or admired. You look at renowned authors like J. K. Rowling and Stephen King and think to yourself, *I want to be like them.* You aspire to make millions as an author, win literary awards, become a household name, and retire in splendor, knowing that your work will be remembered among the greatest contributions to literature of all time.

How to overcome this: While it's good to hope for success as an author, the prospect of external rewards cannot sustain you through the long, challenging process of writing. Most writers are not rich and famous, but they are fulfilled, because they do what they love every day. The most powerful stories come from a place of love, passion, and creativity. Focus on writing the book *you* would want to read—the one that stirs something deep within you. When your motivation is rooted in *meaning* rather than validation, the writing journey becomes more satisfying—and ironically, often more successful.

REMEMBER YOUR *WHY*

Even if you successfully overcome all the obstacles mentioned above, you will still encounter challenges on this journey. Some days, you may not feel like writing. You might wonder why you're doing this at all. You might even face discouragement from those around you who believe you should find a "real job." Regardless of the opposition you face, you can equip yourself to confront it and become a bulletproof writer by remembering your why.

Your why is the fuel for your creative fire. It's the reason you picked up this book in the first place. It's the reason you feel compelled to take these story ideas out of your head and bring them to life. Your story *matters*—to you and to your future readers. *Why?*

Take some time to reflect on that question and come up with your own why.

Perhaps it's something like this:

- This story reflects a struggle I overcame in the past, and I hope my readers learn from my experience.
- This story is both humorous and inspiring; I believe it will brighten the lives of my readers.
- This is a story I wish I could have read while growing up.

Once you know your why, I encourage you to write it on a sticky note and place it on your desk where you'll see it every day. Continuously remind yourself of why you show up repeatedly to do the creative work that brings your vision to life. It matters to you!

If you know why your story matters to you, why it matters to your characters, why it matters to your readers, and why it matters to the world, you will be empowered not only to write it but to share it with others and let your creative light shine.

Every day, I receive letters from writers in my online community who are achieving their writing dreams and reaching levels of success they never thought possible. If these writers could reach and surpass their goals to make their author dreams a reality, guess what? So can you!

If you're still here with me on the penultimate page of this book, it means you're already leaps and bounds ahead of most people. Why? Because you're in the game, while most people aren't even trying. You have massive, ambitious goals—and guess what? Those goals are not crazy. They're just big enough to match your ambition.

But here's the truth: It's not about what you *say* you'll do; it's about what you actually do. The early mornings. The late nights. The day-to-day grind that nobody claps for. Stop worrying about how far away the end result feels. Instead, fall in love with the process. Every rejection? That's feedback. Every draft? That's progress. Every single move you make today, tomorrow, next week—it's all compounding into something unstoppable.

You possess all the time, talent, and knowledge you need, and I'm so proud of you for staying committed to your creativity and crafting a compelling story that will touch the hearts of thousands of readers one day. Now you just need to take action. So stop overthinking, start writing, and always remember to *make your story matter.*

ACKNOWLEDGMENTS

While writing can feel like an extremely lonely art at times, the truth is this: None of us can do it on our own. So many incredible people have helped to bring this book to life, and I want to take a moment to express my deepest gratitude to them.

First, I want to thank the entire *Make Your Story Matter* community on YouTube. If you had told me ten years ago that I would one day help over half a million writers worldwide rediscover their love for storytelling, I would have laughed. And yet, here we are. Every single video you've watched, every livestream you've joined, every moment you've spent on my channel, has meant the absolute *world* to me. It's safe to say that this book would not exist without your enthusiasm and support—so thank you, from the bottom of my heart.

A million thanks to my superstar agent, Stacey Glick, whose constant support and enthusiasm for this book made me believe in it even more. From day one, you understood my passion and vision like nobody else, and I truly feel like I won the literary-agent lottery to be able to work with you.

Make Your Story Matter has been brought to life thanks to the amazing team at BenBella Books. My endless gratitude goes to: Glenn Yeffeth (for believing in this book from the very beginning), Claire Schulz (for being so intentional about preserving my vision and voice), Clara Tamez (for guiding this book through the publishing process with such grace), Kellie Doherty (for being a marketing mastermind), Kim Broderick (for her incredible attention to detail), and Jason Arias (for the fabulous cover design). Many thanks also to Ariel Jewett, Sarah Modlin, Madeline Grigg, Lindsay Marshall, Rachel Phares, Alicia Kania, Susan Welte, and the rest of the BenBella team. You are all rock stars.

Last but definitely not least, thank you to the friends and family who inspired me to write this book and have believed in my dreams longer than I've believed in them myself. My incredibly creative and talented sister, Katie, who has been writing with me and cheering me on since we were kids. My amazingly supportive and whip-smart mom, who never tired of rereading this book and finding ways to make it better each time. My moonshot-thinker dad, who first encouraged me to start a YouTube channel, back when I didn't even know what I would make videos about. My life would be empty without the three of you. Also a big hug of gratitude goes to Brooke and Amy, for listening to me rant, flail, and occasionally whine over the making of this book. I'd be lost without your friendship.

And finally, thank *you.* For choosing to pick up this book and dedicate your time to honing your writing skills. I hope it has helped you rediscover your natural storytelling instincts and inspired you to pick up your pen or laptop and create something. Remember: *Your story matters.* Now go out there and make your voice heard.

NOTES

1 Markowsky, G. (n.d.). *Information theory: Physiology*. In *Encyclopedia Britannica*. https://www.britannica.com/science/information-theory/Physiology.

2 van der Kolk, B., as cited in Forte Labs. (n.d.). *The Body Keeps the Score summary*. https://fortelabs.com/blog/the-body-keeps-the-score-summary/.

3 professormattw, "George Land and the NASA Study," *ProfessorMattW.com*, August 19, 2024, https://www.professormattw.com/post/george-land-and-the-nasa-study.

4 Keysers, C., et al. (2004). *SII/PV Activation during the observation and experience of touch*. Neuron, 42(1), 335–346. https://www.sciencedirect.com/science/article/pii/S0896627304001564?.

5 Dispenza, J. (2018). *How to brainwash yourself for success & destroy negative thoughts!* Impact Theory Podcast: https://www.youtube.com/watch?v=La9oLLoI5Rc&t=147s.

6 Sirois, F. M. and T.A. Pychyl. (2013). *Procrastination and the priority of short-term mood regulation: Consequences for future self.* Social and Personality Psychology Compass, 7(2), 115–127. https://doi.org/10.1111/spc3.12011.

7 The Naked Scientists. (2016, October 31). *The science of suspense* [Interview with Dr. Keith Bound]. The Naked Scientists. https://www.thenakedscientists.com/articles/interviews/science-suspense.

8 Truffaut, F. (1985). *Hitchcock: Revised Edition* (R. Scott, Trans.). Simon & Schuster, (Original work published 1966).

9 Tobin, V. (2018, April 25). *The science of the plot twist: How writers exploit our brains*. The Conversation. https://theconversation.com/the-science-of-the-plot-twist-how-writers-exploit-our-brains-95748.

10 MasterClass, "Ron Howard Teaches Directing." https://www.masterclass.com/classes/ron-howard-teaches-directing.

DOWNLOAD YOUR COMPANION WORKBOOK

Make Your Story Matter is designed to walk you through every single step of the storytelling process and leave nothing to guesswork. If you haven't already downloaded your companion workbook, you can do so now by scanning the code below.

https://abbieemmonsauthor.com/mysm-companion-workbook

This companion workbook can be used again and again for every new project you write. Simply print it and fill it out by hand, or open with your PDF editing software of choice. Once you've completed the workbook, you'll have a failproof road map that will guide you along the journey of bringing your story to life.

ABOUT THE AUTHOR

Abbie Emmons has been writing stories ever since she could hold a pencil. What started as an intrinsic love for storytelling became her lifelong passion. For over eight years, Emmons has been sharing her wisdom on her YouTube channel, where she teaches writers how to make their stories matter by harnessing the power and psychology of storytelling to transform their ideas into masterpieces.

A self-taught expert with years of rigorous study in the writing craft, Emmons has discovered an essential truth: "Story is the best teacher of story." Drawing on her passion for psychology and neuroscience, she has made it her mission to decode the "story instincts" we all naturally possess. Her groundbreaking approach unlocks the hidden structure and emotional depth that make stories impactful.

What started as a personal quest to improve her writing skills has overflowed into a vibrant online community of more than half a million passionate writers who have connected with her creed to "make your story matter." Emmons went on to launch Abbie's Story University, an online learning platform that has attracted thousands of students worldwide. Through monthly live lectures and in-depth courses, Abbie's Story University offers comprehensive instruction on creative writing, editing, publishing, and more, nurturing a thriving community of writers dedicated to honing their craft.